DRUG WARRIORS
AND THEIR PREY

DRUG WARRIORS AND THEIR PREY

From Police Power to Police State

RICHARD LAWRENCE MILLER

PRAEGER

Westport, Connecticut
London

Library of Congress Cataloging-in-Publication Data

Miller, Richard Lawrence.
   Drug warriors and their prey : from police power to police state /
Richard Lawrence Miller.
     p.   cm.
   Includes bibliographical references and index.
   ISBN 0–275–95042–5 (alk. paper)
    1. Narcotics, Control of—United States. 2. Narcotic addicts—
Government policy—United States. I. Title.
HV5825.M57   1996
363.4'5'0973—dc20   95–9306

British Library Cataloguing in Publication Data is available.

Library of Congress Catalog Card Number: 95–9306
ISBN: 0–275–95042–5

First published in 1996

Praeger Publishers, 88 Post Road West, Westport, CT 06881
An imprint of Greenwood Publishing Group, Inc.

Printed in the United States of America

The paper used in this book complies with the
Permanent Paper Standard issued by the National
Information Standards Organization (Z39.48–1984).

10 9 8 7 6 5 4 3 2 1

Everywhere in the world I dread that same self-deception which holds that "it can't happen here." It can happen anywhere. It becomes unlikely only where the mass of the population is aware of the threat, where there is accordingly no relapse into lethargy, where the character of "totalitarianism" is known and recognized from its very inception and in each of its aspects—as a Proteus which is constantly putting on new masks, which glides out of your grasp like an eel, which does the opposite of what it claims, which perverts the meaning of its words, which speaks, not to impart information, but to hypnotize, divert attention, insinuate, intimidate, dupe, which exploits and produces every type of fear, which promises security while destroying it completely.

Karl Jaspers[1]

CONTENTS

PREFACE: THE DESTRUCTION PROCESS

One does not need . . . collective pathology as in the Nazi era, in which legal institutions still appeared to function but had in fact acquired some aspects of madness. The potential for such madness is present even in ordinary times and places.

Otto Walter Weyrauch[1]

This book uses a case study to explore the process by which society can destroy an ordinary group of people. In the United States the process has already been applied against Japanese-Americans and against African-Americans. Both those examples prove that the process can be halted when a society awakens from a delusion in which a group of ordinary people is targeted for destruction.

That is fortunate because American history provides yet one more example of ordinary people targeted for destruction. That example was underway while this book was written, and indeed is the reason why this book was written.

In the United States during the 1990s drug users were targeted for destruction. I believe the effort to be more than a mistake; I believe it to be a catastrophe. Not everyone agrees with me. Indeed, the war against drug users enjoys such wide popular support that many Americans intent on saving their country from drug users may have difficulty believing anyone could sincerely oppose that war. Attitudes toward a war, however, can depend on the perspective from which it is viewed. Two motion pictures illustrate the power of perspective. In 1934 Leni Riefenstahl directed *Triumph of the Will*. A half century later Oliver Stone directed *Salvador*. Both films treat the same subject: People convinced of their superiority rescue a country threatened from within. One film presents the rescuers' perspective. The other presents the rescue as seen by those on the

THE CHAIN OF DESTRUCTION

Each element in the chain is linked together, although one element may predominate at a particular time. Later links are supported by earlier ones.

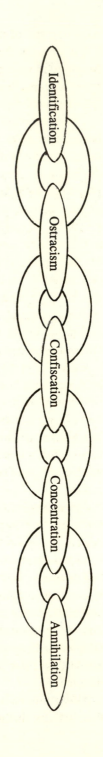

receiving end of the noble effort.

I write from the viewpoint of those on the receiving end. I tell a story about people who want to destroy their neighbors. These people are not monsters. In every way imaginable they are ordinary persons. But they have become entwined in a destruction process at great cost to themselves and their society.

The destruction process is basically the same anywhere. Certain things must be done in order to eliminate a large group of persons from society. On the facing page is a diagram inspired by Raul Hilberg's monumental study of the destruction process as applied to the Holocaust.[2] Elements of destruction can be visualized as a chain. Once the targeted group is identified, members can be ostracized from community life through boycott of social and business relations (including job dismissals), and through revocation of legal rights. The next link in the chain of destruction is property confiscation, followed by concentration of the group's members into geographical localities. The final element of destruction is annihilation, by prevention of birth and infliction of death. Birth can be prevented through regulations affecting marriage and childbearing, including compulsory contraception and sterilization. Death can be inflicted by indirect or direct means. Indirect means include withholding of medical care. Direct means include death squads and central killing operations (camps).

Each link in the chain will be examined by a chapter in this book. When this book was written, the identification, ostracism, and property confiscation aspects of the war on drug users were well established and proceeding smoothly. The concentration element was at mid-point, and the annihilation element had begun. The latter two elements were in "prototype" stage rather than "full production," but necessary mechanisms were in place. There was no reason to doubt that full production could be reached. And we know the destruction process can accelerate suddenly.

Americans who experience the drug war as mental Muzak may be startled to learn that the destruction process has progressed so far. Few important drug dealers, let alone "narcoterrorist kingpins," are being processed. The majority of victims are ordinary people minding their own business.

Elsewhere I have argued that mass murder is probable once a society decides to eliminate a group of ordinary people, as was the case in Nazi Germany. The process allowing such an outcome in the war against drug users is underway. That is one reason why I feel unease about the growing popular support for eliminating drug users in America. Nonetheless, although the destruction process can lead to mass murder, the process can be abandoned. Its fulfillment is not inevitable.

I hope this book will help illuminate what drug warriors are doing and why their activity threatens all Americans.

DRUG WARRIORS AND THEIR PREY

1

IDENTIFICATION

> Is nazism a German problem only? Is its menace over for the world at large, both as an instrumentality of Germany's national politics and as a supra-national appeal to the meanest in human nature? . . .
>
> Are the Jews the only minority that is threatened by nazism and all it stands for? Is it too academic to ask: what minority is next to be singled out—or is it a group that is still to be molded into and elevated to the rank of a minority?
>
> Max Weinreich, 1946[1]

If we wish to destroy drug users we must detect them. In the United States during the 1990s, characteristics of drug users were popularly considered so blatant as to make detection simple. But in this chapter we shall find that characteristics of drug users are not blatant at all. Indeed, in most cases their behavior is so indistinguishable from that of other citizens that police are often unable to detect a drug user without removing and analyzing part of the person's body. Such means of detection implies that popular images of drug users are stereotypical instead of accurate. Decades of scientific research verify that implication. Drug users look and act like everyone else.

HOW SCIENCE DESCRIBES DRUG USERS

Legal status of a drug has little relation to its effects. Alcohol is one of the most powerful intoxicants. Yet it is legally available to adults, where the far milder drug marijuana is forbidden. Nicotine falls within scientific criteria describing Schedule I controlled substances, which are forbidden even for medical use in hospitals, and tobacco smoking kills far more persons than do all illicit drugs combined. Yet not only is tobacco legal, but its production is encouraged by the U.S. Department of Agriculture and by farm organizations whose members are dedicated to family values. Historically, coffee drinking has been a death-penalty offense in the old Near East, where opium use was considered a sign of manliness.[2] Legal status of a drug is determined by its standing in a culture and by what people believe about its users. Those factors have nothing to do with chemistry.

Each society accepts certain kinds of drug use as normal. In the United States, drinking beer is so normal that beer is considered a beverage rather than a dosage form of the mind-altering drug alcohol. Coffee is considered a beverage rather than a dosage form of the stimulant caffeine. Both these drugs can cause problems if abused, but most users partake of them in ways that improve their lives. One drug user may prefer illegal marijuana to legal alcohol, but that illustrates personal taste, not personality disturbance. An American heroin-using professional hounded into prison is no less competent than a heroin addict allowed to work as a physician in Britain. Our point is that drug use is normal. Most people are drug users. Indeed, judged by typical behaviors among America's citizens, drug use is a criterion of normality. Americans who do not use drugs are abnormal.

Because drug use is normal and because the legalistic label "illicit" has nothing to do with chemistry, we should not be surprised that scientists working since the 1800s have detected no difference between illicit drug users and the rest of the population. Researchers find no significant difference between the grade-point averages of college students who use illicit drugs and those who do not.[3] Few differences of any kind emerge between drug users and nonusers in high school and college populations.[4] An esteemed narcotics expert wrote about "professional and clerical workers as well as laborers who worked regularly for years despite their use of as much as 40 grains of morphine daily."[5] A classic examination of heroin users declared, "There are many addicts we studied who continued at their jobs, with sufficient industry and deportment to satisfy their employers."[6] Still another researcher described heroin addicts he encountered: "Most were working-class whites who held steady jobs, bought their drugs with money from their salaries, and led unobtrusive lives in suburbs far removed from what most of us think of as the world of the addict."[7] A District of Columbia police official declared that around 1971 "more than 100 officers were taking heroin. How did we learn about them? Not because their performance was poor. . . . We took urine specimens."[8] Physicians who use opiates have been allowed to continue treating patients because no impairment of professional ability was evident.[9] Through the 1980s investigators repeatedly found heroin addicts leading ordinary lives while steadily employed at middle-class jobs.[10] "Good health and productive work," said a renowned authority in the 1980s, are "not incompatible with regular use of opioids."[11] Marijuana users can perform accustomed tasks without measurable disability.[12] Even some automobile driving experiments show no reduction in skill after using marijuana. Such findings prompted one driving skill researcher to muse, "This result is puzzling because of the elaborate efforts made in this study to maximize marihuana intoxication."[13] No significant psychological difference distinguishes LSD users from everyone else.[14] Results are similar with cocaine research. If a portrait of the general population excludes drug habits but includes other personal characteristics (income, education, family life), there is no way to tell who is a drug user and who is not. Drug users act the same as everyone else.[15] Scores of interviews demonstrate that the subject's drug use escaped notice from the interviewer.[16] A standard medical reference book notes, "Even large doses [of morphine] . . . do not cause slurred speech or significant motor incoordination."[17] One of the most respected medical authorities notes, "Without laboratory technics, even skilled clinicians cannot distinguish between patients maintained on methadone and patients who are drug free."[18]

Drug warrior claims about drugs costing the workplace billions of dollars are incorrect. In 1989 President George Bush said drugs in the workplace cost our society $60 billion to $100 billion a year. But the White House extrapolated that claim from a single survey done in 1982, a survey reporting that daily marijuana users had incomes twenty-eight percent lower than non-daily users.[19] The income differential might have explanations other than drug use. For example, losing a job is known to encourage drug abuse,[20] and losing a job can reduce someone's income. Persons twenty-five years old who smoke marijuana daily might also be persons who dropped out of high school when fifteen years old or persons alienated from society who choose to drift from one town to another. Those factors can affect income. We should also note that President Bush devised his cost estimate by comparing a group of uncommonly heavy marijuana smokers to a group of more typical casual smokers. He did not compare users to nonusers. The survey cited by the White House found no income difference between nonusers and casual users of marijuana, heroin, and cocaine.[21] As we shall see, casual users far outnumber abusers. In terms of income, the survey showed illicit drug users to be ordinary people, but President Bush misrepresented the findings. Lastly we should note that the survey figures used by President Bush measured employee income, not accidents or lower productivity or health benefit claims or anything else that could be interpreted as a cost to society. By the same reasoning, the president could have argued that unemployment or a low minimum wage costs our society $60 billion to $100 billion a year. The president's claim about drugs in the workplace was fabricated.

Control of variables such as those just noted (education, drifting from town to town) is one of the trickiest aspects of research into drug users' income. Comparing the income of an abstinent brain surgeon to the income of a heroin-using dishwasher tells us little about the drug's effect on income. An abstinent dishwasher may also earn less than the surgeon. Some researchers have been careful to control non-drug variables and have, in effect, compared surgeons to surgeons and dishwashers to dishwashers. Those findings are contrary to propaganda about drug users. One researcher found "results that suggest increased use of marijuana or cocaine is associated with higher wages."[22] Other researchers found "drug users actually received higher wages than non-drug users."[23] Such findings do not mean that persons seeking higher incomes should start using illicit drugs, but such findings do mean that drug use alone does not depress income.

Scientific data that confound propaganda about drugs in the workplace go beyond income. One study published by the federal government showed illicit drug users at Utah Power & Light having lower health benefit costs than nonusers.[24] Another study published by the federal government found that Georgia Power Company employees who tested positive for illicit drugs had higher promotion rates compared to the entire workforce and that marijuana users had absentee rates thirty percent lower than those of other employees.[25] According to supervisor evaluations, hospital employees using illicit drugs performed as well as nonusers.[26] (These were hospital employees whose urine showed evidence of illicit drug use, not employees who acted intoxicated while on the job. On Monday morning there is no reason to expect an employee to be any more impaired by Friday night's marijuana cigarette than by Friday night's glass of beer, even though evidence of use can be found in Monday's body fluid work-up.) Still another study found "the net productivity effect for all marijuana users (both those who engaged in long-term or on-the-job use and those who did not) was positive."[27] If drug use typically caused employees to become unsatisfactory, drug testing would be unnecessary: An incompetent worker can be disciplined or fired regardless of drug use. The purpose of workplace drug-testing is to target satisfactory employees for punishment. The purpose is to identify ordinary people who can be victimized. Urine tests fulfill the same function that the yellow star did for Jews in Nazi Germany, identifying them for ostracism because nothing about their appearance or behavior differed from that of other ordinary people.

Job performance of illicit drug users, licit drug users, and nonusers is about the same. This has been documented in the United States for over a century.[28] President John F. Kennedy provided a classic example. Even though he started with physical health that was less than robust, Kennedy's "promiscuous" use of amphetamines and a self-injected opiate caused no apparent decline in job performance.[29] Employers have encouraged workers to use amphetamines, cocaine, opiates, marijuana, and nicotine *on the job* to improve productivity,[30] and coffee breaks are still routinely provided to encourage employees to dose themselves with caffeine. Whether such policies have been wise is an issue we need not address here. The point is that until the war on drug users became popular, employers welcomed drug use by employees. Such employees were considered desirable and normal. The kind of workers who used drugs fifty years ago were no different from the kind who use drugs today. Attitudes toward them have changed, but they are still ordinary people.

A top federal drug war official did not cite job performance as a reason for firing drug users; instead, the official urged employers to fire drug users simply because "using drugs is a criminal activity."[31] Even drug czar William Bennett admitted that a non-addicted drug user "is likely to have a still-intact family, social and work life. . . . Non-addicted users still comprise the vast bulk of our drug-involved population. There are many millions of them."[32] Bennett was counting only users of illicit drugs. If we include users of caffeine, alcohol, and nicotine, we boost the total far higher. Including such drugs is not a trick: Their basic effects are no different from some outlawed preparations. Chemistry of licit drugs does not assure that users' behavior will be benign. The relationship of alcohol to violence is well known. During a cigarette shortage in Europe after World War II, some nicotine addicts lied and stole to obtain tobacco. Some traded away personal treasures, even traded away food despite their already poor nutrition.[33] Some reports say women resorted to prostitution in order to smoke tobacco.[34] If nicotine addicts lose their supply, they may act in ways associated with persons addicted to heroin or cocaine, but none of those drugs inherently degrades users.

Most evils blamed on illicit drugs are actually caused by "set" or "setting." "Set" is the general personality of a user, including momentary moods. Plenty of psychopaths smoke tobacco, but cigarettes did not turn those users into psychopaths. The same holds for heroin and other drugs. Scientists report that even PCP (phencyclidine or "angel dust") fails to live up to its notorious reputation of transforming docile people into unstoppable killing machines. Persons who behave violently while using PCP have a history of violence when not using PCP.[35] "Setting" is the environment in which a drug is used, and includes laws governing its use. A careful student reported that "almost three-fourths of the economic cost of drug abuse is incurred because drugs are illegal: police protection, legal defense, productivity losses for those who are career criminals instead of legal workers, productivity losses for those in prison for drug crimes."[36] Exorbitant drug prices encouraging burglary might disappear if the illicit trade in drugs changed to a legal setting. Most violence blamed on illegal drugs is actually due to their illegality. Dealers cannot enforce contracts through courts, nor report theft of inventory to police, nor collect insurance on those losses. Instead, dealers use violence to discipline the marketplace. The same violence was seen during alcohol Prohibition and disappeared afterward. Today few grocery store owners shoot customers attempting to buy beer. Few beer distributors competing for the same territory gun down innocent bystanders. Few police are killed in raids on taverns. Few houses on residential blocks have twenty-four-hour traffic from persons buying six-packs of beer. Crime did not end with Prohibition, but streets and neighborhoods became safer and more pleasant. Changing the setting of drug use can make a tremendous change in community life.[37]

A scientific consensus holds that drug use is normal, that sexual activity is normal, that credit card spending is normal. A person may choose forms of those activities that set the person apart as abnormal. But those are expressions of abnormality, not causes of it. Drugs do not cause abnormality any more than sex or credit cards do. For example, many natural products have mild drug effects. To help get work done a Bolivian farm worker can chew coca leaves or drink coca tea as a stimulant. Such use has no more hazard than other routine activities and, moreover, is integrated into the user's life in a constructive way. Someone who instead chooses a highly refined drug extracted from coca leaves—such as crack cocaine—may use the drug in a way that damages health and cuts the person off from other experiences in life. In a general sense, an abuser of cocaine is no different from an abuser of alcohol; both engage in dangerous behavior in an effort to cope with greater or lesser psychological distress. The abuser was abnormal before encountering the drug; the drug did not make the abuser abnormal. Specific circumstances may differ for each abuser, but abusers behave in ways that clearly set them apart from nonabusers. Behavior of a hospitalized alcoholic certainly differs from that of a moderate drinker. That difference, however, cannot be measured by a urine test. At a given time, a person who uses a drug in a wholesome way can have a body fluid concentration just as high as an abuser's. Abnormality can be detected only by observing behavior.

Abusers of a drug are far less common than users. Even with a powerful drug such as crack, some researcher report that fully two-thirds of crack smokers do not exhibit addictive behavior.[38] And crack users are but a fraction of cocaine users. Researchers find that about ten percent or less of cocaine users (a population including all crack smokers) are abusers,[39] and the percentage of addicts is smaller yet. Moreover, the more powerful a drug is, the less appeal it has to a general population. Special individuals with special needs might enjoy crack often, but most citizens would prefer a milder preparation and would use it occasionally rather than continuously. As the 1990s began, the National Institute on Drug Abuse found that between 98,293,000 and 107,537,000 Americans were current users of alcohol. Between 50,413,000 and 56,981,000 were current tobacco cigarette smokers. Between 8,918,000 and 11,669,000 were current users of marijuana. Between 307,000 and 798,000 were current crack users.[40] Neither price nor availability accounts for the overwhelming consumer rejection of crack. A drug's appeal depends not on its chemistry but instead on how many needs it satisfies in a person's life.

Although federal drug policy dogma accepts the invalid "gateway" theory that tobacco use leads to marijuana use, and marijuana use leads to crack use, the government's own census of drug users challenges that theory. If using a mild drug often produced desire for a stronger drug, we would not see drugs decline in popularity as their strength rises; the trend is opposite of what the gateway theory claims.

Characteristics of drug users have been discussed at length because most citizens get their information about drug users from drug warrior propaganda. Most Americans are no better informed about drug users than most Germans were informed about Jews. A few pages of prose cannot undo incessant hate propaganda, whether the pages of prose appeared in Bavaria during the 1930s or in America during the 1990s. The preceding discussion may not persuade skeptical readers, but at least they can become acquainted with the scientific consensus that drug users are ordinary people.

HOW THE LAW DESCRIBES DRUG USERS

The law's challenge is to find something about drug users that sets them apart from other ordinary people. The so-called war on drugs is, after all, a war on ordinary people. This is clear from the war's strategy and tactics. Drug czar William Bennett declared, "Users who maintain a job and a steady income should face stiff fines. . . . These are the users who should have their names published in local papers. They should be subject to drivers' license suspension, employer notification, overnight or weekend detention, eviction from public housing, or forfeiture of the cars they drive while purchasing drugs."[41] U.S. Attorney for Western Missouri Jean Paul Bradshaw II agreed that casual users must be a law enforcement priority. Upon taking office, he pledged that he would be "hitting the users hard."[42] A few months later, a Missouri county prosecutor hailed passage of a sales tax to finance a county drug squad. "I'm excited," he said. "It gives us an opportunity to do something about dopers and dealers."[43] In exasperation that most users find illicit drugs to be a boon rather than a bother, our government has made users a primary target of criminal proceedings. Bureaucrats want to punish millions of Americans to illustrate not the hazard of using illicit drugs, but the hazard of getting caught.

This strategy contrasts starkly with federal alcohol prohibition in the 1920s and 1930s. Manufacture and sale were illegal, but users were never targeted. Federal law allowed people to buy, possess, and consume alcohol. No effort was made to criminalize people for the status of being an alcohol user, and acts inherently associated with that status remained legal.

Most criminal offenses involve actions: *hitting* a person, *stealing* some money. If no action occurs, no offense occurs. Drug use is more difficult to criminalize on the basis of action; few users are detected in the act of taking a dose. Chances are small that anything about the user's subsequent behavior will be criminal. And of course any subsequent criminal behavior can be prosecuted through laws already in effect against such action. So a way must be found to criminalize drug use regardless of whether any criminal act results from drug use.

Those who make war on drug users criminalize the physical bodies of victims, and one's physical body is as inescapable as the genealogy that Nazis used to identify Jews. The crime of drug use is thereby a "status crime." The crime occurs because of what the person is, instead of what the person does. American jurisprudence traditionally abhors status crime because it punishes ordinary people who are minding their own business. Most status crimes are age related. A juvenile can be prosecuted for drinking beer in a tavern even though such an act is legal for an adult patron. Such prosecution is rare because little support exists for imprisoning teenagers who attempt to behave as adults. The rarity of such prosecution demonstrates that even though criminal sanctions are not triggered unless the juvenile commits the act of drinking, prosecutors and courts understand that the person is actually being punished for juvenile status, not for the act of drinking. An adult would be unmolested by the law. Other examples of status crimes are prohibitions against gun ownership by felons, and escalation of punishment for repeat drug offenders. It is not the act but the actor's status that creates a crime or worsens a punishment. A federal statute[44] creates a lesser-known category we may call "status immunity," allowing police officers to violate drug laws while enforcing them. For example, an undercover officer can legally share a marijuana cigarette with someone even though the companion can be arrested for accepting the officer's generosity. Police laboratories in California and Florida manufactured crack that undercover agents sold to customers who were then arrested.[45] Police in auto theft squads do not steal cars as a law enforcement technique, nor do homicide units encourage murders, but experience demonstrates that drug laws can rarely be enforced unless enforcers violate those laws. Drug squad immunity to prosecution goes beyond violation of drug laws, and outer limits of permissible law-breaking have yet to be established.[46] When prosecutors decide whether to charge someone as a drug offender, the decision is based not on the person's action, but on the person's status as an ordinary citizen or as a drug squad member.

Using an illicit drug is not only a status crime but probably the most sweeping status crime in American jurisprudence. No age exemption exists, and prosecutions are frequent.

The reason drug use has to be a status crime is because a user's actions do not reveal use. Most users behave normally. Even the minority who act abnormally cannot be identified as users through their abnormal actions. A person may be dizzy or irritable or slovenly for reasons other than drug use. Those who make war on drug users face the same challenge confronted by those who made war on Jews. If neither actions nor physical appearance can target victims, how can victims be detected?

The law identifies drug users through their blood. Also through their excreta. Drug warriors believe that blood of illicit drug users differs physically from that of other persons. Although that belief is reminiscent of Nazi doctrine about Jews, drug warriors can measure the physical difference scientifically. They do not have to depend on arbitrary and pseudoscientific schemes such as the Nazis used. A sample of blood or excreta can be drawn from anyone, and objective physical evidence of drug use can be detected. By law this detection process is the means through which someone is determined to be an illicit drug user.

This detection process also shows that illicit drug use is a status crime. All that matters is a person's blood and excreta. All that matters is the makeup of a person's physical body. Drug law does not care if an illicit user is a beloved schoolteacher who improves a community or a vicious psychopath who tortures victims to death. Criminality is determined solely by the offender's physical body. Drug law mimics Hitler. "Unlike other anti-Semites, Hitler made no distinctions between German and foreign, rich and poor, liberal, conservative, socialist, or Zionist, religious or non-religious, baptised or unbaptised Jews. In his eyes, there was only 'the Jew.' . . . 'The Jew' represented evil incarnate, performing for Hitler much the same function as the Devil does for many Christians."[47]

The law does not care if tests used to detect illicit drug users fail to demonstrate that users are impaired. The law does not care if users behave in ordinary ways. A statute creating a status crime targets ordinary people. That is its purpose. If illicit drug users acted in ways that distinguished them from nonusers, a status crime statute would be unnecessary.

The status nature of drug user offenses is further demonstrated by assorted medical treatment provisions found in anti-drug-user laws. Laws typically allow a victim to pay for medical treatment instead of undergoing prosecution. Being diseased is a status, not an act. Criminal laws do not allow defendants to undergo medical treatment instead of prosecution for the "disease" of burglary or check forging. Drug use is a unique criminal offense in that it is defined as disease. Moreover, the offender is defined as sick without any diagnosis by a physician. This is "bill of attainder" medicine. In former times legislatures could pass a bill of attainder by which a specific individual or a generally described group was declared guilty of a crime or deprived of some benefit without a trial. The practice led to so much abuse that the United States constitution forbids it.

The attainder principle is used in anti-drug-user law, however, forcing victims to pay large sums for "therapy" recommended by no physician and too often conducted by persons who would not be trusted to perform a tonsil exam. Typical counselors in such programs are ex-users. Such credentials alone hardly qualify anyone to offer counseling: "Ex-users are usually failed users. If they didn't understand drugs when they were using them, why should they be expected to understand them now?"[48] (Further illustrating drug warriors' selective disregard for conventional medicine, when acupuncture was endorsed by neither the U.S. Food and Drug Administration nor the American Medical Association, courts nonetheless ordered drug offenders to undergo that unproven therapy to "cure" illicit drug use. Yet the same courts could cite lack of FDA and AMA endorsements when forbidding other patients to use marijuana on a physician's recommendation.) Court-ordered "treatments" are an important source of revenue for substance abuse programs (as are workplace drug tests identifying competent workers who must undergo "rehabilitation" in order to keep their jobs). "The bulk of published studies suggest that compulsory counselling . . . could not work. . . . It is easy to understand why. Psychotherapy at its best is an intimate personal encounter. The most protected feelings are exposed and examined. The difference between voluntary and forced psychotherapy is the difference between making love and rape."[49]

In a discussion of drug war policy, a county prosecutor told me that government must prevent citizens from engaging in addictive behavior even if they desire the behavior, that the state should hurt such persons through criminal punishments to prevent such persons from hurting themselves. Here drug warriors introduce legal thinking new to American jurisprudence; as one court said in 1988, "A legal duty to guarantee the mental and physical health of another has never before been recognized in law."[50] The drug war, however, is not the first time a regime blended medicine with criminal justice. In 1938 a Nazi medical writer declared, "National Socialism means something fundamentally new for medical life. It has overcome an idea that was central to medicine of the recent past: the right to one's own body. Through this victory, the relationship of the physician to his patient has taken on an entirely new dimension."[51] Decades later, one of the foremost students of Nazi medical policy noted, "The responsible Nazi doctor could no longer tolerate substances that damaged the society as a whole, even if certain individuals found them pleasurable."[52] Nazis declared that citizens have an "obligation to be healthy."[53] Habits that had been commonly accepted became subject to criminal sanctions. For example, in 1944 the Nazi regime outlawed tobacco smoking on municipal buses and trains.[54] The Nazi legal doctrine of "subverting one's own person" eventually expanded beyond questions of physical health to questions of intellectual activity. Confiding doubts about the regime in one's diary became a death penalty offense. "'Subverting one's own person' typified the regime's relentless and illogical encroachment on the citizen's autonomous behaviour."[55]

Status crime reduces legal requirements that must be met before punishing someone: Authorities need not prove that a victim has done anything at all. Once the principle of status crime is accepted, like other legal principles it expands to the limit of logic. For instance, under Nazi law "a person taking an object not belonging to him is not therefore necessarily a burglar—only the nature of his personality can make him such."[56] A contemporary observer of Nazi courts noted, "Motives, general disposition, criminal antecedents and personal character largely replace objective characteristics" such as witnessed acts.[57] Courts were not asked to determine whether a particular act occurred but to determine whether a defendant had a general criminal nature. Nazi officials "took measurements of all the features of prisoners and if their biometric characteristics seemed to jibe with some other known criminal they were immediately earmarked as congenital offenders. You may be sure that whenever a prisoner's nose was a little longer than that of the ordinary Aryan type he was found to be a congenital criminal and held indefinitely in preventive detention."[58] In addition, as the *Frankfurter Zeitung* noted in June 1938, "It is becoming legal practice also to take the outstanding characteristics of the accused's clan into account."[59] A defendant's own actions diminish in importance while actions of family members increase in importance, providing insight about the defendant's latent nature. Status crime encourages judges to base criminal sanctions on medical criteria, criteria based on examination of persons other than the defendant. Indeed, as we shall see in the next chapter, American drug control law has taken the principle a step further, punishing relatives of a defendant even if they commit no offense.

Because the bill of attainder approach to medicine defines a drug user as both criminal and sick, an accused person is virtually defenseless when confronted by a malicious prosecutor. A county prosecutor in Missouri seized the sports car of a college student accused of marijuana possession.[60] In a radio broadcast the prosecutor ridiculed a suggestion that the seizure was influenced by the thousands of dollars it brought his agency. The prosecutor claimed the action was altruistic, designed to encourage the defendant to enter therapy. No physician had diagnosed the defendant as needing therapy, but the law's bill of attainder diagnosis allowed the prosecutor to portray his greed as compassion. Such action was possible only because anti-drug-user law defines offenses as both sickness and crime—a prosecutor cannot seize the car of a tobacco smoker or a hypertensive person to encourage those persons to enter therapy. In the sports car example, the student was exonerated of the criminal charge, but the law allowed the prosecutor to keep the car (which he did not return until the innocent owner promised to make no complaint about the prosecutor's conduct). We may ask why anti-drug-user laws permit prosecutors to seize property from persons found innocent of any crime. Subsequent chapters will examine such economic brutalization in detail, along with other legal consequences caused by defining drug users as both criminal and sick.

Ironically, defining a drug user as sick generates support for the drug war among family and friends of victims. Although consequences that befall victims can be more serious than if they were simply defined as criminal, the medical bill of attainder allows family and friends to view the person as sick rather than criminal. Instead of being outraged by injustice, they are grateful that law officers captured the victim in time to offer help. A mother who wanted her daughter to enter a drug treatment program turned the daughter in to police. The daughter received a 7½-year sentence without parole and was ordered to enter treatment upon release.[61] "Our goal is not to send everybody to jail to hurt them. Our goal is to help them," said one rural Missouri drug squad officer.[62] His Kansas City colleagues agreed after a crack bust: "The sting was meant to catch users and get them help, said Sgt. Don Birdwell."[63] When parents of a twelve-year-old girl were jailed after she reported their drug use to police, a police spokesman declared, "She did the right thing. We don't see this as turning in parents. We would rather view this as someone requesting help for their parents."[64] In 1985 the chairman of a White House–endorsed conference on drug abuse declared, "We, as parents of all nations, must say to our local law enforcement officer, 'If my child, my loved one, or my friend breaks the law by using illicit drugs, please arrest him or her.'"[65]

Unquestionably, some drug abusers can benefit from medical treatment. But criminal sanctions are unnecessary to provide anyone with medical treatment. If a person is unable to make a rational decision to seek aid, a civil court can order the person to undergo treatment. Drug warriors simply use the medical bill of attainder to deceive the public into thinking the drug war is intended to help needy citizens rather than victimize ordinary ones. An irony in this approach to medicine is that our limited treatment resources are devoted to unwilling recipients, while persons seeking aid must wait for treatment slots.

Not all drug offenses are status crimes. Users typically possess a supply of their drug, and the act of possession is criminal. Users typically share their supply with friends, and an act of sharing is drug dealing—considered to be a sale regardless of whether compensation changes hands. Users who do not wish to enrich the criminal underground may grow their own marijuana. The act of cultivation is a crime. Such acts, however, are all inherent to the status of drug user. By analogy, it is like not only prosecuting someone for having the status of Jew, but also prosecuting the act of attending synagogue, eating certain foods, possessing Judaic religious paraphernalia. Such acts cannot be relied upon to identify someone as Jewish, but a Jew can be relied upon to have committed one or more such acts. Criminalizing acts inherent to status directs attention to acts in order to disguise the fact that the basis of persecution is status. Such trickery disguises the fact that ordinary people are being victimized for ordinary behavior. Perhaps not everyone engages in the criminalized ordinary acts, but neither does everyone commute to work on city buses or attend movies that include vulgar dialogue. Nonetheless, such ordinary acts could be criminalized if one wanted to persecute people for the status of having low income or high artistic appreciation.

Legal definition of victims helps determine who will make war against them. For example, a genealogical definition in Germany helped recruit clergy who kept genealogical records. A medical definition in the United States recruits physicians, nurses, and other health care providers, transforming them from helpers into hunters. The Rockhurst College Employee Substance Abuse Policy Statement says, "Faculty and staff seeking help for alcohol or drug abuse are encouraged to contact the Counseling Center" but also says, "The College administration will, with the assistance of the security department, report any illegal activities to the Kansas City, Missouri Police."[66] Employee Assistance Programs put workers' physical and mental records into large data bases that can be informally accessed by police.[67] In many states health care professionals are supposed to report drug-using pregnant women to government authorities,[68] and state social service agencies routinely report drug-using mothers to police.[69] When California's Child Protective Services receives a toxicology test showing that a hospital patient has been exposed to illicit drugs, the state agency has turned over those results to police, resulting in prosecutions.[70] A prosecutor said newborns in county hospitals would be screened for exposure to illicit drugs, and positive tests made mothers liable for drug prosecutions.[71] Missouri enacted a law in 1991 giving physicians immunity from civil suits filed by patients for breach of professional confidence in reporting drug users to state agencies.[72] Likewise, Nazi law ordered German physicians to inform government agents about patients who might be likely candidates for involuntary racial hygiene therapy (sterilization), and protected physicians from civil suits for that breach of professional confidence.[73] A 1991 article in the *Journal of the American Medical Association* noted that open communication between physician and patient affects patient health, and that "state intrusion" chills such communication "particularly in sensitive areas where patients' concerns frequently need to be elicited, [and] has direct negative implications for the provider-patient relationship and the quality of care."[74]

Evidence exists that AIDS-reporting laws may have enabled police in Missouri to obtain access to confidential patient records.[75] If police can now examine medical records of patients with the legal disease of AIDS, police can just as easily examine medical records of patients with the illegal "disease" of drug use. A patient in a Nevada hospital reported undergoing what was described as an AIDS blood test, but the sample was also used to screen for marijuana use. When the test showed positive for marijuana, a police visit followed.[76] The Georgia Court of Appeals has held that cocaine metabolites in urine prove the crime of cocaine possession.[77] The function of health care personnel as agents of social control rather than healing is also apparent when drug defendants undergo court-ordered "therapy" to avoid jail. Those involuntary patients encounter health care personnel serving the legal system rather than serving the patient, enforcing social values through medical means. Such a philosophy of medicine powered Nazi racial hygiene, in which individual patients could be forced to suffer if their suffering promoted public policy goals. Drug treatment personnel can and do transfer their patients to hellish prisons if the "treatment program" is unsuccessful. Health care personnel have become police agents. They do not advertise their role as bluntly as the SS nurse "in white gown with a stethoscope *and* a rubber-truncheon."[78] Nonetheless, an American drug user who turns to a physician can no more expect protection than a Jew who turned to a clergyman.

Unlike German clergymen, health care providers make money from persons they victimize. In addition to money received from victims ordered to pay for drug abuse treatment, in Missouri the law requires any physician who attends pregnant patients to provide *state-approved* drug advice to "all patients."[79] On its face, the statute language includes all the physician's patients, pregnant or not, male or female. But even if limited to pregnant women, a patient seeking a blood pressure reading can be forced to pay for an extended office call that includes a drug education talk or be charged for a drug education booklet handed to her by the receptionist. The drug war boosts physician income. It also boosts income of medical laboratories. Urine testing is estimated to be a billion-dollar business.[80]

The medical definition of victims recruits friends and family as police agents. As we have seen, parents and children are openly encouraged to report one another's drug "sickness" to police, ostensibly to obtain medical help. The "patient" may also be stripped of employment, of the family house, and a decade or two of life through a mandatory prison sentence, but such brutalization is rationalized with the excuse that things would have gone even worse for the drug user if "help" had been delayed longer.

Just as persons targeted by Nazis could occasionally step aside through Pseudo or Real Liberation (as Nazi jargon described the process), similar possibilities exist in the United States. In Germany Pseudo Liberation was based on facts, Real Liberation on grace. Persons identified as drug users can undergo Pseudo Liberation if repeated analyses of their physical bodies find no evidence of illicit drug use. The fact of abstinence allows those individuals to escape definition as drug users, and sanctions against them can cease. The equivalent of Real Liberation through grace occurs when someone uses drugs licitly. Someone who daily smokes two packs of tobacco cigarettes and drinks several cocktails may have a serious chemical abuse problem but through grace can escape definition as a drug user because those drugs are legal. The law defines drug abuse in terms of the substance used, not in the way it is used. A teetotaler who avoids tobacco but smokes marijuana once a month may have no drug problem at all, but the law allows such a person to be maltreated demoniacally.

Even Hitler made exceptions for Jews he favored, and drug warriors likewise exempt favored persons from penalties. Federal narcotics commissioner Harry Anslinger admitted he discreetly supplied illegal drugs to a wealthy and beautiful woman he admired, to a U.S. Navy officer, and to a powerful member of Congress (later identified as Senator Joseph McCarthy); Anslinger moreover threatened to prosecute a reporter who discovered the practice.[81] "It was widely understood that if you were really important and got mixed up yourself, a member of your family hooked, for instance, the Commissioner could quietly arrange a safe supply of your drug of choice for you."[82] The most typical exemption, however, occurs when police provide users with drugs for personal use as a reward for turning in drug-using acquaintances.

As the war on Jews progressed, the definition of Jew broadened to sweep up more victims. In the war on drug users, ever more citizens are swept up as ever more drugs are made illegal. At one time elite athletes who used steroids and other performance-enhancing drugs were role models for youths. Anti-drug-user laws have transformed such athletes into disgraced criminals. Their behavior did not change. The law did. Hollywood movies once portrayed tobacco smokers as persons filled with zest for life. Now tobacco smokers become criminals if they light up in certain places. Criminal sanctions against nicotine users do not yet approach the harshness directed against users of some other drugs, but not long ago adult tobacco users faced no sanctions at all. Just as Nazis raised standards of "racial" purity higher and higher, thereby maintaining a pool of victims, so too do drug warriors demand that blood from citizens be tested again and again until it fails to meet some new arbitrary standard of purity.

HOW DRUG WARRIOR RHETORIC DESCRIBES DRUG USERS

Drug users are defined not only by law but by rhetoric from politicians, bureaucrats, community leaders, news media, and entertainment media. The public depends on such rhetoric for its knowledge of drug users. Parallels between rhetoric against Jews and rhetoric against drug users are striking. Although the basis of drug war law is that users are ordinary people, drug war rhetoric portrays them very differently. Vilification of drugs users is continual. That rhetoric serves to loosen inhibitions against attacks on ordinary people, excusing legal and extralegal sanctions that might otherwise seem unconscionable.

Nazis who made war on Jews portrayed them as communists. The same is said of drug users. President Richard Nixon and Vice President Spiro Agnew popularized the image of marijuana users as procommunist war opponents.[83] Drug warriors go further yet, declaring that drug use itself is a communist plot. The administration of California Governor Ronald Reagan credited "subversive elements" with using drugs to promote college campus unrest.[84] In 1980 New York Governor Hugh Carey denounced the "Russian design to wreck America by flooding the nation with deadly heroin. . . . I am not overstating the case."[85] The end of the communist empire was not accompanied by an end to drug use in America, but public credibility of drug warriors remained unimpaired.

Jews were portrayed as the source of most crime in Nazi Germany. So, too, are illicit drug users portrayed as the source of most crime in America. "Drugs, food stamps and guns are synonymous," said an Arizona detective. "If you find one, you'll find the others."[86] U.S. Supreme Court Justice Anthony M. Kennedy, joined by Justices Sandra Day O'Connor and David H. Souter, declared, "Studies . . . demonstrate a direct nexus between illegal drugs and crimes of violence."[87] Many robbers and thieves are illicit drug users, but that does not mean that drugs turn users into criminals. Let us consider "set" once again, this time in the context of crime. The "set" or general personality of a robber includes a rejection of important social norms. We should not be surprised if illicit drug use is one expression of such a personality, any more than we should be surprised that such a person carries a hot temper or a dangerous weapon. Quick-tempered persons, however, are not inherently burglars. Gun owners are not inherently muggers. And drug users are not inherently criminals. One student has noted declining crime as per capita use of drugs rises.[88] Neither tobacco nor marijuana turn a user to crime; nor do alcohol or opiates. The British practice of providing opiates to addicts was not accompanied by an increase in criminal behavior among recipients. Nor has the similar American practice of providing methadone been accompanied by an increase in criminal behavior; indeed, advocates of methadone programs claim the trend is quite the opposite. Supply of a particular drug may have nothing to do with crime. For example, a summer 1972 dock strike accomplished a feat that still eludes drug squads: The heroin supply plummeted in Eastern cities. Although street prices rose by 500 percent, crime rates did not change. Many heroin addict criminals simply switched to other cheaper drugs; their addiction to heroin did not cause their criminal behavior.[89] Neither Amsterdam nor Alaska, where marijuana use by adults has been tolerated, has experienced a crime wave from those citizens. "Crack did not induce users to commit crimes," said Michael S. Gazzaniga, Professor of Neuroscience at Dartmouth Medical School. Noting estimates of 200,000 crack users in New York City alone, Gazzaniga commented, "If the drug produced violent tendencies in all crack users, the health-care system would have to come to a screeching halt. It hasn't. In fact, in 1988 the hospitals in New York City (the crack capital of the world) averaged only seven crack-related admissions, city-wide, a day. The perception of crack-based misbehavior is exaggerated because it is the cases that show up in the emergency rooms that receive public notice."[90] "Aggression is not linked to marijuana, not to heroin, and if it's linked to crack cocaine, there's not much evidence," reports Albert J. Reiss, Jr., the William Graham Sumner Professor of Sociology at Yale University. "In all the studies—from rats to lawyers—alcohol is the only thing you can find linked to violence."[91] Many criminals use drugs, but they are a minority of drug users. The entire population of drug users is no different from the general population: a few saints, a few more sinners, but a vast majority of ordinary people.

Jews were called disease carriers; so are drug users. Crack-using prostitutes may spread sexually transmitted disease, but prostitutes were known as a source of such affliction long before crack existed. Reckless intravenous drug injectors may spread AIDS with unsanitary sharing of needles, but typically such persons began demonstrating self-destruction and lack of concern for others long before injecting drugs. Hospital patients receive intravenous drugs every day with no risk of contracting AIDS from the needles. Needles do not cause AIDS. As in so many cases of drug war rhetoric, we see the technique of citing someone with a problem, with the invalid assertion that drugs cause such a problem. But perhaps the most dangerous disease attributed to Jews and drug users alike is the disease of their status, of Jewishness or drug using itself. Just as Aryan populations were always at risk from contamination by Jews, so are pure Americans at risk from an epidemic spread by drug users. "The casual adult user is in some ways the most dangerous person because that person is a carrier," said drug czar William Bennett.[92] "First use invariably involves the free and enthusiastic offer of a drug by a friend," Bennett said. "This friend—or 'carrier,' in epidemiological terms—is seldom a hard-core addict. . . . A non-addict's drug use, in other words, is *highly* contagious."[93] Such rhetoric, **Douglas N. Husak** has pointed out, argues that

> Jones's use of marijuana should be prohibited because it might induce him to try cocaine, which might cause him to become addicted, which might lead him to become poor, which might make him more inclined to commit a crime. Each additional link in this causal chain decreases the chance that the ultimate harm will occur. . . .
>
> Bennett's rationale adds even more distance between the anticipatory offense and the ultimate harm to be prevented. Smith's problem-free and casual use of a recreational drug should be prohibited because it might lead Jones to experiment with a drug that might make his behavior more likely to conform to the (already lengthy) causal scenario described above. . . . If Smith's life has not been adversely affected by his use of drugs, why worry that Jones might mimic it?[94]

Like Bennett, U.S. Senator Joseph Biden (D-DE) has talked of "the epidemic of illegal drug use."[95] But to call drug use an epidemic is incorrect. People can become sick against their will, despite the most stringent precautions. Marijuana and other drugs are not delivered by mosquitoes or bad water supplies. Drug use is a voluntary decision. It is no more an epidemic than is choosing a lunch of unhealthy fast foods instead of juice and sprouts. Drug use is spread by exchange of information, not exchange of body fluids. And even that information sharing is no more a cause of drug use than news reports of the day's police blotter are a cause of crime. "Epidemic" may be a gripping metaphor for drug use, but drug warriors mean it literally, and they are wrong. Their rhetoric has important public policy implications, however. "It is part of Western tradition that epidemics warrant stringent measures to protect the public. During epidemics of various contagious diseases over the last few centuries, it has seemed legitimate for authorities to quarantine ships, prevent people from entering and leaving towns on pain of death, seize and incarcerate people who show signs of the disease, and, in extreme cases, kill people suspected of transmitting the disease."[96] Epidemic rhetoric promotes harsh measures against victims.

Jews were portrayed as sexually loose, and so are illicit drug users. Says a marijuana authority: "As for homosexuals, a growing number have found this drug an ideal releaser of restraints, and use it to sidetrack the usual inhibitions, suspicions, and guilt associated with socially unapproved sexuality,"[97] The authority adds, "The homosexual magazine *Queens' Quarterly* made the relationship of the use of cannabis and the gay sexual scene quite clear."[98] One drug addiction authority describes marijuana parties thusly: "Exhibitions of perverted sexual practices ('circuses') are not an uncommon feature at 'tea parties.'"[99] What is said of marijuana is also said of crack cocaine: "We are told that women who use crack become sex-crazed; 'toss-ups' for 'strawberries' who lie around crack houses indulging in all kinds of promiscuous sex, including bestiality. Journalists tell us that men crack users report crack makes women so sexually excitable they will do anything. The implications for sexually transmitted diseases are obvious."[100] As justification for closing the federal medical marijuana program to new patients, Public Health Service director James O. Mason said that patients using marijuana therapeutically "might be less likely to practice safe behavior" in sexual activity and thereby spread AIDS.[101] A radio "public service announcement" in the 1990s had fictional dialogue in which a character got intoxicated on drugs and caught AIDS because no one bothered to take precautions in a sexual encounter. The announcement ended with the slogan, "Get high, get stupid, get AIDS."[102] This sort of thing is straight out of Julius Streicher, even managing to combine the theme of disease with immorality. Regardless of whether casual sexual encounters and multiple partners are right or wrong, wise or unwise, such conduct violates traditional middle-class values. That is why drug warriors promote a sexual theme, because it portrays drug users as outside the boundaries of legitimate society, a portrayal helping to inflame the public. In reality, of course, drug users are ordinary people whose sexual habits are shared by the general population.

Rhetoric describing Jews as immoral is duplicated in descriptions of drug users, who supposedly are always ready to lie and cheat in order to obtain drugs. Worse yet, users supposedly seek to recruit naive citizens into the rotten drug culture, sometimes giving free samples of drugs until a new user is hooked and must then pay exorbitant prices to the "benefactor." The pusher myth is popular, but scientific investigators have not found dealers who are willing to give away a product for which there is an insatiable cash demand. Dealers have trouble maintaining sufficient inventory and turn away potential customers. Scientific investigators have found far more users who warn naive associates away from drugs than users who seek to persuade others to use drugs. Unquestionably some drug users lie and cheat to get what they want, but such behavior has less to do with chemistry than with the personality set of a particular user and the illegal setting of drug use, which restricts a user's access to a drug.

Another common rhetorical theme holds that drug users are crazy. News stories abound of drug users engaged in bizarre and frightening behavior, from LSD users staring at the sun until they are blinded to PCP users who run naked in the streets while throwing dogs over fences. Some stories, such as the LSD sun staring, are fabricated.[103] Yet the lie is readily believed. A person intoxicated by any drug may behave in strange ways. Yet investigators typically find that an intoxicated person who acts in a frightening or bizarre manner is a person whose personality and behavior were abnormal before taking the drug. Unquestionably, too many persons who become drunk on alcohol become violent toward other persons. Yet the percentage of alcohol users who are affected in that way is extremely small. It is the same with users of any other drug.

Nonetheless, one of the most clever rhetorical techniques says that even normal-acting drug users are crazy because they like to take poison. The technique is particularly insidious when applied to drugs officially recognized as medicinal, such as morphine or cocaine. When used on a physician's advice they are called pharmaceutical agents. When used without a physician's advice they are called poison. A newspaper article describing crack cocaine said, "Because it is smoked, it attacks the pleasure centers of the brain almost immediately."[104] Cocaine "attacks" the brain, but other inhaled substances such as nicotine, ether, or nitrous oxide are not described as poisons. President Reagan called drugs "blood pollutants" and vowed, "We won't let people who are poisoning the blood of our children to get away with it."[105] Rev. Cecil L. Murray of Los Angeles opposed lifting criminal penalties against illicit drugs: "To legalize it, to condone it, to market it—that is to put a healthy brand on strychnine. . . . [W]e cannot make poison the norm."[106] Jesse Jackson agreed, "Drugs are poison."[107] President Bush concurred, saying drugs "have no conscience. . . . They just murder people."[108] A drug may become toxic if a high enough dose is taken. So may other substances. People have died from drinking too many glasses of water at one sitting. Drugs can be beneficial if a proper dose is taken. If a person experiences a physical or psychological benefit from a proper dose, that hardly means the person is crazy. To call a substance "poison" because overindulgence can be harmful is a rhetorical trick, a deceit intended to make the public believe that even ordinary-seeming drug users are crazy and dangerous. "Poison users" are portrayed as not only suicidal but homicidal. Responding to a magazine article about drug offenders receiving sentences harshly disproportionate to harm from the offense, one perturbed reader declared, "It's frightening to think that some people actually want certain criminals set free so that they can continue to poison our society."[109] Speaking of such disproportionate sentences, a judge admitted that convicts "may not have any [prior] criminal records, but these are people who smell out a chance to make a buck selling poisons that murder our babies."[110] Jesse Jackson declared, "If someone is transmitting the death agent to Americans, that person should face wartime consequences."[111] In *The Scapegoat*, René Girard notes poison rhetoric as a classic technique of scapegoating ordinary people: "The accusation of poisoning makes it possible to lay the responsibility for real disasters on people whose activities have not been really proven to be criminal. Thanks to poison, it is possible to be persuaded that a small group, or even a single individual, can harm the whole society without being discovered."[112]

The standard line is that drug users are doomed. Civil libertarian William O. Douglas quoted the following description of drug users:

> The teeth have rotted out; the appetite is lost and the stomach and intestines don't function properly. The gall bladder becomes inflamed; eyes and skin turn a bilious yellow. In some cases membranes of the nose turn a flaming red; the partition separating the nostrils is eaten away—breathing is difficult. Oxygen in the blood decreases; bronchitis and tuberculosis develop. Good traits of character disappear and bad ones emerge. Sex organs become affected. Veins collapse and livid purplish scars remain. Boils and abscesses plague the skin; gnawing pain racks the body. Nerves snap; vicious twitching develops. Imaginary and fantastic fears blight the mind and sometimes complete insanity results. Often times, too, death comes much too early in life. . . . Such is the plague of being one of the walking dead.[113]

Drug users are unfit and will not survive competition with nonusers. "One must not have mercy with people who are determined by fate to perish." Such thinking, expressed by Hitler in 1942,[114] may be a factor in brutality directed against drug users. They are doomed anyway; it is not like merciless deeds are done to citizens who can expect to lead a life worth living.

After Nazis had spent years cutting Jews off from jobs, education, food, and shelter, Nazis cited the subsequent squalor of ghetto life as proof of Jewish inferiority. A similar technique is used by drug warriors. When drug warriors seek images of drug use and its effect on a community, they do not dispatch camera crews to film factory workers unwinding on Monday night with marijuana so they can be rested and productive when they arrive on the assembly line Tuesday morning. We do not see pictures of stockbrokers or business executives or high school teachers, all admired by their communities, all of whom relax with an illicit drug at bedtime. We do not see pictures of the neat working-class neighborhoods, great mansions, or huge commercial enterprises that are the environments of typical illicit drug users. Instead we see pictures of slums, human degradation, and heavily armed police storming a drug house. Crack is blamed for unpleasant living conditions in certain areas of the city where I live. I recall these same areas exhibiting serious problems such as unemployment, absentee slumlords, and gangs of young thugs long before crack was invented. Although drug war leaders admit that most drug users are white, middle-class, employed, engaged in wholesome family life, and exhibiting no problem attributable to drug use, nonetheless visual images of drug users emphasize squalor. Citizens deprived of love, respect, opportunity, and hope may develop abusive relationships with people and with drugs, and such citizens may be more visible in some districts than in others. But to blame drugs for the condition of those citizens and their neighborhoods is to ignore reality.

As a corollary to the Nazi allegation that urban blight demonstrated Jewish inferiority, anti-Semitic rhetoric also argued that Jews caused blight. Likewise, drug warriors blame users for urban blight today. A county prosecutor told me that neighborhood residents harbor little anger toward drug dealers, who simply meet a popular demand. Instead, residents are enraged at drug users who provide the demand, blaming them for problems associated with the illicit trade—without users there would be no trade. When speaking with citizens concerned about drug activity in their neighborhoods, I too have found rage directed at users. If, however, profit margins were less obscene, if courts enforced dealer contracts, if police and insurance companies investigated and compensated losses when dealers were victimized by criminals, if government encouraged prudent and conservative business people to be dealers (instead of encouraging reckless and improvident sociopaths), neighborhoods would experience no more harm from sales of marijuana than they do from sales of tobacco. In other words, if the illicit drug trade were legalized, problems associated with that commerce would disappear. Neighborhoods are degraded by drug laws, not by drug users.

Just as Nazi cinema reinforced anti-Jewish stereotypes, American movies and television reinforce false stereotypes about drug users. In Germany, gratuitous anti-Semitic scenes were routine even in movies where the plot had nothing to do with that topic. Likewise, President Nixon bragged about convincing Hollywood producers to insert anti-drug-user messages in dramas: "Approximately 20 television programs throughout the country are going on this fall dealing with the drug problem in one way or another, and dealing with it not in the way of just a straight-out sermon but in terms of that subtle, far more effective, method of approach where a story is told and the individual—and usually the young individual—watching the program becomes interested in the story and, therefore, they get the message."[115] Nixon met with forty-eight television producers, including representatives from programs such as "Dragnet," "Hawaii Five-O," "The Storefront Lawyers," "I Spy," "Zig Zag," "Felony Squad," "Silent Force," "The Name of the Game," "The FBI," "Dan August," "Dial Hot Line," and "Room 222." Nixon also got anti-drug themes introduced into "The Young Lawyers," "Mod Squad," "Marcus Welby, M.D.," and "Matt Lincoln." "Dragnet" producer Jack Webb began working on a series dramatizing federal drug squads.[116] The practice of inserting anti-drug-user messages into episodes of popular television programs continued into the 1990s, with even "Startrek: The Next Generation" including a scene where a bewildered adolescent asked how anyone could be crazy enough to use drugs. Drug users have long been a staple of police dramas. For years such programs have portrayed drug users as violent, irresponsible criminal deviants, in contrast to cool professional police officers whose investigative techniques are inspired by devotion to civil liberties. Researchers have consistently found that the more someone watches television, the less understanding the person has of real life.[117] Hollywood's continual lies about drug use are a significant element of public support for the war on drug users. Those lies are even a basis for drug war legislation: Congressional debate on the necessity for harsher drug war measures cited material from the fictional television series "Miami Vice."[118] The office of drug czar William Bennett declared, "The television and film industries have already done a great deal, but they must do more."[119] A *Washington Post* book review noted that the Disney Channel "did more" by editing history to support the drug war, eliminating sequences in "The Making of Sgt. Pepper" in which former Beatles band members said they were not harmed by marijuana or LSD.[120]

Like Nazis, drug warriors even portray their victims as murderers. Nancy Reagan declared, "If you're a casual drug user, you're an accomplice to murder."[121] President Bush agreed: "Casual drug use is responsible for the casualties of the drug war. . . . Dabblers in drugs bear responsibility for the blood being spilled."[122] "Drugs do deal death," U.S. Representative Bill McCollum said.[123] Pregnant women who use drugs are accused of trying to kill their children.[124] A Partnership for a Drug-Free America ad said that anyone who buys marijuana is responsible for murders of police.[125] By characterizing drug users as murderers, drug warriors promote a public climate that will tolerate any level of harshness against users. Even courts are affected by such rhetoric: "It is fair to conclude from federal sentencing trends of the past twenty years that where drug law violations were formerly treated in district courts like property crimes they are now treated like violent crimes."[126]

As with Nazi actions against Jews, drug warrior actions against users are made more palatable through rhetoric portraying victims as nonhuman. "We will no longer tolerate those who sell drugs and those who buy drugs," said President Reagan. "All Americans of good will are determined to stamp out those parasites."[127] "We're talking scum here," a drug cop told one reporter. "Air should be illegal if they breathe it."[128] "One 'reality'-based crime program (Night Beat, WNYW-TV, 12/92) took us to a police briefing, where the chief of a narcotics unit *on camera* tells his assembled officers—not once but twice—'Remember, you are dealing with the scum of the earth.'"[129] One researcher of police attitudes found that "when confronted with the violence they sometimes inflict [against drug offenders], they justify themselves by asserting that their victims are not really human: 'they're scum,' 'they can't feel pain,' and so forth."[130] One official described prisoners under his command: "Those aren't people—they have to be handled quite differently."[131] Such an attitude can be deadly, as demonstrated by the source of that particular description, an SS murderer.

In Nazi Germany top scholars, who relied on government-funded research for personal income and professional prestige, put a scientific veneer on anti-Semitic rhetoric. So, too, do scientists in the United States receive government money to make reports that drug warriors cite as proof of their hate rhetoric. Such reports created a climate allowing one physician to say in the *Journal of the American Medical Association*, "The average drug abuser steals to maintain his or her habit, and the amount stolen or damaged ranges from $100 000 to $1 000 000 [*sic*] per year per drug abuser."[132] Under the definition commonly used by the medical profession, including the American Medical Association, a drug abuser is simply someone who self-administers a drug without supervision by a physician.[133] Given the millions of illicit drug users who fall within that definition, the claim that most steal or damage $100,000 to $1,000,000 a year is patently inaccurate. Yet hate rhetoric gives the claim enough credibility to merit publication in a prestigious medical journal.

A common theme runs through propaganda against Jews and drug users. They are portrayed as an ever-growing group dangerous to the nation; self-preservation requires a war on them. "The first premise of successful propaganda within one's own people is the conviction that the war has been forced upon it," said a respected Nazi work on military science. Only then will the citizenry be "ready to devote itself fully and completely to the struggle. On this basis the government has to propagate a great idea which as a guiding star shows the way."[134] Nazi rhetoric claimed the Jewish threat grew ever more serious as one anti-Jewish measure after another was enacted. In the 1940s an outside observer not caught in the madness might have wondered what more could possibly be done, yet at the same time many Nazis actually believed the war on Jews had not even begun. When the Nazis took power, they claimed that "Jews had captured control of the government, the press, the professions, the arts, economic life, and worst of all, through intermarriage, had made great inroads in corrupting the biological purity of Aryan racial stock."[135] In contrast to Nazi propaganda, as the war on Jews began, German government statistics reported that Jews comprised less than eleven percent of physicians, less than three percent of judges and prosecutors, barely one-half percent of elementary and secondary teachers, and about one percent of the general population.[136] (These statistics are reported solely to demonstrate the exaggeration of numbers in Nazi propaganda. Even if the propaganda numbers had been correct, there would have been no reason to fear these ordinary people.) A July 1933 headline in the prominent German newspaper *Volkischer Beobachter* proclaimed, "70,000 JEWS IMMIGRATED INTO GERMANY WITHIN THE LAST 15 YEARS."[137] Not only was that claim false, in reality the Jewish population was declining. Frankfurt had 107 Jewish births in 1933. In 1934 Jewish births numbered 67, deaths 314.[138] Two years later most districts in Upper Bavaria, Bremen, Silesia, Anhalt, and Mecklenburg were "Jew-free."[139] Although the government could have hailed such disappearance of the Jewish population as proof that the war on Jews was succeeding, instead the Jewish threat was portrayed as worsening.

In a similar way, those who make war on drug users claim the targeted group is powerful and growing larger. "A substantial majority of Americans appears to believe that drug abuse is rampant somewhere in the United States, but most do not seem to have direct knowledge of or contact with such abuse in their own life experiences."[140] Numerous surveys have shown drug use declining in the United States from the late 1970s to the 1990s, yet warriors proclaim the situation to be more serious than ever. In 1989, literature promoting a drug war sales tax in Kansas City declared, "'Crack' Cocaine is being sold like fast food, on every street in our city,"[141] a lie so big and repeated so often that voters believed it and enacted the tax sought by the county prosecutor. As we shall see, drug users are not organized and powerful, but instead are isolated and helpless while being hunted and caught by private and public agencies. Upon capture, victims are stripped of their livelihoods, their possessions, their children—even stripped of decades of their lives through mandatory prison sentences. Prisons are so overflowing with drug offenders that billions of dollars are being appropriated to build more. Legislators continually devise new laws to criminalize conduct that was previously law-abiding. Police continually demand and receive more "tools" from judges and lawmakers. Yet in 1992 an adviser to the mayor of Kansas City told me, "There is no drug war. We haven't started to do anything yet, it's all talk." The county prosecutor, who boasted about his record of successful drug prosecutions, agreed: "There never was a war on drugs. . . . George Bush had unwittingly taken a great step forward by having William Bennett put this strategy together. Then he lost all of his momentum and—to me—all of his credibility by basically ignoring it. To be sure, the spin doctors and the political positioners had tried to put a gloss on the drug control strategy to make it look like something is going on. However, it is not."[142] U.S. Representative Charles Rangel (D-NY) declared, "We haven't even fired the first shot in the war on drugs."[143] Millions of victims already, billions of dollars spent each year, with warriors demanding more and more from a public that is portrayed as unwilling to get serious about fighting drug users. Obviously warriors measure success neither by body count nor budget bloat. Instead, they measure success by unquestioning obedience from the public, the legislatures, and the courts. "Submit," drug warriors cry, "and we shall make you free."

Nazi rhetoric claimed Jews intended to destroy middle-class values, even intended to murder middle-class citizens. Although drug users fit the profile of the average American, drug warriors continually claim that users threaten average Americans. Portrayals of political radicalism, sexual immorality, criminal violence, repudiation of the work ethic, and other images we have discussed have a common theme of challenge to middle-class values. That is the reason drug war authoritarians emphasize those images, to terrify the middle class into accepting the need for drug war laws that reduce the accountability of government to the people.

At one time drug users were not singled out for discrimination. Mainstream alcohol temperance advocates, for example, directed their ire at alcohol commerce and expressed sympathy for alcohol abusers. In the latter nineteenth century, productive opiate addicts were cherished members of the community and their affliction was viewed with compassion. Certain groups who used certain drugs were hated. But hatred directed against Chinese opium users in the 1870s, African-American cocaine users in the 1890s, Mexican marijuana users in the 1930s, and hippie LSD users in the 1960s had little to do with their drug use, although drugs associated with those groups were outlawed as a means of harassing them. (A Chinese worker could hardly be imprisoned for industrious-ness, but leisure time opium smoking was a habit largely limited to Chinese immigrants who could then be jailed in order to create job openings for white males.) As the twentieth century progressed, certain types of drug users, such as heroin addicts, were stereotyped as gutter derelicts. But disdain directed against such Americans related to the junkie lifestyle; the stereotype served more as a warning against drug use than as an attack upon users.

A dramatic change occurred in the 1980s. For the first time, all drug users came under attack for their drug use alone, not because they were members of some group hated for another reason. As in Germany fifty years earlier, fearful citizens had elected a national leader who promised to restore the nation to past levels of glory. As in Germany, citizens yearned for a simple explanation of problems confronting the nation. President Ronald Reagan and his spouse Nancy Reagan announced that drug users were threatening America. As the perceived threat from communism dwindled, the president pumped up the perceived threat from drug users to justify authoritarian governmental actions that had earlier been justified as a response to the communist threat. Previous experiments with criminal law, using drugs as a cover to attack specific hated groups, had given government officials the necessary experience to widen the swath to all illicit drug users immediately upon President Reagan's order. The sudden acceleration of effort was matched only by the effort's effectiveness. Decades of anti-drug propaganda directed against hated groups had created a climate of ignorance and fear, allowing the public to accept the notion that all users of any illicit drug, not just members of particular groups using particular drugs, merited suppression.

A national coordinator of anti-drug-user rhetoric emerged, an organization called Partnership for a Drug-Free America. Its propaganda helped convince the public that drug users are not ordinary people, that instead they are dangerous enemies who must be eliminated. Partnership rhetoric promoted a climate making brutalization of ordinary people not only acceptable but virtuous. In 1990 almost $1 million a day in free advertising was being donated to Partnership.[144]

Philip Morris, Anheuser-Busch, RJR Reynolds, American Brands, DuPont, Johnson & Johnson, SmithKline Beecham, Hoffman-LaRoche, the Proctor & Gamble Fund, the Bristol-Myers Squibb Foundation, and the Merck Foundation have all been important sources of money for Partnership propaganda.[145] Those groups are manufacturers (and affiliated foundations) of tobacco, alcohol, and pharmaceuticals. As one student of Partnership activity notes, "Partnership advertises, in effect, against having chemical competitors to alcohol and tobacco."[146] Nor does Partnership propaganda discuss the competition that marijuana could provide to expensive medical pharmaceuticals.

Partnership's goal is not drug education but drug propaganda. The group states forthrightly that its purpose "is to reduce demand for illegal drugs by using media communication to help bring about public intolerance of illegal drugs, their use and users."[147] In describing anti-drug publicity, drug czar William Bennett's office said, "One laudable example is the Partnership for a Drug-Free America's campaign to encourage negative attitudes toward drugs and to label drug users as unpopular losers."[148] Deputy drug czar Herbert Kleber declared, "The Partnership has changed the attitude of the whole country towards drugs."[149]

Said an observer in 1933, "I would say that Nazi propaganda is much too transparent to work were it not for the fact that it very often does work."[150] A Partnership ad declared, "Boys and girls used to use straws to sip sodas at the drug store. Now they cut the straws in half and use them to snort drugs deep into their nostrils. Times have changed. Our children need our help."[151] The typical American child does not snort cocaine. The headline of another Partnership ad said, "The last thing an addict needs from you is understanding,"[152] implying addicts need intolerance and hatred, so we need feel no guilt about nurturing such attitudes. Over a picture of a line of cocaine powder, a Partnership headline declared, "To millions of American workers, it's considered a lunch line."[153] In reality, few workers use cocaine during the workday. Errors and distortions in Partnership propaganda have been widely noted by drug policy experts, but the public knows little of these deceptions. A Partnership ad stated that marijuana users showed the same brain-wave pattern as someone in a coma. That statement was incorrect. When challenged, a Partnership spokesperson acknowledged, "We kind of got left standing bare naked on the ice with that one."[154] The huge headline of another ad shouted, "Cocaine can make you blind," but only at the end of many lines of small print anti-drug rhetoric did Partnership reveal the seemingly factual headline as metaphor: "Cocaine really does make you blind to reality."[155] The ad's headline deceived anyone who failed to read all the way through. When asked about a Partnership ad claiming that crack will kill anyone who lacks the enzyme pseudocholinesterase, a scientific consultant to the group admitted that "we have no evidence to support that."[156] Nor did the consultant even know how many people lack the enzyme. A 1990 Partnership ad claimed, "Last year, 15 million Americans used cocaine."[157] The ad, however, was designed in 1987;[158] thus it could not be referring to 1989. The latest authoritative figures available when the ad was run were from a 1988 National Institute on Drug Abuse estimate showing 8.5 million cocaine users, about half the number that Partnership claimed.[159] The ad also claimed that in 1989 "5 million of those who survived required medical help." The actual number of cocaine emergencies treated nationwide was closer to 62,000.[160] Partnership exaggerated the problem by a factor of eighty. When challenged on these numbers, a Partnership spokesperson admitted the numbers were "plain wrong" and suggested they were "extrapolated from a *Newsweek* article or something."[161] Partnership refuses to run ads correcting or retracting factual inaccuracies, so the general public remains unaware of distortions.[162] Aside from errors and distortions, Partnership's campaign ignores truths long known to serious researchers, such as roles that poverty, joblessness, lack of love, and lack of hope play in drug abuse. If a persuasion campaign relies upon emotion and inaccurate data, questions must arise about the campaign's message.

Describing the Partnership campaign as "some of the best advertising I've seen," a Partnership spokesperson declared, "The ads really stick in your mind and get straight to the point."[163]

A distinguished student of Nazi ways noted, "Propaganda is not a substitute for violence, but one of its aspects. The two have the identical purposes of making men amenable to control from above."[164] Partnership's orchestrated campaign of fear propaganda was important in that respect because many persons find fear unbearable, and transform fear into the more comfortable emotion of anger. Promoting fear promotes hatred. And hatred promotes brutality.

By the summer of 1989, the orchestrated hate campaign not only had succeeded in making drug users the nation's number one problem cited by Gallup poll respondents, but seventy-five percent of teens and almost fifty percent of adults said they were ready to volunteer their time to fight the menace. "In key ways today, the American people are in a wartime mode and sense a national emergency in the drug crisis," said George H. Gallup. "The U.S. public overwhelmingly endorses a get-tough approach." Crime, unemployment, and inflation trailed far behind drugs as problems of concern.[165] A CBS News/*New York Times* poll taken at about the same time showed that sixty-four percent of respondents felt drugs were the nation's top problem.[166] "There is virtual unanimity that drugs are the No. 1 problem," said a Missouri county prosecutor.[167] "People are so fed up with the problem they're ready to do anything they can to control it," one Kansas City politician declared.[168] A. M. Rosenthal, a long-time senior executive of the *New York Times* (which carried large amounts of Partnership propaganda) declared,

> Inevitably the time will come when the people of the country will no longer stand for it. They will seek the solution in death penalties and martial force. They will stop caring how many prisoners are crowded into a cell or how they are treated, just as long as they are off the streets. They will support judges and legislators and politicians who understand their sense of hopelessness against drugs and who will support repression as a national policy. Repression will satisfy a totally understandable and justifiable public sense of fury and frustration.[169]

Although Partnership for a Drug-Free America is an umbrella organization for hate rhetoric against drug users, media outlets are fully capable of promoting such rhetoric on their own accord. "'If this is a war,' declared NBC's Tom Brokaw on the subject of drugs, 'we're all soldiers.'"[170] Introducing an anthology of Partnership ads, ABC's Peter Jennings declared that the media "have all joined as partners dedicated to the proposition that not one more person should start using illegal drugs."[171] *Washington Post* publisher Katherine Graham has said, "the media must all get together and do something about this [illegal drug] problem, and these wonderful [Partnership] ads are most effective."[172] Without consulting their columnist, *Post* editors altered a signed opinion piece criticizing Drug Abuse Resistance Education (DARE), a popular school program that has police officers tell young students about drugs, and that enjoys generous funding from public and private sources. The alterations eliminated some criticisms of DARE and introduced praise provided by a DARE representative.[173] In 1990 a Georgia newspaper printed "drug coupons" and asked readers to put the names of possible drug users on the coupons and forward them to the sheriff's department.[174] In 1994 one journalist complained, "For a magazine writer, criticizing the drug war is like disagreeing with your editor—it could mean the end of your career."[175] Recognizing the power of editors, a DEA (Drug Enforcement

Administration) official sent a complaining letter to every local editor who ran a signed opinion piece by columnist William F. Buckley, Jr., in which Buckley had questioned brutal actions taken against marijuana users by the DEA.[176] Although the documentary *The Panama Deception* won an Oscar for its skeptical look at the U.S. arrest of Panama's president for drug dealing, the Public Broadcasting System refused to let American viewers see it.[177]

Media typically give routine coverage to government drug warrior announcements without presenting dissenting views. A companion technique is to refuse media access when dissenters request it. Advocates of reform get few opportunities to make a case in newspapers or on the airwaves, and normally are expected to do so in a debate format—relinquishing part of their time to drug warriors in the interest of "fairness." Such a policy also allows drug warriors to prevent reformers from having access to the public; if a suitable drug warrior will not agree to debate a reformer, then in the interests of fairness the public cannot be allowed to hear the reformer.[178] Although television stations broadcast Partnership propaganda free of charge as a "public service," broadcasters have refused to accept paid commercials offering another viewpoint on this public controversy.[179] Aside from evidence of media bias, such behavior demonstrates a religious fervor where believers in the drug war need to hear continual praise. Such a need suggests that despite outward bluster, believers have so many doubts about their conduct that they cannot confront questions about it.

Such attitudes are shared even by research institutions. Although most careful scientists who study illicit drugs share a consensus that dangers and effects are grossly exaggerated by drug warriors, most funding for research on drug users comes from agencies promoting the drug war, and they are more accommodating to research proposals that will probably support the agencies' mission. Federal rules explicitly forbid government funding for some types of research challenging drug war dogma, such as investigation of whether AIDS risk can be reduced by providing sterile injection equipment to intravenous drug addicts.[180] The Reagan administration sought to stop federal funding of any scientific project examining social origins of drug abuse.[181] The gravy train for scientists promoting the drug war is no less lucrative in money and fame than the anti-Jewish gravy train that scientists clambered aboard in the Third Reich.

If research challenging the drug war is permitted, getting the research findings published in mainstream scientific journals is difficult. Some scientific journals, like the popular media, seem to have an editorial policy promoting the drug war. Analysts examined "cocaine baby" research reports in files of the Society of Pediatric Research. In eighty-one percent of reports claiming that cocaine harmed fetal development, medical personnel failed to determine if the pregnant women used cocaine. In seventy-five percent of reports claiming that cocaine caused no harm to fetal development, the scientists confirmed cocaine use by the pregnant women. Despite additional factors making reports of cocaine's benign effect on fetal development more reliable than "cocaine baby" reports, the analysts found that medical journals generally refused to publish reports that pregnant women could safely use cocaine. The analysts concluded that journals preferred politically correct reports that would help scientists get research grants from government agencies.[182]

In addition to promoting inaccurate perceptions of drug use, political bias in scientific journals has a more insidious peril. Scientific rhetoric can camouflage the political basis of research and shield it from the wide scrutiny that political claims must normally withstand. Reporters, columnists, and citizens who would skeptically dissect statements from a president or senator may naively accept statements from "drug scientists." Camouflage provided by scientific rhetoric enabled outrageous claims from "racial scientists" to be accepted not only in Nazi Germany but in areas of the world free from totalitarian inhibitions on dialogue.[183] In the United States, some scientists fear personal consequences from honest reporting about illicit drugs: "One of the people we asked to write for this book replied that after long thought he had to decline, because he feared the effect on his ability to support himself and his family if he said what he really thought about psychedelic drugs."[184] One of the world's foremost experts on heroin reported, "The Department of Justice banned my book, *The Great Drug War*, from inclusion on a government archive computer disk that contained a wide array of recent significant drug research. . . . A department official explained to an amazed friend that the book had to be stricken from this allegedly objective group of writings because, he had discovered, 'it disagreed with government policy.'"[185] After federally funded researchers found the DARE program to be both ineffective and a drain on funding for better school programs, DARE fought against publication of the report, and the Justice Department refused to publish the research results. The director of the Center for Research in Law and Justice at the University of Illinois–Chicago described DARE's action as "repugnant, out of line and very unusual." After the *American Journal of Public Health* obtained the report and decided to print it, "DARE tried to interfere with the publication," a *Journal* spokesperson told a reporter. "They tried to intimidate us."[186] When a Joint Chiefs of Staff think tank found no link between heroin supplies and crime rates, the authoritative report was not published.[187] Indeed, the text of the federal Anti-Drug Abuse Act of 1988 implies that any scientific support for drug legalization will be ignored by lawmakers: "The Congress finds that legalization of illegal drugs, on the Federal or State level, is an unconscionable surrender in a war in which, for the future of our country and the lives of our children, there can be no substitute for total victory."[188] An editor at one book publishing house expressed personal support for the drug war and told me that a manuscript questioning the drug war, no matter how well done, would be rejected. Reformers sometimes even have trouble being heard at formal conferences having nothing to do with drug policy. Eric Sterling, president of the Criminal Justice Policy Foundation, was asked to be a panel member at a federal conference on violence. As Sterling was about to mount the stage, organizers told him that they had learned he supported drug law reform, and asked him to excuse himself from the panel.[189]

Even if drug law reformers manage to present their research findings to public policy makers, those officials are largely indifferent to facts about the issue. A senior official in one state frankly told me that he was simply demagoguing the issue to get votes. Prosecutors at the Nuremberg trials noted a similar attitude among Nazi conspirators, in which they promoted anti-Semitism not because they were concerned about a Jewish problem but because they felt anti-Semitism would be politically popular.[190]

Drug warriors sneer that talk of drug legalization is trendy, but their claim is rhetoric designed to make fellow warriors feel embattled and thereby whip up support for harsher measures. As an advocate of drug law reform, I give public presentations. In one instance a group of Quakers continually heckled me, their faces twisted like gargoyles as they shouted their hatred. When I noted that the law permitted someone with a marijuana cigarette to be imprisoned for life, one Friend yelled in fury that if such was the law, then it must be enforced—this from a member of a sect famed for its resistance to inhumane law. Another Friend angrily insisted that if drug users denied they were sick, they should be restrained and forced to undergo psychotherapy until cured—this from a lesbian who might easily be targeted for similar treatment because of her sexual identity. As I watched an assembly of pacifist social activists begin to congeal into a mob with its anger directed at me, I did not feel I was part of a trendy and popular movement.

I did feel I was witnessing a result of years of continual hate propaganda. Without such vilification, the war on drug users would be impossible, because citizens would recoil from persecuting people no different from themselves. Drug war propagandists serve the same function that Nazi propagandists served, a function judged harshly at Nuremberg.

The level of hatred against drug users is so great, one federal judge privately told me, that no drug defendant can get a fair trial. Yet I am unaware of this jurist ever making such a statement in open court, where it would shield a defendant from unjust conviction. The level of hatred against drug users is so great that a sitting judge is willing to pass sentence upon defendants who he believes have not received a fair trial. Such attitudes powered the Holocaust.

We have now seen how drug users are identified by science, law, and popular rhetoric. Despite scientific descriptions showing drug users to be ordinary people, law and rhetoric mesh in finding false and arbitrary ways to distinguish those ordinary people from fellow citizens. Although those irrelevant and even imaginary characteristics of drug use may be factually invalid, they serve the social purpose of placing drug users apart from everyone else. Once a group can be identified, it can be targeted for destruction. Hate propaganda such as we have seen in this chapter is an element of ostracism, and ostracism's crucial role in the destruction process is the topic of our next chapter.

2

OSTRACISM

> In the name of a united nation the all-inclusive Third Reich is erecting
> a social and spiritual quarantine as dividing as medieval walls.
>   Anne O'Hare McCormick, 1933[1]

Having seen how a group of ordinary people is identified so it can be destroyed,
we are ready to consider another element of the destruction process: ostracism.
The hate propaganda we examined in the previous chapter not only serves to
identify victims. Its defamations promote public loathing of victims, nurturing an
atmosphere where acts of ostracism become natural. Ostracism seeks to prevent
the targeted group from surviving in normal society. Ostracism can come from
private individuals, such as employers who fire competent drug users. Ostracism
can also come from government, through means such as laws directing physicians
to violate professional confidentiality by reporting patients' illicit drug use to state
authorities. Restricting access to employment and health care are just two of
many ways to impede survival. In this chapter we shall examine how drug
warriors use private boycott and public law to prevent drug users from surviving
in normal society.

Ostracizing a group of ordinary people requires techniques that conflict with
American legal tradition. In another book, I have explored the Nazi legal system.
Its principles are alien to American tradition but have begun to appear, one
principle at a time, in drug law enforcement. Supreme Court Justice Robert H.
Jackson warned, "The principle then lies about like a loaded weapon ready for
the hand of any authority that can bring forward a plausible claim of an urgent
need. Every repetition imbeds that principle more deeply in our law and thinking
and expands it to new purposes. All who observe the work of courts are familiar
with what Judge Cardozo described as 'the tendency of a principle to expand
itself to the limit of its logic.'"[2] If a Nazi principle is accepted in one type of

litigation, judges will apply it to others as well. The logic of Nazi jurisprudence corrodes traditional American legal guarantees because these serve a legal system whose fundamentals differ from those of Nazi law. As more Nazi fundamentals are adopted, assorted democratic guarantees become irrelevant and disappear. In Germany loss of those guarantees eventually corrupted all law enforcement.

LOSS OF LEGAL RIGHTS

Attacks on civil liberties are basic if ordinary people are to be destroyed. Attacks have two premises. First, civil liberties interfere with the destruction effort and must be eliminated. Second, civil liberties are inherently undesirable because they give citizens power to affect government actions. For Nazis the second premise was the more important one. But they publicized the first premise to generate public support for repeal of civil liberties. Rhetoric inflamed the public about alleged danger from Jews so that fear would overcome normal scruples. Actions that are otherwise intolerable can become popular when portrayed as emergency war measures. German leaders used the war on Jews as a smoke screen to generate public support for actions that eventually put all citizens at the mercy of a totalitarian regime.

American drug warriors use a two-track approach to weaken civil liberties. One track exempts drug users from civil liberties protecting other citizens. An additional track expands the definition of drug user. That expansion occurs in two directions. One direction lengthens the list of illegal drugs, so last year's legal conduct becomes illegal this year. The other direction uses new technology to improve detection of drug use in a person's body. For example, Friday night use of marijuana was undetectable by police on a Monday morning in the 1950s, but in the 1990s police body fluid analysis can reveal use. Such technology can increase the pool of victims even if marijuana use declines in the general population. By expanding both the list of illegal drugs and the means to detect their presence in a human body, officials sweep up persons who were once left alone. By stripping civil liberties from more and more citizens, government officials gain more and more power to act on any subject without regard to citizens' desires.

That gain in power is not coincidental to the drug war. The gain is intended by top drug warriors. As with German leaders in the war on Jews, American leaders in the war on drug users find civil liberties inherently undesirable. Unfortunately, too many citizens agree. Many find authoritarianism comforting, liberating them from the stress of making personal decisions about right and wrong. To be righteous, all a person has to do is follow orders. Dictatorships typically enjoy huge popular support.

In evaluating drug warrior attacks on civil liberties, we should first pause to remember why the Bill of Rights exists. It exists because American colonists were so outraged by British police conduct that they overthrew the government. The revolution was a shoot-out with the police. Patriots did not risk their property and their lives for misty ideals. Patriots acted to save themselves from destruction by their own government. A few years later when proponents of a strong national government got the U.S. Constitution adopted, the public immediately demanded a Bill of Rights to ensure that the new regime could never engage in abuses that were standard British procedure.

There is a reason why patriots of the 1700s prized civil liberties so highly. That reason is illustrated by what happened in Germany when the Nazi government repealed civil liberties. A regime that wishes to eliminate guarantees protecting property and lives is a regime that is up to no good. If a regime must attack citizens' property and lives to achieve its goals, the regime merits replacement. Civil liberties are a trip wire alarm against evil.

Evil can appear suddenly, as when Nazis started their regime with wholesale repeal of civil liberties. Or evil can appear so gradually that it seems as normal as smog. Loss of American civil liberties in the name of drugs has been so incremental that some persons can scarcely believe how far drug warriors have moved us toward a totalitarian regime, with assent from judges "so enamored of jurisprudence that they did not even notice that a travesty of justice was being put over."[3]

Because drug warriors so often portray civil liberties as lawyers' tricks used to get defendants out of jail, we often forget that civil liberties are intended to prevent groundless arrest in the first place. Mere arrest can devastate an ordinary citizen. After arrest "police could well be calling all the people in your phone book or professional database, asking if they know you and, when they respond yes, asking them such questions as, 'Do you know anything about this person's involvement with drugs. . . ?'"[4] Explaining one's absence from work can be a problem.

> In all likelihood, your boss already knows. The friendly detectives from the police department have probably already visited your boss, asking if you had behaved in any "unusual" ways which might indicate that you were involved in drugs. . . . In all likelihood, you will be fired. If you argue (quite correctly) that you haven't been convicted of anything, and that one is, in our country, innocent until proven guilty, the boss will probably vaguely refer to something such as "Where there's smoke, there's fire," or "At our company, we can't even risk the *hint* of impropriety."[5]

Such can be immediate consequences of drug squad civil liberty abuses.

One civil liberty under attack is free speech. As noted already, drug war opponents are denied means of communication routinely granted to drug warriors. This denial comes from a private boycott, but that boycott is nearly as effective as denial by government order.

In addition to private boycott, government restrictions on free speech are growing. A classic subterfuge is to bring criminal charges against someone who speaks out against the drug war. As some of President Clinton's cabinet choices discovered, upstanding citizens can easily be in violation of some law. In 1993 the U.S. Attorney in St. Louis issued a press release about a guilty plea in a marijuana case. The amount of marijuana was so small that observers could scarcely believe the offense merited federal action, let alone a press release publicizing it. The press release incorrectly claimed the accused person was St. Louis coordinator for the National Organization for the Reform of Marijuana Laws (NORML).[6] Skeptics suggested that prosecution of the hapless defendant was intended to cripple NORML's St. Louis activity and damage NORML by implying that it is a criminal organization. A letter to the editor questioning antimarijuana laws irked an Idaho drug squad, which went to the letter writer's residence, searched the writer's trash, and arrested the writer when marijuana stems were found. A police spokesman explained that only a person who is a law violator would seek change in the law[7] (an interesting attitude, considering that police and prosecutors continually seek changes in law). Although the official charge was marijuana possession, the Idaho writer was punished for his speech. Similar thinking was seen in 1935 when the SS journal *Das Schwarze Korps* and the Ministry of Justice journal *Die Deutsche Justiz* called for punishment of Jews who complained about a boycott action against Jewish businesses.[8] Punishment not for thwarting the boycott, but just for complaining about it. Prosecution of an Aryan for a 10-pfennig purchase violating the boycott occurred in part because he questioned the policy of zero tolerance for commerce with Jews.[9] When using criminal violations as a subterfuge to punish Americans for questioning the drug war, police follow a well-established model. And the Idaho incident did have a chilling effect on free speech. A newspaper columnist wrote of a Missouri woman who, because of the Idaho action, became afraid to speak against the drug war lest she become a target of police harassment.[10] Such concern is not theoretical. Two days after an Arkansas woman gave a television presentation on legal commercial uses of hemp (which comes from the same plant that yields marijuana), police raided her home on the basis of an alleged anonymous accusation that she possessed marijuana. Despite a thorough search, police found no marijuana. Said the woman afterward, "For a lot of people with jobs and children, they're so afraid that if they speak out at all, those things will be taken away from them. This is part of the way they're keeping people from voicing their opinions, standing up, and trying to change marijuana laws."[11]

Civil forfeitures, discussed in the next chapter, can be used to suppress speech. Missouri police and prosecutors have routinely seized cars and other valuable property of persons later found innocent of any drug law violation. To get the property back, the innocent owner may have to sign an agreement to refrain from criticizing authorities.[12]

Criminal investigations can serve as punishment even if no charges are filed. A U.S. congressman got the Internal Revenue Service to investigate NORML, thereby requiring it to divert some of its limited resources to the IRS inquiry. The reason for investigation was the congressman's anger at NORML's willingness to provide factual information about urine testing, information that could be used to affect test results.[13] Distributing facts about human biology was punished with a government investigation of NORML's finances. In the 1980s, someone was convicted of aiding PCP manufacturing by taking out an advertisement offering information on how the drug is produced.[14] Distributing facts about chemistry is now a felony.

A Drug Enforcement Administration agent described the marijuana information magazine *Sinsemilla Tips* as equivalent to child pornography, and accused the publisher of "hiding behind the First Amendment." Unable to close the magazine by fiat, the DEA raided and harassed the magazine's advertisers, cutting off revenue the magazine needed to stay in business. Eventually the DEA threatened the publisher with criminal prosecution, but said no charges would be filed if the publisher "voluntarily" agreed to close the magazine.[15] The publication folded. The marijuana information magazine *High Times* was victimized by the same tactic. Drug agents explicitly told the owner of a raided garden store, "Your advertisement in *High Times* is what got you in trouble." The garden store owner asked whether such advertising could possibly be illegal and was told, "After today it won't be. [*High Times*] will be closed." The DEA later expressed astonishment when it received an inquiry from the magazine, astonishment because the DEA thought the publication no longer existed.[16] After the raids on advertisers, two-thirds of them removed their business from the magazine. Even customers of *High Times* advertisers were harassed. DEA agents smashed through the door of a customer who was an orchid grower and, backed up by automatic weapons they displayed, confiscated the orchids as "evidence." The search warrant for one garden store raid said the owner's discussion of tomato growing with undercover DEA operatives was cause to suspect illegal drug activity in the store, because "tomatoes" could be a code word for marijuana.[17] Drug agents argued that purchase of garden equipment from merchants advertising in *High Times* justified searches. Identical ads for the equipment appeared in *Greenhouse Grower*, *Fish Monthly*, and *Soilless Grower*. Customers included Kent State University, Lockheed's missile division, and the U.S. embassy in Russia.[18] Perhaps the motive for attacks on *High Times* was best articulated by a Montana police chief who asked local merchants to stop selling the magazine: "The point of the magazine is, 'Hey, let's make pot legal.'"[19]

Drug warriors do not always rely on subterfuge to restrict speech. Sometimes they take direct action. Federal drug czar Robert Martinez threatened to cut off $120 million in federal grants to Stanford University if it failed to dismiss a lecturer who criticized the drug war and who provoked authorities by claiming to be a drug user. Stanford fired the lecturer.[20] Legislation repeatedly introduced in the Missouri legislature during the 1990s sought to punish record dealers with up to life imprisonment for selling phonograph records with lyrics that "might" describe drug use.[21] In 1990 the initial draft of the federal Omnibus Crime Bill declared that questioning the president's drug war policies was treason, subject to standard punishments for that offense.[22] Drug warriors sought to make this book a crime.

Drug warriors have gone further yet, with "imitation controlled substances" laws. These laws criminalize intellectual belief. If a person buys a legal substance such as oregano but believes it to be marijuana, the person is subjected to penalties for marijuana possession although the actual substance is legal.[23] California law even eliminated the requirement that authorities produce physical evidence in such a case.[24] The drug war has introduced thought crime to American jurisprudence. Arguments used for imprisoning people because of their beliefs about drugs can also be used for imprisoning people because of their beliefs about other things. Moreover, arguments used to prohibit harmless personal drug consumption in the privacy of one's own home can also serve to prohibit harmless religious observances at home; Nazis used such arguments for that very purpose. Indeed, the drug war has already mixed criminal sanctions with religion. Many courts order drug users to enter so-called twelve-step programs, which require participants to profess spiritual belief.[25]

Aside from attacks on speech questioning the drug war, government officials use the drug war to attack free speech in general. DEA's acting administrator told Congress, "On the Freedom of Information Act, of course, we are still looking for reform of that area. . . . As you know, it has been a tremendous burden on law enforcement. Of the requests under the Freedom of Information Act and Privacy Act, 60 percent are coming to DEA from the criminal element. . . . We are just overwhelmed by the requests."[26] In addition to the burden free speech imposes on government resources, a deputy associate attorney general told Congress that drug violators use the Freedom of Information Act to learn of investigations against them.[27] Perhaps we shall next be told that foreign spies are using the act to obtain secrets. Drug warriors are forthright about the threat free speech poses to their vision of America.

Houses, personal effects, and physical bodies of Americans were once protected from violation by government agents unless they first observed suspicious conduct or obtained a search warrant after convincing a judge that they would probably find evidence of a law violation. "Framers of the Fourth Amendment were deeply suspicious of warrants," U.S. Supreme Court Justice John Paul Stevens has said. "In their minds the paradigm of an abusive search was the execution of a warrant not based on probable cause,"[28] that is, not based on trustworthy knowledge that a crime has occurred. When writing of the Fourth Amendment, U.S. Supreme Court Justice Robert H. Jackson recalled his experience as a prosecutor at the Nuremberg trials. He said rights against unreasonable search

> are not mere second-class rights but belong in the catalog of indispens-
> able freedoms. Among deprivations of rights, none is so effective in
> cowing a population, crushing the spirit of the individual and putting
> terror in every heart. Uncontrolled search and seizure is one of the first
> and most effective weapons in the arsenal of every arbitrary govern-
> ment. And one need only briefly to have dwelt and worked among a
> people possessed of many admirable qualities but deprived of these
> rights to know that the human personality deteriorates and dignity and
> self-reliance disappear where homes, persons and possessions are
> subject at any hour to unheralded search and seizure by the police.

Jackson said the only protection that citizens have against such arbitrary police state conduct is the exclusion of illegally obtained evidence from criminal proceedings.[29]

In the name of drugs, however, the U.S. Supreme Court removed this protection during the 1980s. The Court ruled that evidence obtained through an invalid search warrant could be used in trials.[30] Police no longer have to demonstrate probable cause to conduct a search; if a magistrate grants a warrant without probable cause, the search is now valid even if the warrant is not. In dissent to this decision, Justices William J. Brennan and Thurgood Marshall declared that the court decided to "give way to the seductive call of expediency" in drug law enforcement and that "the vital guarantees of the Fourth Amendment are reduced to nothing more than a 'form of words.'"[31] Justice Stevens added, "It is the very purpose of a Bill of Rights to identify values that may not be sacrificed to expediency."[32] Nonetheless, even the Supreme Court's blanket authorization of judicial search warrants without probable cause proved insufficient for drug squads. In the 1990s the Drug Enforcement Administration began issuing administrative search warrants, in which police could authorize themselves to make a search without approval from a judge.[33] In a 1990 drug case, the U.S. Supreme Court examined the Fourth Amendment's guarantee that "the people" shall not be subject to unreasonable searches and declared that the phrase "'the people' seems to have been a term of art" and the Fourth Amendment's reference to "the people" does not mean its protection applies to anyone facing criminal proceedings.[34] A century earlier, Justice Joseph P. Bradley warned against such parsing. "Illegitimate and unconstitutional practices get their first footing . . . by silent approaches and slight deviations from legal modes of procedure. This can only be obviated by adhering to the rule that constitutional provisions for the security of person and property should be liberally construed. A close and literal construction deprives them of half their efficacy, and leads to gradual depreciation of the right."[35]

Expedient searches can be physically degrading. In the 1940s, two sheriff's deputies saw a suspect put a pill in his mouth, leaped upon him, pried open his mouth, and choked him to prevent him from swallowing. Failing in those efforts, the deputies took the handcuffed suspect to a medical facility, had him strapped to a table, and over his protests had a physician force the suspect to vomit. After the pill was recovered from the suspect's body, he was convicted of drug possession. The U.S. Supreme Court overturned the conviction, with Justice Felix Frankfurter angrily calling the police actions unconscionable in a free society.[36] Times have changed. In 1985 the U.S. Supreme Court ruled that government agents have authority to hold a person incommunicado, without access to family or legal advice, until the person obeys the agents' order to defecate into a waste basket while they watch, so the feces may be examined for evidence of drug law violation. This authority exists without agents having to show probable cause for suspecting a violation.[37] Noting U.S. Supreme Court approval of "indefinite involuntary incommunicado detentions 'for investigation,'" Justices Marshall and Brennan described such practices as "staggering" and "the hallmark of a police state."[38]

Personal degradation in the drug war extends beyond providing samples of one's body to government agents. With cooperation of school authorities, Indiana police sealed a junior and senior high school complex. Police searched every student and every student's locker for drugs. Several female students were strip-searched; no drugs were found on them. Out of the nearly 3,000 students searched, no drug contraband was found among the junior high students, and just over a dozen high schoolers had marijuana, "drug paraphernalia," or beer. The demeaning raid was filmed by local television. Indignant parents filed a lawsuit. A court ruled that being a junior or senior high school student was sufficient grounds to suspect a child of being a drug law violator, thus searches of students by police require neither a warrant nor observation of suspicious conduct. The U.S. Supreme Court let the ruling stand.[39]

In the 1980s school districts announced mandatory blood and urine tests for all students, with results to be turned over to police.[40] Missouri legislators introduced bills to exempt school officials from civil liability for violating students' civil rights in this regard.[41] One school system made possession of aspirin a suspension offense. A Reagan drug war official who helped write that rule explained that aspirin tablets might contain LSD.[42] At one high school a student was suspended for five days because a teacher saw her give two Midol tablets to a friend experiencing menstrual distress: The school had a zero tolerance policy for possession of nonprescription drugs.[43] Antics of President Jimmy Carter's brother Billy inspired one family to have an unopened can of Billy Beer as souvenir. When a child took the can to her third grade class as a show-and-tell item, she was suspended and directed to receive counseling for illicit possession of alcohol.[44] Drug czar William Bennett demanded especially heavy criminal punishment of children who sell drugs near schools, in order to "prevent dealers from utilizing underage 'drug runners' to circumvent the law."[45] Two analysts of Bennett's policy noted, "It is difficult to think of an appropriate comment on the deviousness of a proposal to punish children in order to discommode the adults who are exploiting them."[46]

The U.S. Supreme Court has ruled that ordinary acts such as traveling on a Greyhound bus are reasonable cause for a drug squad search of all passengers and luggage (Florida v. Bostick, 111 S.Ct. 2382 (1991)). A joker clause in that ruling supposedly upheld the Fourth Amendment's guarantee that citizens and their effects shall be free from unreasonable search—the Supreme Court said that any bus passenger could object to being searched for drugs. The practical effect of such a right to object is nil. Police who conduct Greyhound searches say that refusal of "voluntary" cooperation is deemed suspicious.[47] How many Greyhound passengers will have the courage to say no to cops? And how many have read Florida v. Bostick, 111 S.Ct. 2382 (1991)? Whether drug squads even care is questionable:

> As the officer in charge ascended our front porch steps I again denied him permission to enter the house [without a search warrant]. He opened the door and while stepping through chanted: "Do I have permission to enter? Yes, I do, thank-you."
> "No! You do not have permission to enter!" I screamed.
> "Fine, that's how it will be written in the report."[48]

After a rental Cadillac was stopped for speeding, police asked the driver to consent to a search of the car. A passenger, who was an attorney and identified himself as such, advised the officer that a search was impermissible unless the driver was being arrested. The officer maintained that an innocent person would not object to a search. Reinforcements were called in, and the car occupants were held for a half hour while a drug-sniffing dog was en route. They were forced to stand in the rain while the dog explored the car. No drugs were found.[49] The innocent people were held because police use the Fourth Amendment as a way of testing guilt, not as a check against groundless suspicions. "The citizen's choice is quietly to submit to whatever the officers undertake or to resist at risk of arrest or immediate violence." That was Justice Jackson's earlier analysis of such a situation.[50] A criminologist who witnessed a search agreed. "We may ask why the suspect did not assert his legal rights and demand a search warrant as soon as the door was opened. . . . He was physically coerced (albeit by indirection, since no actual violence was used). Five physically well-constituted, armed men (plus one middle-sized unarmed professor) broke in unexpectedly and stood around with no-nonsense looks on their faces. At that moment, it would have taken an act of heroism to order them out."[51] "Listen," said one blameless person harassed by such a search, "I was a black man traveling alone up in the mountains of Eagle County and surrounded by four police officers. I was going to be as cooperative as I could." Officers delayed him for nearly an hour while going through his belongings.[52] He got off lucky. Searches can take much longer, and can include partial disassembly of a vehicle—which officers may or may not reassemble for the owner.

Justice Jackson warned that such warrantless searches "may be exercised by the most unfit and ruthless officers as well as by the fit and responsible," and added, "We must remember that the extent of any privilege of search and seizure without warrant which we sustain, the officers interpret and apply themselves and will push to the limit."[53] Indeed, regarding the bus searches, a Florida court noted,

> The evidence in this cause has evoked images of other days, under other flags, when no man traveled his nation's roads or railways without fear of unwarranted interruption, by individuals who held temporary power in the Government. The spectre of American citizens being asked, by badge-wielding police, for identification, travel papers—in short a *raison d'etre*—is foreign to *any* fair reading of the Constitution and its guarantee of human liberties. This is not Hitler's Berlin.[54]

Drug war rulings that citizens can exercise a civil liberty if they are aware of it actually take the liberty away. Missouri police who wish to search a private automobile for drugs routinely tell a motorist, "We have to search your car, okay?" Few motorists realize their assent transforms illegal harassment into a lawful police investigation. The Fourth Amendment is supposed to prevent certain activities by government agents, not allow such activities until a knowledgeable and courageous citizen refuses to cooperate. Viewing the Fourth Amendment as a rule of court procedure misses its point. The Fourth Amendment is supposed to guarantee that police will never delay a Greyhound bus and hold all its passengers simply to satisfy a local constable's idle curiosity about whether any drugs might be on board. When the Fourth Amendment no longer assures that law-abiding citizens can travel unmolested and without delay, a substantial loss of civil liberties has occurred. U.S. Supreme Court Justice Jackson wrote in 1949:

> Only occasional and more flagrant abuses come to the attention of the courts, and then only those where the search and seizure yields incriminating evidence and the defendant is at least sufficiently compromised to be indicted. If the officers raid a home, an office, or stop and search an automobile but find nothing incriminating, this invasion of the personal liberty of the innocent too often finds no practical redress. There may be, and I am convinced that there are, many unlawful searches of innocent people which turn up nothing incriminating, in which no arrest is made, about which courts do nothing, and about which we never hear.[55]

A search of 100 buses produced seven drug arrests.[56] That is seven accusations, not seven convictions. Denver police estimated they searched 2,000 air travellers in 1990. They arrested 49. A drug squad at the Pittsburgh airport searched 527 air travellers in 1990, and arrested 49. Buffalo, New York, drug agents searched 600 air travelers in 1989, and arrested 10. Nashville authorities refused to provide search numbers, saying "It might stir up the public and make the airport officials unhappy because we are somehow harassing people. It would be great if we could keep the whole operation secret."[57] Using the drug offender profile, in 1989 Houston drug agents handcuffed 60 airport travelers and took them to a hospital, for X-rays to determine whether they were smuggling drug containers inside their bodies. X-ray exams exonerated 56 of them.[58] In 1985 Justices Marshall and Brennan noted that travelers subjected to degrading drug searches were typically innocent.

> One physician who at the request of customs officials conducted many "internal searches"—rectal and vaginal examinations and stomach pumping—estimated that he had found contraband in only 15 to 20 percent of the persons he had examined. It has similarly been estimated that only 16 percent of women subjected to body-cavity searches at the

border were in fact found to be carrying contraband. It is precisely to minimize the risk of harassing so many innocent people that the Fourth Amendment requires the intervention of a judicial officer.[59]

In a state judicial decision upholding courtroom use of drug evidence obtained by "unlawfully assaulting, battering, torturing and falsely imprisoning the defendant," the court said the way to discourage such conduct is for victims to file civil suit against drug squad officers.[60] Gung-ho officers, however, face no deterrent from civil suits: "A federal jury found that a search of a woman's body cavities for drugs by Pampas, Texas police violated her civil rights, but absolved the city of liability and awarded the woman no money."[61] A criminologist agreed about lack of practical redress: "If a policeman can give some reason to his *organizational superiors* (including the district attorney) for conducting a search, in practice the worst punishment he can suffer is loss of a conviction. If a search yields no incriminating evidence, those who are illegally searched are usually pleased to drop the matter."[62]

The drug war's notion that a citizen can sign away Fourth Amendment rights upon a government agent's demand is mischievous. Amendments Thirteen and Nineteen are written as forcefully as Amendment Four. As part of a plea bargain, can a citizen agree to be sold into slavery? To save the family home from forfeiture, can a mother agree not to vote again? Court rulings inspired by the drug war suggest that the answer is yes.

Another loss of former Fourth Amendment rights is transformation of medical records into police records. Medical records may be in the custody of a physician, but they are the property of patients who paid serious money to generate those records. In the name of drugs, laws direct physicians to give government agents access to that patient property. Patients may not even know that their property, as intimate as a diary, is being examined by government agents.

The drug war has eliminated the Fourth Amendment's former guarantee that citizens' houses are to be secure against penetration by government agents. Because the U.S. Supreme Court has ruled that an anonymous telephoned accusation is sufficient grounds to issue a search warrant,[63] only government agents of unusual incompetence are unable to generate sufficient grounds to enter any house. A student of Nazi police methods wrote, "Even anonymous tips were usually followed up, and significantly enough, whether the name of the accuser would (if available) be made public was left to the police. In other words, the extent to which an individual had recourse to legal defence, even when the charges were false or carelessly laid, was determined by the Gestapo."[64]

When drug war police inform a judge of an anonymous accusation against a citizen, the judge thereby has permission to issue a warrant for police to search the citizen's residence. These searches are indistinguishable from Nazi raids, involving physical and verbal abuse of house occupants while accompanied by massive destruction of personal property. Someone targeted in a raid recalled, "One thing I've noticed about the police is that they get very hyper at times like these. Some of them were shaking like a leaf, they were so excited."[65] A witness to one raid reported that after bursting through a front door, one officer used an axe to demolish the door from inside. In the same raid, after the witness saw a suspect knocked unconscious, one officer continued to strike the unconscious man in the head.[66] Eighty members of a Los Angeles drug squad used sledgehammers to search two duplex units for drugs. After demolishing the units, officers found only a small quantity. They left behind a spray-painted sign, "LAPD RULES."[67]

Normally such conduct becomes awkward only when drug squads hit the wrong person or wrong address. A couple at a root beer drive-in was terrorized by drug officers who erroneously thought the couple might have received illicit drugs. "A man grabbed me with both hands around the neck . . . and started to squeeze. Another grabbed a handful of my hair and yanked out a handful of it. . . . I think I swore at them, and the fellow who had been choking me said, 'Watch it, buddy, or it will get tougher. You haven't seen anything yet.'" Afterwards a police spokesperson commented, "Well, we just can't be right all the time."[68] In one "search" of a wrong address, "doors were ripped off cabinets, televisions were overturned and an air-conditioning unit was uprooted. . . . According to the couple, police smashed the toilet into small pieces, pulled drawers out of the bedroom dresser, pulled objects off shelves and dumped the contents of boxes and containers. The house was in chaos Friday. Powdered detergent, beans and artificial bacon bits had been dumped on the kitchen floor. Dishes, pots and pans had been strewn about."[69] Compare to a Nazi search: "Gestapo men turned the whole place upside down. They pulled out drawers and tore the beds apart. They even emptied the salt container onto the table and poked through the ashes in the stove, searching for something they could use to incriminate my father." Another Gestapo search: "They even sifted through the salt box—it looked like Sodom and Gomorrah when they got done."[70] A child's memory of a Nazi visit in 1938: "Men were standing there with axes in their hands, all dressed in black. They ran around axing all our furniture and throwing things out the window. They smashed the closet door and broke all my toys."[71] A child's memory of an American police visit in 1990: "I saw people standing in the hall and others running into the kitchen and upstairs. I didn't know what was going on. Next thing I knew, I was at the police station getting yelled at all the time. They kept asking me questions. I kept telling them I didn't know. . . . After returning home I found most of my toys and things were broken or missing. They haven't been replaced because Mom and Dad can't afford it and the cops say they didn't do it."[72] Police have been known to urinate on property they leave behind.[73]

Federal agents boarded a university professor's boat and searched the engine with a fire axe, split open the fuel tank, drilled thirty holes through the hull above and below the waterline, and tore out the interior woodwork. Finding nothing, the agents allowed the owner to have the boat back. The $24,000 craft was a total loss.[74] Victims reported that masked members of a Texas drug squad, dressed in black and brandishing automatic weapons, smashed into two homes in a predawn raid and terrorized the families. The raid, however, had been conducted at the wrong addresses.[75] An innocent victim in Illinois saw "men running up the hall dressed like hippies with pistols, yelling and screeching. I turned to my wife. 'God, honey, we're dead.'" The federal narcs held the couple in bed at gunpoint. After tying up the man, one agent put a pistol to the victim's head and warned, "You're going to die unless you tell us where the stuff is." A later report of the incident noted books strewn on the floor and garments torn from hangers. Law officers departed after their leader realized their error.[76] When a drug squad bashed through the door of another innocent Illinois family's home, the crippled mother fainted. The narcs stopped her spouse from helping her and held one child at gunpoint to thwart the child's attempt to phone for help. After the fruitless house search was completed, the mother received emergency therapy at a mental hospital. The drug squad explained that they could make mistakes; they were human after all.[77] "I was asleep about three A.M.," said yet another innocent Illinois victim, "when the agents rushed in and pushed me against the wall." While they put a gun to his head, "walls were smashed and windows were broken, and stereo equipment, a shotgun, golf clubs, and a camera were confiscated." The victim was held incommunicado for over three days, forbidden even to contact a lawyer while police interrogated him. They never told him what crime he was suspected of, and eventually released him without filing charges. Police had searched the wrong address.[78] FBI agents, who are sometimes more restrained in raids, nonetheless did $350 worth of damage when they simply smashed through the front door of a residence without asking to be let in. Being at the wrong address, they failed to find anything they were looking for, and apparently spent time listening to the absent occupant's audio cassettes and watching a videotape. Said the astonished resident, "I just wonder how many other mistakes they made." Had the FBI hit the right address, the owner would have been punished with the $350 expense of repairing the door regardless of whether charges resulted from the search; in the present case the FBI offered to help pay for the damage.[79] We have no reason to believe drug squads behave differently when they attack the wrong residence than when they strike the intended one.

In contrast to chaos occurring when officers have suspects in custody and have all the time needed for leisurely inspection, consider what a criminologist observed while accompanying a drug squad's surreptitious illegal search of a room when the occupant might return unannounced at any moment: "The officers, who by my observation were skilled at searching without changing the appearance of the room, had been looking mainly through drawers. They rearranged the little they had upset and the three of us went downstairs."[80] Clearly, vandalism is unnecessary while conducting a search and is instead intended as extralegal punishment of victims. One prosecutor admitted as much:

> When you ask for a warrant knowing that it's going to be quashed, when you know it's bad to begin with, you can still get one issued in most counties, make the search and have it thrown out later. You've busted in the guy's house and ransacked the joint, or you've impounded his car and torn the insides out of it. So the warrant is quashed, so what? He's off on the charge which was BS to begin with, but you've really made his life miserable.[81]

Vandalism by drug squads is so common that it seldom merits press coverage. Typically the only mention occurs when squads vandalize an "innocent" citizen's property. "Innocent" is put in quotation marks because *every* instance of vandalism is directed against an innocent person. No case has been proven in court when a raid occurs; the ostensible purpose of the raid is to determine if enough evidence exists even to file charges against someone currently presumed innocent.

Degradation of victims goes beyond physical abuse of property and persons. "At two o'clock Tuesday morning, March 7, I was awakened and faced by two men with pistols, who had come into the house. . . . These two men were accompanied by two others in civilian clothes. . . . My wife asked them to turn about while she dressed, but they refused. She was compelled to remove her night gown at the point of a revolver and stand naked before the intruders. When she protested they said, 'Don't be theatrical'."[82] In another nighttime raid, police rousted a couple from their residence. The woman was clad only in a tee shirt. She obviously had no weapon and could have been placed in a police vehicle if authorities were concerned about an escape attempt. Instead they kept her outdoors and repeatedly ordered her to raise her arms over her head, thereby exposing her buttocks and pubic area to onlookers.[83] One of these raids occurred in the 1930s during the war on Jews. The other occurred in the 1980s during the war on drug users. Similarities in technique were due to similarities in purpose: not merely enforcing the law, but attacking the psyches of targeted victims.

Some victims lose more than their property and dignity. "When they raided us they didn't identify themselves and I thought we were being robbed, so I threw a bottle down the stairs at this guy and he shot me. I caught a dum-dum in the leg which blew apart my femur. I still carry fragments of the bullet."[84] Masked members of a California drug squad raided the home of an elderly man. "The 64-year-old retired ranch foreman suffered bruises and facial cuts when he was pinned to the floor while drug agents tore his house apart." They failed to find the drug manufacturing operation they were seeking on the basis of a false accusation.[85] In what apparently was a midnight raid on the wrong address, a California drug squad shot the innocent resident, causing wounds that required six weeks of intensive care.[86] In another 1992 California raid where officers burst in without identifying themselves, an elderly wife started screaming, "Don't shoot! Don't shoot me!" Her husband suddenly appeared with a handgun, and officers killed him. No illegal drugs were found on their property.[87] Relying solely on the word of a paid informant who later explained he had been so drunk he could not remember the right address, a Boston drug squad raided the home of a retired Methodist preacher and chased him into his bedroom, where three police officers pushed him to the floor: "Boston's coroner said it was a heart attack, brought on by sudden and extreme stress. Rev. Accelyne Williams, a slender 75-year-old man, spent his final moments doubled over, vomiting, his hands bound behind his back with a tight strip of plastic, totally confused about what was happening to him. . . . He had literally been scared to death by shouting, storming anti-drug troops." No drugs were found.[88]

When reviewing accounts of drug squad raids—language used by drug agents, their screaming, their sweating, their frantic physical activity—my impression is less that they are seeking law enforcement than that they are seeking a perverse sexual gratification.

Police and public housing authorities combine forces for mass searches that would be inconceivable in high-rent high-rises. Though less damaging physically than drug squad raids of specific residences, mass searches can bring other types of harm to tenants as buildings are sealed while each apartment undergoes a "housing inspection." One person reported that police forbade him to leave the apartment until it was searched. Hours later the search occurred and the person was allowed to leave—but he had missed a job interview. The search helped keep him unemployed. Some tenants who complain about repairs report that landlords notify police that drug activity is present in the apartment. The drug war becomes a tool in landlord-tenant disputes.[89] These types of mass searches, by authorities using writs of assistance, were a cause of the American Revolution in the 1700s, and helped produce the Fourth Amendment.

Our brief review of drug war effects on the Fourth Amendment shows that the following acts are considered cause to believe a citizen is a criminal: attending high school, traveling on a Greyhound bus, being the target of an anonymous accusation. In the name of drugs, many other acts and personal attributes now indicate criminal activity and comprise a "profile" that narcotics police use to pinpoint possible drug offenders who should be detained and searched:

> having a pale complexion[90]
> having a dark complexion[91]
> having a Hispanic appearance[92]
> being between the ages of twenty-five and thirty-five[93]
> acting nervous[94]
> acting calm[95]
> carrying $100 bills[96]
> carrying $50 bills[97]
> carrying $20 bills[98]
> carrying $10 bills[99]
> carrying $5 bills[100]
> wearing a pager[101]
> wearing casual clothing[102]
> wearing a black jumpsuit[103]
> wearing clothing with a bulge in it[104]
> wearing "a lot of gold jewelry"[105]
> wearing perfume[106]
> being a female who wears platform shoes[107]
> being a female who carries a condom in her purse[108]
> running up large electric bills[109]
> having a heat source in a house[110]
> having window coverings that hinder someone from peering inside a residence[111]
> having a telephone answering machine message recorded by someone other than the person who is the phone subscriber[112]
> owning a dog[113]
> having a home security system[114]
> having a recreational vehicle motor home[115]
> driving a rental car[116]
> driving with an unfolded road map[117]
> driving a car with out-of-state license plates[118]
> having McDonald's fast food bags on a car floor[119]
> "scrupulous obedience to traffic laws"[120]
> failing to twist around in car to watch as a marked patrol car passes routinely in the opposite direction[121]
> "sitting very erect" in a car[122]
> being a foreigner without friends or relatives in the United States[123]

being a foreigner who does not speak English[124]
returning from a visit to Mexico without having bought souvenirs[125]
visiting for only a short time in a city where illegal drug sales occur[126]
flying from Los Angeles to Detroit[127]
flying from Los Angeles to Atlanta[128]
flying from Ft. Lauderdale to Atlanta[129]
flying from Dallas to Atlanta[130]
flying from Atlanta to Kansas City[131]
flying from Miami[132]
flying from Chicago[133]
flying from Detroit[134]
flying to and from New York City[135]
flying to and from San Juan, Puerto Rico[136]
flying to or from any city[137]
arriving at an airport and buying a ticket shortly before one's flight
    departs[138]
paying cash for an airline ticket[139]
buying a one-way ticket[140]
buying a round trip ticket[141]
buying a first class ticket[142]
buying more than one ticket when the itinerary could have been served
    by one ticket[143]
making a trip on more than one airline[144]
flying nonstop[145]
changing planes[146]
having no luggage claim checks affixed to your plane ticket envelopes[147]
carrying luggage lacking identification tags[148]
incompletely filling out an airline baggage identification tag[149]
having a cellular telephone in a suitcase[150]
having American Tourister luggage[151]
having new luggage[152]
having no luggage[153]
traveling with a companion[154]
traveling without a companion and meeting no one at the destination
    airport[155]
acting as if you are looking for a person you expected to meet at the
    destination airport[156]
being among the first passengers off an airplane[157]
being among the last passengers off an airplane[158]
being among the middle group of passengers off an airplane[159]
arriving in the early morning[160]
looking at one's wristwatch[161]
lacking a confirmed hotel reservation[162]
using a telephone soon after leaving an airplane[163]

walking quickly[164]
walking slowly[165]
leaving an airport without loitering[166]
leaving an airport from an exit offering no public transportation[167]
leaving an airport by taxicab[168]
renting a motel room under a name that seems Hispanic or African-
    American[169]
renting a motel room adjoining one of a traveling companion[170]
using cash to pay for a motel room[171]
looking at a police officer[172]
not looking at a police officer[173]
"looking around at other people"[174]

Basically, drug warriors argue that being a citizen is sufficient cause to suspect a person of criminal conduct, thereby constricting civil liberties protections for that person. That situation is hard to distinguish from the legal status of citizens in Nazi Germany.

Nonetheless, drug squads sometimes feel their search authority is too limited, and find ways to evade remaining limits. Police can give license trouble to hotels if they are labeled as gathering places for "undesirables," such as drug users. "Consequently, . . . hotel managers will give keys to policemen that permit them to make searches while the occupant is out of the room, some hotel owners will permit the vice control squad to tap into their switchboards."[175] A criminologist watched police make a secret warrantless search of a hotel room, looking for evidence of a drug violation. "As one policeman commented: 'Of course, it's not exactly legal to take a peek beforehand. It's not one of the things you usually talk about as a police technique. But if you find something, you back off and figure out how you can do it legal.'"[176]

In the 1700s the state's dominance over an individual in criminal proceedings was regarded as so overpowering that the Fifth Amendment guaranteed that citizens would not have to incriminate themselves through compelled testimony. In contrast, drug warriors argue that the power of an individual citizen is so overwhelming that government agents must be able to coerce self-incrimination. One method is through urine tests after arrest for any crime. Results can be used to prosecute a person for "internal possession" of a drug, or even for earlier possession outside the body.[177] At one time the U.S. Supreme Court forbade such prosecutions. Justice William O. Douglas explained, "Words taken from his lips, capsules taken from his stomach, blood taken from his veins are all inadmissible provided they are taken from him without his consent. They are inadmissible because of the command of the Fifth Amendment. That is an unequivocal, definite and workable rule of evidence for state and federal courts."[178] In the name of drugs, however, police are now allowed to use physical bodies of suspects (that is, the status of what suspects are, rather than the conduct of what they do) to convict them of drug offenses.

Police access to medical records has already been discussed in the context of illegal search, but the purpose of such a search is to prosecute a patient through information given to a physician, that is, through self-incrimination. Missouri's 1990 Omnibus Drug Control Bill required physicians to test all pregnant women for drug use and to report positive results to the state, thus potentially allowing arrest and jailing of those women. California has similar statutes. A South Carolina hospital cited such requirements when turning over confidential medical records to police, who then arrested patients for drug use; some patients "were handcuffed and put in leg shackles or handcuffed to hospital beds during the arrests."[179] Taxes on illegal drugs exist in some states. Such tax laws typically require revenue authorities to keep a careful record of users and dealers who pay the tax. Not everyone is convinced that such lists would be inaccessible to police. That is probably one reason why users and dealers fail to pay such taxes, because to avoid violating the tax law they must confess to violating the drug law. For that reason, in 1969 the U.S. Supreme Court ruled that federal taxing of illegal drugs violated Fifth Amendment guarantees.[180] Even a scheme closing such tax records to police was ruled unconstitutional.[181] Nonetheless, after 1969 citizens continued to be convicted for failing to pay state taxes on illegal drugs.[182] The same principle would be at work if laws required citizens to give a statistical agency a confidential report of any crime they commit. Forcing someone convicted of a drug offense to pay such a tax has also been held to violate the Fifth Amendment's prohibition of double jeopardy.[183] Warned one court, "Although the Montana statute labels the assessment as a 'tax' . . . a state cannot evade the prohibitions of the federal constitution merely be changing the label of the punishment."[184]

Plea bargains are another method of compelling self-incrimination. If an accused person will confess to a crime, perhaps even a crime that was not committed, other charges are dropped. Mandatory sentencing laws expedite the plea bargain process. Mandatory sentences give prosecutors, rather than judges, the power to determine what level of punishment shall be administered upon conviction for a criminal act. One act can violate multiple drug laws ranging from misdemeanors to felonies. "Mandatory" punishment for that one act is optionally determined by the prosecutor who draws the indictment. If a prosecutor threatens a person with long imprisonment unless the person confesses to a lesser crime, such a confession is coerced. Yet in the name of drugs, courts refuse to recognize the coercion. Plea bargains also neatly erase the Fifth Amendment's guarantee of trials. If an accused person can receive graver charges and greater punishment upon demanding a trial, a trial is no longer a right. Through plea bargains, drug warriors have gained a power similar to one seized by the Gestapo. Drug warriors cannot choose from a range of punishments as broad as that available to the Gestapo. But within perimeters of the permissible range, drug police and prosecutors have broad power to administer punishments.

Prosecutors perceive those perimeters as broad indeed, illustrated by a case in which drug war principles leaked over to banking regulation. A banker agreed to a plea bargain involving a $10,000 fine. Subsequently the prosecutor took a job with the Treasury Department and imposed a $1,035,000 Treasury Department civil fine on the basis of that guilty plea.[185] The banker contended the subsequent fine was imposed because the prosecutor wanted a harsher punishment than the court would approve. Because the plea bargain negotiations promised no further punishment, the civil fine was rescinded; but if there is no plea bargain, police authorities can now enhance judicial punishment. Another parallel to that Nazi practice occurs when prosecutors refuse to return cash or other assets seized from defendants who are later found innocent by a jury. A New Jersey prosecutor asked why he should have to "peel off a roll of $20 bills to a crack dealer that a jury won't convict."[186] Drug squads can now make decisions of guilt and punishment without being subject to court review, just as German courts lacked jurisdiction over "political" actions by the Gestapo.

The most vivid example of prosecutors' power to administer punishment is civil forfeiture of property. We shall closely examine that example in the next chapter, as it plays a key role in destroying a targeted group of people. For our present purposes, we need merely note that drug war measures give prosecutors power to seize "drug-related assets" unless the property owner can prove the property has no drug connection. Proving a negative can be difficult. Moreover, targeted property owners typically lack the knowledge or resources to navigate the arcane procedures of forfeiture appeals, and lose their property by default. Civil forfeitures can occur without the property owner being convicted of any crime. In 1992 the Missouri legislature considered a bill to require conviction for a drug crime before prosecutors could seize a citizen's property. I was in the capitol on the day that a powerful chairman condemned the bill as "a drug dealer's wet dream." The bill was not enacted. The next year another legislator became alarmed that requiring involvement of a prosecutor put too many limits on drug squads, and introduced legislation to give police officers power to do property forfeitures themselves.[187] That was a power enjoyed by the Gestapo, a power that Nuremberg Military Tribunal prosecutors treated as a crime against humanity.[188]

Civil forfeiture evades the Eighth Amendment's ban on excessive fines. In misdemeanor cases, government agents have taken property worth thousands of dollars even though the criminal fine might be fifty dollars. Because police and prosecutors can keep the property they seize or sell it and keep the proceeds, civil forfeitures are an important producer of government income. Civil forfeitures can also operate as a shakedown racket, with prosecutors offering to drop a criminal case if the accused person will turn over property wanted by government agents.

An important aspect of civil forfeiture is that it can be used as an administrative punishment when prosecutors lack enough evidence to file charges, let alone convict someone of a crime. Court approval of property transfer can be unnecessary, as when accused citizens turn over property to a drug squad in return for having charges dropped. Losing a car or house or the family farm can be a tremendous blow to any citizen, let alone one who is innocent of a crime. In the name of drugs, police have been given the power to administer that punishment. Technically, because the forfeitures are conducted under civil law rather than criminal law, they do not violate Fifth Amendment guarantees against deprivation of property without due process of law. The process of law is duly used by drug squads, just as Nazi government agents followed the law in their seizure of property from Jews who were not convicted of a crime. At the postwar Nuremberg trials, prosecutors argued that such property seizures were inherently unjust, and characterized the seizures as crimes against humanity.[189] American police and prosecutors now wield the same property confiscation punishments enjoyed by the Gestapo.

Until trials are generally no longer required, as a stopgap measure police and prosecutors seek to limit defendants' abilities to escape conviction. Prosecutors need not disclose the identity of secret informers used to build a case unless the defendant can prove that such unidentified informants have information needed by the defense[190]—a hard standard to meet. As we shall see in the next chapter, civil forfeiture can strip an accused person of assets needed to hire a lawyer. Admittedly, courts do appoint counsel to represent impoverished defendants, but drug defendants do not always get top quality representation; in one Missouri drug war case the judge appointed an Alzheimer's disease patient as defense counsel.[191] In addition, the sheriff selected the jurors. The defendant spent 8½ years in prison before authorities conceded the conviction was flawed. Were the Sixth Amendment obeyed in drug war cases, such innocent persons might be exonerated after a few days of trial rather than after a few years of prison.

Even drug defendants who are exonerated can remain targets of vindictive prosecutors. A man's construction business collapsed when he was indicted for cocaine conspiracy. His loss of income left him unable to pay his house mortgage, and he lost his home. Because he was unable to afford an attorney, the court appointed one. After the jury acquitted this innocent man of all charges, prosecutors demanded that he reimburse the government $150,000 for fees and expenses submitted to the court by his court-appointed attorney.[192]

The Eighth Amendment's prohibition of excessive bail is evaded by the Comprehensive Crime Control Act of 1984.[193] The purpose of bail is simply to assure that a defendant will appear for trial. The Eighth Amendment is designed to prevent judges or prosecutors from jailing an unpopular but dependable defendant for months because the person could not meet an outrageous bail. This important guarantee limits time that a person not convicted of a crime must spend in custody. The guarantee is also important for the outcome of a trial; persons unable to make bail are more likely to be convicted than persons who remain free before and during trial.[194] The 1984 law evades those guarantees, however, by prohibiting release of a defendant if a court finds probable cause before trial to believe that the defendant committed a drug offense carrying a prison term of ten years or more. Such a defendant is arbitrarily defined as dangerous to the community, and dangerous defendants are not entitled to bail. Because every indictment must be supported by probable cause, and because more and more drug offenses carry ten-year prison terms, prosecutors now have wide discretion to prevent pretrial release by fine-tuning indictments. Skillful legal counsel can help such a defendant achieve pretrial release by demonstrating the defendant factually poses no danger to the community, but not all drug defendants have such legal representation. In a six-month period, among 889 defendants held under the 1984 law only 185 achieved pretrial release.[195] By using evasions (noted later) of the Fifth Amendment guarantee against double jeopardy, drug prosecutors have even devised a way to transform pretrial release into punishment. In this procedure, a defendant pays a bail bondsman to obtain pretrial release on state charges. This can be a substantial sum; if bail is $50,000, a bondsman typically receives $5,000 from the defendant. The $5,000 is non-refundable. In order to punish the defendant, state prosecutors can then drop the case, and federal prosecutors can file charges instead. If federal bail is permitted, the defendant must pay a bondsman again. Either way, the defendant has paid a substantial sum to the first bondsman for nothing.

Amendment Eight prohibits cruel and unusual punishments, but drug offenders receive savage retribution for offenses having trivial impact on society. Later in this chapter we shall examine such retribution in our discussion of civic duty, but if the Eighth Amendment were respected such discussion would be unnecessary.

Amendments Nine and Ten are intended to assure that citizens cannot be criminalized for engaging in ordinary behavior. While evaluating the language of an early narcotics law, Justice Oliver Wendell Holmes declared, "Only words from which there is no escape could warrant the conclusion that Congress meant to strain its powers almost if not quite to the breaking point in order to make the probably very large proportion of citizens who have some preparation of opium in their possession criminal."[196] An amendment to the U.S. Constitution was required to overcome the Tenth Amendment's ban on federal interference with alcohol commerce. And even the alcohol prohibition amendment left unmolested Ninth and Tenth Amendment protections of alcohol purchase, possession, and consumption. Throughout the alcohol prohibition era, federal law permitted citizens to consume the drug. Subsequent judicial interpretation, however, reduced the Ninth and Tenth Amendments to the status of Nazi Germany's Hindenburg Exceptions. Hindenburg Exceptions permitted certain kinds of Jews to function in normal society—until public sentiment demanded action against them. Certain kinds of drug users are allowed to function in American society, such as those who choose to smoke tobacco. That exception can be eliminated at any time by legislative action, as was eventually done to the "large proportion of citizens who have some preparation of opium" and to persons who smoke marijuana. Indeed, a special clarifying section was required in the 1970 Controlled Substances Act because otherwise the biological effects of nicotine would have subjected users to penalties specified for heroin users. Formerly courts consistently ruled that under the Ninth and Tenth Amendments Americans had an absolute right to use drugs. A 1932 Supreme Court decision upholding a prosecution for failing to pay taxes on an illegal morphine sale declared, "The statute is not aimed at sales of the forbidden drugs *qua* sales, a matter entirely beyond the authority of Congress."[197] As we have seen, tax laws were used as a subterfuge to get around civil liberties protecting drug use. Nonetheless, when the Supreme Court at last ruled such tax laws to be unconstitutional in 1969, Congress outright banned use of illicit drugs. Subsequent challenges based on the Ninth and Tenth Amendments have always failed. In the name of drugs, federal courts have eliminated the right to be left alone. Government agents have enthusiastically exercised their new power, supervising citizens' tastes in music, sexual conduct, and other personal choices. Growing calls are heard for government to force obedience to precepts of Christian fundamentalists, who openly describe democracy as a violation of God's law.[198] The drug war made these new governmental interventions possible. More interventions become possible as more civil liberties are extinguished.

Citizens terrified by drug warrior propaganda readily accept drug warrior attacks on civil liberties. In September 1989, a *Washington Post*/ABC News poll found almost two-thirds of respondents ready to sacrifice "a few" freedoms in the name of drugs. Over half felt search warrants should not be required if police wanted to enter a citizen's home to look for drugs. Over two-thirds wanted police to stop and search automobiles at random in hopes of finding drugs. Almost three-fourths wanted criminal penalties to prohibit motion pictures with scenes of illegal substance use.[199] The hidden drug warrior agenda is sharply illustrated by comments from African-Americans, whose social and economic well-being depend on strict protection of civil rights. According to an Atlanta official, African-Americans frightened of drugs said, "To hell with rights. Just kick ass and take names." A Chicago activist concurred, "I'm all for whatever tactics have to be used. If that means they are trampling on civil liberties, so be it."[200] Thus does the drug war encourage African-Americans to repudiate the laws that liberated them, resuming the repression of African-American communities in the name of drugs, a restoration of repression that would never be permitted by courts in the name of race.

Evasions of civil liberties ultimately reduce our ability to hold government officials accountable for their behavior. Nuremberg Military Tribunal prosecutors argued that Nazis behaved criminally when they refused to punish police for harming citizens. Nuremberg prosecutors demolished Nazi excuses that sound eerily familiar a half century later, if "drug user" is substituted for "communist": Police "culprits were not experienced . . . , victims were Communists . . . , victims had been obstinate and insubordinate, . . . communism had an especially strong hold" in cities where police used harshness.[201] "Nazi conspirators adopted and endorsed a large body of unwritten laws exempting the police from criminal liability for illegal acts."[202] Nazis argued that political acts by police and other government officials were exempt from outside accountability.[203] Said one Nazi commentary: "Measures of the Political Police can be checked only by their own channels of administrative supervision. . . . There can be no legal backing for a court decision. Any agency outside of the Political Police must lack the necessary expert knowledge for a decision."[204] It is no coincidence that such Nazi reasoning was used by America's top drug warrior, President George Bush, when he pardoned his Iran-Contra associates for violations of criminal laws. Bush reasoned that because these officials were promoting White House policy, their actions were political and exempt from legal accountability. The drug war's transformation of civil liberties into empty ritual makes abuses of power possible in areas far removed from drug laws. Throughout the Nuremberg tribunal's examination of acts by Nazi police, prosecutors, and judges, we find the theme that civil liberties infringements are criminal. That theme derives from American recognition that law does not create fundamental rights; such rights exist apart from any written law (a principle explicitly stated in Amendment Nine of the U.S. constitution). What counts is not a piece of paper purportedly authorizing police actions. What counts is the impact that such actions have on ordinary citizens. What counts is the suffering experienced by victims.

CIVIC DUTY AND THE EDUCATIONAL NATURE OF LAW

Because civil liberties are but one expression of a democratic tradition designed to prevent government activities such as a drug war, drug warriors embrace two broader principles attacking that democratic tradition. One principle holds the law's purpose to be protection of the state, not citizens. Elsewhere, in describing Nazi jurisprudence, I have called this principle "civic duty." The other drug warrior principle holds that statutes and regulations merely provide examples of how to accomplish a law's social purpose, and those examples do not limit actions officials can take. In my study of Nazi jurisprudence, I called this principle "the educational nature of law."

In drug prosecutions, civic duty is used to justify abuses once considered indefensible. Let us examine three typical examples.

One example is perjury. In a sworn statement, a top drug squad officer of the Missouri Highway Patrol told a judge he had delivered marijuana to a man in the Ozarks, and the judge thereupon granted the officer's request for a warrant to search the man's house and farm. In fact no such delivery had been made, but after obtaining the search warrant, the officer disguised himself in a United Parcel Service uniform, made the delivery, and conducted the search. When the officer's perjury was revealed, a court ruled that it was trivial and the search warrant was valid.[205] A New York county judge found false police statements in a wiretap application to be "negligent, not reckless," so the case based on the wiretap could proceed. A state appeals court reviewing the case found the false statements "at the very least . . . showed a reckless disregard for the truth" but sustained the conviction based on the wiretap.[206] In the interest of gaining drug convictions, civic duty permits law officers to lie about events that have not happened.

Another example of civic duty is civil commitment, used to imprison persons if a prosecutor lacks enough evidence to obtain a conviction. Because drug statutes define illegal drug use as sickness, a prosecutor can get a court order forcing a person to undergo therapy through "civil commitment." Such a person is locked up. Although ostensibly a medical patient rather than a prisoner, frequently such persons are housed in prisons where they share cells with convicted criminals. Because civil commitment is considered beneficial therapy rather than punishment for crime, the patient is not entitled to a lawyer during commitment proceedings. Moreover, civil commitment can be for an indeterminate time, until therapists pronounce the patient cured. Because many drug abuse therapists claim that a patient may go into remission but can never be cured, someone receiving *therapy* for drug use can be locked away far longer than someone receiving *punishment* for drug use. For these very practical reasons, prosecutors like to say that drug use is a disease.

Several factors illustrate that civil commitment is a sham to expedite punishment in drug cases. A New York law declared that a drug user accused of a crime (a simple arrest met that criterion) could be locked away under civil commitment.[207] In that context civil commitment is not therapy but rather a tool to intimidate drug users during police interrogation. In addition, civil commitment is ostensibly used when a person is unable to make a rational decision for self-preservation. For that reason it is rarely used outside the context of drug indictments. After all, most sick people want treatment—indeed, so many want treatment that lack of health care became a major political issue in the 1990s. Civil commitment is used only when a person is unable to make a rational decision. Traditionally, such an irrational person would not be held criminally accountable for actions during that state of mind, so civil commitment should automatically dismiss criminal drug use charges, but such does not happen. Moreover, if "therapy" is unavailing on such an irrational patient, that failure should prove continuing incapacity, but instead therapeutic failure becomes an excuse to resume criminal drug use proceedings.

That resumption is an innovation in American jurisprudence. Traditionally, criminal proceedings are directed against past behavior. A failed drug patient, however, can be prosecuted because authorities are dissatisfied with prospects for the person's future behavior. When a regime imprisons citizens because of what they might do someday, the regime is following the Nazi concept of civic duty.

Formerly, civil commitment was rare. Formerly, it nurtured incapacitated citizens if they needed medical help. Civic duty has transformed civil commitment into a method of imprisoning citizens convicted of no crime. In the transcript of one civil commitment proceeding, I counted only 500 words; a single sheet of paper could hold the facts and discussion of them among the committed person, the person's spouse, a police matron, a public defender, a prosecutor, and the judge (who used profanity while issuing the commitment order).[208] Participants at a 1985 White House–endorsed drug war conference said such hearings placed too great a burden on prosecutors and called for the process to be expedited and used more often.[209] A senior speaker at the same conference also said that a single unconfirmed drug-positive urine test should be enough grounds for civil commitment.[210] The statistical principle expressed by Bayes's theorem shows that the number of innocent persons falsely accused will soar if drug use is low in a population. Suppose 0.5 percent of a population uses heroin, and a urine test is 98 percent accurate. In 10,000 tests there will be 49 true positives and 199 false positives—the vast majority of positives are false even though the test is 98 percent accurate. Moreover, a *confirmed* drug-positive urine test fails to demonstrate drug use. Even Georgia's supreme court has admitted that someone who does not use cocaine can have a positive urine test if the person has been breathing near a cocaine smoker.[211] The same holds true for breathing near a marijuana smoker.[212]

Still another example of civic duty is mandatory sentencing. Police and prosecutors often claim that civic duty requires harsher sentences than judges wish to impose against drug users. Recognizing that judges do not always impose sentences demanded by police and prosecutors, legislatures have passed laws mandating those sentences for certain offenses. (The *prosecutor*, however, can agree to a lesser sentence. Such authority thereby creates another plea bargaining tool. An assistant U.S. attorney praised the prosecution options created by mandatory sentences: "They induce people to cooperate and the ability to bargain around them enables us to dispose of a lot of cases at an early stage.")[213] One effect of mandatory sentencing is to impose longer sentences on petty offenders and shorter sentences on "drug kingpins," because kingpins can reveal their knowledge about the drug trade in return for a favorable plea bargain. Petty offenders have no useful information to reveal and are unable to make such deals. An undercover agent seeking an LSD buy was told by the dealer's girlfriend, an eighteen-year-old high school student, where to meet the dealer. She received a ten-year sentence for conspiracy. The dealer received five years because he had information to barter with prosecutors.[214] Such disparate sentences for a drug offense involving a man and woman are nothing unusual, and are boosting the percentage of females in the prison population.[215] Arguably, the systematic effect of such mandatory sentencing is sexist. Another effect of mandatory sentencing is to encourage release of violent offenders, whose crimes do not carry mandatory sentences, in order to make room in prisons for nonviolent drug offenders. Former Minneapolis police chief Tony Bouza expressed exasperation at mandatory drug sentences: "The result was to leave no room for rapists, killers, burglars, muggers, and other recidivists, for whom there were no mandated sentences."[216] A Florida prosecutor agreed: "It's not leaving any beds for the killers and rapists."[217] The public safety question raised by such a practice is obvious, but the *Journal of the American Medical Association* has noted a little-recognized consequence: Prison overcrowding caused by mandatory sentencing has made tuberculosis a growing public health threat, as infected inmates circulate among prison employees while incarcerated and among the general community upon release.[218]

One of the most interesting uses of mandatory sentencing targets a specific racial group. Cocaine hydrochloride powder can be processed to produce crack. To get a given effect, a user must ingest a larger quantity of powder than of the processed product, but either format can create the same effect. As one researcher explained, whether a person uses powder or crack, "it's still the same cocaine molecule."[219] Indeed, federal courts have noted scientific findings that cocaine and crack are the same thing.[220] "It's like distinguishing between scotch and bourbon," noted one judge. "Alcohol is alcohol. Cocaine is cocaine."[221] Nonetheless, a mandatory sentence of five years is required for selling 500 grams of powder—a $50,000 crime—or 5 grams of crack—a $100 crime.[222] Unlike cocaine powder, crack is generally viewed as a drug used by African-Americans—an incorrect perception; scientists have found that African-Americans are no more likely to use crack than Hispanics or whites. Social and environmental factors, not race, make crack a "drug of choice."[223] Courts have agreed that the purpose of harsher mandatory sentences for crack possession is to discriminate against African-Americans;[224] one judge protested that such mandates are "directly responsible for incarcerating nearly an entire generation of young black American men for very long periods."[225] Yet most judges calmly perform their civic duty by meting out harsher penalties to African-Americans. Noted one commentator:

> Read the following sentences.
> "Crack is ruining America's inner cities."
> "Crack is killing policemen, overburdening courts and filling jails beyond capacity."
> "Crack is devastating thousands of families."
> "Crack is putting the lives and well-being of our children at risk."
> Now delete the words *crack is* and insert the words *niggers are.*
> Isn't this the secret message of the Just Say No campaign?[226]

A federal judge concluded, "Prosecutors in the federal courts are selectively prosecuting black defendants who were involved with crack, no matter how trivial the amount, and ignoring or diverting whites when they do the same thing."[227] As we have seen elsewhere in this chapter, racial discrimination in drug law enforcement goes beyond crack. An aide to federal drug czar William Bennett explained, "It's easier and less expensive to arrest black drug users and dealers than it is whites."[228] In 1991 the U.S. Sentencing Commission found that prosecutors applied mandatory sentences to about half of cases with white defendants but to two-thirds of cases with African-American defendants.[229]

Mandatory sentencing eliminates the independent exercise of authority by judges in criminal cases. Nuremberg prosecutors condemned elimination of judges' independence[230] and entered mandatory sentencing as part of the evidence of crimes against humanity.[231] A judge removed from office by the Nazis recalled that "in important criminal cases," the Nazi district attorney would "inform the presiding judge prior to the trial of the punishment which would be sought and point out that this sentence would be expected of him."[232] Procedure is little different in important American drug war cases. Upon conviction, under mandatory sentencing judges must obey the sentencing decision of the prosecutor, who prearranges the sentence by fine-tuning the indictment. Nuremberg prosecutors described "prearrangement of sentences between judges and prosecutors" as criminal.[233]

Mandatory sentencing guidelines are ruthless. A first offense of simple marijuana possession now carries a five-year federal penalty.[234] Escalator clauses take advantage of the repetitive nature of drug use. First-time possession of crack can be punished by five to twenty years if the amount exceeds five grams. A second offense brings the same punishment if the weight exceeds three grams. And a third offense brings the same punishment if the weight exceeds one gram. "Three felony convictions for drug offenses carries mandatory life with no parole, and it is a felony to commit a drug offense within 100 feet of a pinball or video arcade containing more than 10 games."[235] Possession of a marijuana cigarette is such a felony. Federal law permits a $10,000 fine for possessing one marijuana cigarette.[236] An Oklahoma man received a life sentence for felony possession of marijuana, 0.005644 ounce.[237]

The war on drug users has even brought forth the Nazi principle of applying punishments that were not in force when a crime was committed. For example, on the basis of evidence found in a 1985 search, a man was charged in 1991 with committing a federal marijuana offense. In the intervening years the penalty had been increased to mandatory life imprisonment without parole, and he was sentenced under that law, which was not in force at the time he committed the offense.[238] As we shall see in the next chapter, the Racketeer Influenced and Corrupt Organizations Act (RICO) covers offenses such as possessing marijuana. Two or more offenses constitute a "pattern of racketeering," and brutal penalties apply. Just as a pool of victims can be enlarged through defining today's legal conduct as illegal tomorrow, harshness faced by victims can be intensified by statutorily defining their behavior as dangerous instead of allowing a court to evaluate their conduct. The RICO pattern can include illegal actions that occurred before RICO was passed. Courts have held that RICO is not ex post facto because actions covered in the pattern were already illegal; RICO merely imposes penalties that did not exist when the acts were committed.[239] Someone who risked a small fine for a marijuana violation committed before RICO was passed can now face loss of the family car, house, or farm because that violation was afterward defined as felony racketeering. For most of American history such retrospective increase of criminal penalty was forbidden.

In 1798 the U.S. Supreme Court's classic definition of ex post facto included "every law that *aggravates* a *crime*, or makes it *greater* than it was, when committed" and "every law that *changes the punishment*, and inflicts a *greater punishment*, than the law annexed to the crime, when committed."[240] In the name of drugs, however, increasing penalties retroactively is no longer considered ex post facto. A citizen who commits a minor infraction today can face unlimited retribution from prosecutors years later. Courtesy of the drug war, that retribution need not come through RICO. For example, using a case of a convicted drug dealer who made a false statement on a 1986 home loan application, the Justice Department persuaded a federal judge to approve forfeiture of the house because such a false statement became punishable by forfeiture in a 1989 law.[241] Under that precedent,[242] an apartment owner lost his building because of an alleged loan application misrepresentation, and a woman lost her home because the real estate broker handling the loan application made an incorrect statement on it. Amazed court clerks asked one victim's lawyer, "Are they going through everyone's bank records?"[243] Possibly. As we shall later see, bank clerks who spot such inaccuracies can collect up to twenty-five percent of proceeds from sale of forfeited houses. Such are the consequences of opening ex post facto proceedings through RICO.

Another element of RICO has special interest for our inquiry. Nazi judges were concerned less about the specific act committed by a defendant and more about a defendant's "criminal nature." The question was not so much, What punishment is appropriate for this act? The question was, How does this act fit into a pattern of conduct? A Nazi judge based a sentence less on a defendant's individual act than on a pattern of conduct that included the act. RICO introduced that element of Nazi jurisprudence to America. Prior to RICO, a judge would view a defendant's criminal record as a series of individual acts. RICO asks judges to find a pattern in those acts, a pattern that reveals the racketeering (criminal) nature of a defendant. Under RICO a defendant is not punished for individual acts, which may be trivial, but for what those acts reveal about the defendant's antisocial nature.

Some judges question civic duty. The Ninth Judicial Circuit has formally declared that mandatory drug sentencing is "forcing the courts in many instances to impose sentences which are manifestly unjust."[244] That sentiment has been duplicated in resolutions from all other circuits and from the Criminal Law Committee of the Judicial Conference.[245] In a survey of forty-eight federal judges, thirty-eight criticized mandatory minimums. "The minimums are grossly excessive," said one judge. Another comment was, "They are rotten. They are ruining the system. They are one of the worst things that have happened. . . . They are grossly unjust."[246] Judicial protests against civic duty have been noble but feeble. In one drug case the judge told the convicted person, "It looks like you have a pretty good violation of the fifth amendment here, but my hands are tied."[247] In another case a judge "demanded immediate resentencing for Charles if mandatory minimum sentences are repealed."[248] Upon handing down a life sentence without parole for a first offense, a judge called the requirement "preposterous."[249] U.S. District Judge William W. Schwarzer "cried as he sentenced Richard Anderson, a first offender, to 10 years in prison with no parole. The 49-year-old longshoreman made the mistake of driving an acquaintance to a Burger King for $5. Little did Anderson know he was participating in an undercover deal involving 100 grams of crack. Judge Schwarzer called the sentence 'a grave miscarriage of justice.'"[250]

Judges may express regret and even weep while performing their civic duty, but few just say no. Few defy the corruption of the Eighth Amendment produced by mandatory sentencing. Few demand use of executive clemency to correct injustice. Few ask legislators to reform the laws. Few give speeches demanding action. Few dare to choose justice over civic duty. The same attitude was found among German judges who implemented Nazi goals. "It is not known whether as many as ten judges in the whole Reich have voluntarily resigned since the installation of the Nazi regime. Even judges who are aware that they are powerless to protect citizens against arbitrariness have stayed on."[251] Continued service to Nazi justice was not based on fear: "Not a single case is reported in which a judge who resigned was sent to a concentration camp, or even lost his pension." Benign consequences of the few resignations "were known and widely commented on by the judiciary" in Nazi Germany.[252]

Said U.S. Supreme Court Justice Stevens, "No impartial observer could criticize this Court for hindering the progress of the war on drugs." He called the Court a "loyal foot soldier in the Executive's fight."[253] Allegiance to civic duty rather than the U.S. Constitution can be seen in the statement of Justice Harry A. Blackmun: "Given the strength of society's interest in overcoming the extraordinary obstacles to the detection of drug traffickers, such conduct should not be subjected to a requirement of probable cause."[254] So, too, can civic duty be seen in the Court's holding that a Michigan statute requiring life imprisonment for simple drug possession is cruel, but not unusual, so such a penalty does not violate the Eighth Amendment.[255] By such reasoning, the branding of human beings, a standard punishment during the 1700s, might never have ended because despite its cruelty it was not unusual. The intellectual acrobatics in the Michigan statute decision may be world-class, but the artistry is based on a lie required by civic duty: Michigan's statute was unusual indeed; the next toughest penalty for drug possession was Alabama's five-year mandatory minimum.[256] In the name of drugs, the decision also ignored the Court's long-standing rule forbidding cruel punishments regardless of whether they are unusual.[257] When a defendant pleaded that a year in prison was excessive for marijuana possession, a federal judge replied, "This argument . . . should be made to the legislature, not to the courts."[258] If, as this jurist maintains, courts should no longer evaluate whether penalties are cruel or unusual, Eighth Amendment protections no longer exist. Under such reasoning, judges are reduced to their function in Nazi Germany, merely certifying that proper forms are followed when police and prosecutors brutalize victims.

One of the most brutal aspects of civic duty is its disregard of mitigating circumstances. A marijuana cultivator brought his father along on a trip to a marijuana patch, where police arrested both. Although the father denied involvement in the cultivation, he pleaded guilty on advice of his lawyer. The sixty-year-old retired coal miner with black lung disease had no criminal record, but received a 6½-year mandatory sentence.[259] Disregard of mitigating circumstances leaks over to prosecutions themselves. Tragic examples come from sick persons who face felony charges for medical use of marijuana. "I'm an end-stage renal patient on kidney dialysis 3 days a week. I was growing and using marijuana as a medical herb. I was arrested and charged with felony cultivation. When the police entered my home they found one marijuana plant. I live in a trailer and they brought in so many police that some had to wait outside. Several weapons, flak jackets, ski masks, and an assortment of vehicles were present. . . . My neighbors thought I killed someone. . . . I was taken to jail in hand-cuffs."[260] Said another victim,

> My home was raided on September 27, 1991. It was a "no-knock" search for marijuana cultivation. I have no left leg and my hips have been replaced along with my knees, left shoulder and an elbow. I have had a kidney transplant also, and I smoke marijuana for nausea, which comes from the pharmaceuticals I am prescribed.
>
> The animals put me on the floor and tore my home apart. They found a bong, a copy of High Times, and NORML information. They gave me a citation and walked out.
>
> They left my home with no door on it, and me on the floor. It took me about 40 minutes to find a way to get off the floor.[261]

A Florida couple suffering from AIDS was convicted of three felonies for using marijuana to alleviate their symptoms. The husband recalled, "12 heavily armed men battered down our front door, held a gun to my wife's head, ransacked our trailer, then threw us in jail. A dozen vice cops seized two scrawny marijuana plants. The police turned this two-bit bust into a daring drug raid covered on the local news. A hard-line prosecutor transformed these two small plants into three major felony charges."[262] A physician advised a terminally ill Alaska woman to smoke marijuana. Federal drug agents arrested her and her husband for cultivating marijuana. Said the husband:

I could not let my wife go to Federal prison for five years. It would have been her death sentence. We lost our savings and our home. We could fight no more and were forced under duress to sign a plea agreement with the Federal government.

My wife pled guilty to a federal misdemeanor possession charge. She was sentenced to three years probation, a $1,000.00 fine, and one month in jail. At her sentencing, the judge stated there was no evidence to indicate distribution [drug dealing] and that she had a serious ongoing medical problem.

As part of the agreement, I was forced to plead "no contest" to the level "C" state felony of simple possession of one pound of marijuana, for which I received four years in prison with two years suspended.[263]

On recommendation of physicians, a paralyzed Oklahoma man began smoking marijuana to relieve muscle spasms. Police raided his residence and found enough marijuana to indict him as a presumed drug dealer. The quantity was two ounces. Because the wheelchair-bound man had two pistols in his bedroom, he was charged as an armed drug offender. An Oklahoma jury gave him life imprisonment plus sixteen years. The judge reduced the sentence to ten years, and the paralyzed man was sent to prison.[264] A California drug squad arrested a seventy-year-old man for cultivating marijuana used by his fifty-eight-year-old companion for chronic pain relief that avoided side effects of prescription drugs. Authorities informed her that because she was not married to her companion, she would be forced to testify against him. Rather than harm him through her testimony, she committed suicide. Given the circumstances, a judge ruled that the elderly man need serve only nine months in prison.[265] In St. Louis a cancer patient attempted suicide after being convicted of marijuana cultivation.[266] An Idaho drug squad SWAT team descended on a sixty-one-year-old terminal prostrate cancer patient who was using marijuana to relieve his suffering. Upon finding eight plants in the house, along with eight ounces of dried marijuana, authorities indicted the dying man as a felony drug violator and tax evader (he had failed to purchase tax stamps that Idaho requires for illegal cultivation of marijuana). The drug squad confiscated the van he had used for transportation to the hospital where he got cancer treatment, 270 miles away.[267] A man in rural Kentucky used marijuana to treat his glaucoma, a medical need confirmed by an ophthalmologist. State police raided his farm and found 138 marijuana plants plus two pounds of harvested plant. He was indicted as a drug dealer but successfully demonstrated at his trial that the amount of marijuana in question was reasonable for a person needing it to treat glaucoma, and he was convicted only of simple possession. Noting the man had no previous arrests, the judge gave him a year in maximum security prison without parole and approved forfeiture of the man's entire farm as a drug asset. Said the federal prosecutor, "Until those laws are changed, we must enforce them to the full extent of our resources."[268] A Missouri multiple sclerosis patient declared that marijuana "lets me walk without the aid of a cane or walker"[269] but was charged with felony cultivation. A reporter was unable to get a comment from the county prosecutor's office, although a sheriff's deputy "said he sympathized with Gregurich's medical problems and his need to use marijuana. 'But it's still against the law of the state of Missouri.'"[270] Soon thereafter, a Missouri Highway Patrol spokesperson urged defeat of legislative efforts to make marijuana available to patients through their doctors. Rather than grant access to a drug that could improve the condition of people who are physically unfit, drug warriors demand that unfit people be rounded up and imprisoned. The drug war has brought Nazi medical practice to America.

A Florida drug squad even fulfilled civic duty by arresting a seriously ill patient, prone to internal bleeding, who used marijuana with permission of the federal government:

> I explained that I was using marihuana supplied by the government, legally, for medical purposes. I was told that it didn't matter, since marihuana was illegal under Florida law.
>
> I was placed under arrest and taken to jail. While entering the police station, I tripped on a concrete step, fell, ripped open a blood vessel, and began to hemorrhage. No blood was visible, but my ankle was swelling, and I could not walk. The police officers surrounded me, ordered me to rise, and started pounding their nightsticks into their hands.

Several days later charges were dropped, but the drug squad declined to return the victim's federally approved medical marijuana.[271]

As in Nazi Germany, civic duty is not limited to criminal law. Disabled persons convicted of drug offenses can no longer claim protections provided by the Americans with Disabilities Act.[272] Massachusetts police seize food stamps and Medicaid cards from drug suspects.[273] Civic duty is also cited to justify administrative actions such as mass urine tests for employees. The U.S. Supreme Court upheld such a program in the U.S. Customs Service on grounds that drug-using Customs officers would be susceptible to bribes, or unwise use of firearms, or leniency in drug searches, or leaking sensitive information. Dissenting Justice Antonin Scalia scoffed at those excuses. "What is absent in the Government's justifications," he noted, "is the recitation of *even a single instance* in which any of the speculated horribles actually occurred: an instance, that is, in which the cause of bribe-taking, or of poor aim, or of unsympathetic law enforcement, or of compromise of classified information, was drug use. . . . Out of 3,600 employees tested, no more than 5 tested positive."[274] Scalia said the real reason for mass urine tests of thousands of productive employees innocent of any drug offense "is what the Commissioner himself offered in the concluding sentence of his memorandum to Customs Service employees announcing the program: 'Implementation of the drug screening program would set an important example.'"[275] In other words, requiring employees to submit their urine was a test of whether employees had the proper public spirit to cooperate in such a program, not a test for a nonexistent drug problem in their workplace. The program tested employees for civic duty, not for drugs. The same reasoning was used by a Nazi court excoriating a citizen for lacking enough sense of civic duty to make voluntary donations to a Nazi welfare scheme.[276] Also in Nazi Germany, failing to attend a Festival of Labor was a firing offense: not because such failure had anything to do with job performance, but because it demonstrated lack of civic duty.[277] Not voting in a Nazi election was another grounds for dismissal by an employer[278] or for expulsion from a profession. A Nazi court disbarred a lawyer with this ruling: "Through his failure to participate in the election, not only did he give evidence of his own lack of loyalty to other members of the community, but also this conduct of the defendant was such as to raise doubts about the solidarity of the German legal profession and its commitment to the Führer and the state."[279] The election's outcome was assured; the point of voting was to demonstrate one's support of community values. The German workplace had no room for anyone who lacked a sense of civic duty.

Civic duty explains otherwise baffling actions from government agencies uninvolved with law enforcement. For example, the Missouri Department of Revenue controls drivers' licenses. In 1993 the bureau drafted legislation to revoke licenses for non-driving drug offenses, such as possessing marijuana at home. The state highway patrol did not draft this bill, nor did the attorney general's office, nor did any drug squad. Even though the driver's license bureau had no stake in the issue, it felt a civic duty to show support for hurting drug users.

Civic duty requires more and more actions to be criminalized, lest any citizens be left unmolested for attitudes that government officials wish to stamp out. If police want to extinguish a particular attitude toward life, statutes cannot keep up with every act that expresses the attitude. Because new expressions keep appearing no matter how many others are explicitly criminalized, eventually the legal system must embrace the educational nature of law.

The educational nature of law means that specified offenses are illustrative only; other actions can be criminal if they violate the law's spirit. United States prosecutions are still formally limited to specified offenses; that which is not forbidden is permitted. Even though American courts do not acknowledge the principle as openly as Nazis did, police are getting the message. In 1992 Kansas City, Missouri, police set up a fake crack house selling imitation crack. Customers were thereupon arrested, even though police admitted they did not know if such purchases violated any law. Police explained that victims merited arrest even if their actions were legal.[280] Such forthright application of the educational nature of law is inspired by the war on drugs, but as in Germany, once the principle is established, its application will cover more and more areas of citizen conduct.

Judges use the educational nature of law to put their thumbs on scales when weighing amounts of seized drugs. Weight can determine whether an offense is a misdemeanor or felony and determine mandatory sentences. Marijuana stalks have negligible drug content and have industrial value for production of cloth, paper, and other products. For those reasons, stalks are exempted from prohibition and are legal to possess. Nonetheless, courts hold that if stalks are found in a quantity of seized street marijuana, they should be included when weighing the amount. The same practice holds for marijuana seeds, which also have low drug content but possess commercial value as a source of vegetable oil and animal feed. Possession of seed is legal regardless of drug content if it has been rendered sterile so it cannot be used to cultivate marijuana. Only viable seed is illegal. Yet most courts do not require germination tests; any seeds in a plastic bag of street marijuana are included when weighing.

Judges also use civic duty to put their thumbs on the scale by permitting arbitrary statutory schemes that falsify weights. When LSD is distributed on blotter paper, the drug's weight may measure in milligrams or even micrograms. Statutes, however, require the blotter paper itself to be added to the drug weight. This is like sticking a slice of ham in the middle of a fresh roll of butcher paper and charging a customer for fifteen pounds of ham. By adding in the weight of inert blotter paper, the U.S. Supreme Court ruled that someone who possessed 0.005 gram of LSD could receive a mandatory sentence for possessing 5.7 grams.[281] In one federal case involving $30 worth of LSD, the inert carrier weight was used to charge the defendant with possessing $11 million worth of LSD.[282] Prosecutors thereby transformed a $30 misdemeanor into a felony carrying a thirty-year minimum sentence. In 1993, the U.S. Sentencing Commission responded to such extremes by modifying the LSD weighting rule, but the rule remained arbitrary. For example, with LSD in a glass vial, only the drug's weight counts, not the inert vial's weight also.[283] Nonetheless, courts fulfill their civic duty by upholding the arbitrary scheme. The same occurs with marijuana. Federal sentencing rules specify:

In the case of an offense involving marihuana plants, if the offense
involved (A) 50 or more marihuana plants, treat each plant as equivalent to 1 KG of marihuana; (B) fewer than 50 marihuana plants, treat
each plant as equivalent to 100 G of marihuana. *Provided*, however,
that if the actual weight of the marihuana is greater, use the actual
weight of the marihuana.[284]

Actual weight is used only if it produces a maximum sentence. Otherwise, fake
weights are used to maximize the sentence. In one case, the plants weighed only
10 grams each, but the judge used the statutory weight of 100 grams to pass
sentence on the basis of ten times as much marijuana as was actually confiscated.[285] A Michigan law required a life sentence for anyone convicted of possessing
650 grams of any substance containing a mixture of cocaine. Because no degree
of purity was required to trigger that mandatory penalty, no particular amount of
cocaine was required.[286] The same principle is used in federal sentencing rules
for other drugs:

A mixture weighing 10 grams containing PCP at 50% purity contains
5 grams of PCP (actual). In the case of a mixture or substance
containing PCP or methamphetamine, use the offense level determined
by the entire weight of the mixture or substance, or the offense level
determined by the weight of the PCP (actual) or methamphetamine
(actual), whichever is greater.[287]

By criminalizing acts explicitly protected by statute (such as possessing
cannabis stalks) and by enhancing penalties through arbitrary statutory criteria
(such as adding the weight of legal blotter paper to the weight of illegal LSD or
falsifying the weight of confiscated marijuana), courts embrace civic duty and the
educational nature of law.

The educational nature of law, along with civic duty, encourages ruthless
conduct in dealing with members of a group targeted for destruction. In 1982 the
U.S. Supreme Court ruled that a 40-year prison sentence was reasonable for
distributing 9 ounces of marijuana worth $200 (a quantity roughly equivalent to
a carton of cigarettes).[288] Forty years for a $200 crime. Another Missouri man
faced 10 years in prison for selling $25 worth of cocaine, plus another 25 years
for selling $20 worth. Thirty-five years in prison for a $45 dollar crime. The
prosecutor portrayed the result as compassionate, claiming that a long incarceration would help the man stop using cocaine[289] (as if drugs are unavailable in
prison). Simple possession of drugs at home already carries a harsher penalty
than endangering lives through drunk driving, and in 1990 the governor of
Alabama demanded that any marijuana user be imprisoned for one year.[290] In

1991 the U.S. Supreme Court upheld the reasonableness of mandatory life imprisonment for simple possession of drugs.[291] Indeed, the law considers drug offenses to be worse than murder. The average federal sentence for homicide is less than 7 years. A nineteen-year-old with a clean record received 10 years for carrying crack for a drug dealer.[292] A drug offender serving a 20-year mandatory minimum sentence had an uncle who was murdered; the murderer served 7½ years.[293] A Missouri man was sentenced to 5 years for killing a child and an additional 9 years for selling cocaine.[294] A Missouri judge gave a 30-year sentence to a crack cocaine offender with no previous criminal record; a few hours earlier the same judge gave 21 years to a recidivist murderer.[295] All these cases represent customary practice. There is nothing unusual about them. In 1992 the federal *minimum* sentence for LSD possession was 10.1 years (first offense). Compare to the *maximum* sentences for the following first offenses: rape 7.2 years, kidnapping 5.2 years, theft of $80 million 5.2 years.[296]

Civic duty has progressed so far in drug cases that judges now sentence people who are found innocent of a charge. A federal appeals court explained: "A not guilty verdict simply indicates that guilt was not proved beyond a reasonable doubt; it does not establish that the defendant played no part in the charged conduct. Conduct underlying the acquittal may be used in sentencing."[297] A defendant found guilty of selling 1 ounce of cocaine faced 20 months in federal prison. Federal prosecutors instead demanded a 20-year sentence for conspiracy to distribute cocaine, even though the defendant was found innocent of that charge.[298] A jury convicted someone for selling 1.44 grams of crack but found him innocent of possessing another 5.63 grams with intent to sell. The charge on which the twenty-year-old first-time offender was convicted carried a maximum of 16 months' imprisonment. Nonetheless the federal judge handed down a 5-year sentence based on the 5.63 grams.[299] Not only can people be sentenced for "crimes" of which they are acquitted, but in the name of drugs people can be sentenced even if they are never charged with a particular crime.[300] While conducting his first cocaine deal, a nervous defendant bragged about fictitious past experience. On the basis of those imaginary crimes, the judge lengthened the defendant's sentence by fifty percent, even though he was never charged with any of them.[301]

Despite judicial savagery, we continually hear police and prosecutors complain about lenient judges. The spirit of those complaints is reminiscent of *Judges' Letters*, the publication in which Nazi authorities exhorted judges to outdo one another in harshness.

Just like their Nazi predecessors, American prosecutors are now allowed to appeal a sentence if they consider it too lenient.[302] Prosecutors got an appeals court to lengthen a sentence because a judge took under consideration the three small children of the convicted woman; the appeals court said imprisonment is expected to harm family life, and there was no reason to give the woman better treatment than anyone else received.[303] On appeal from prosecutors, a higher court lengthened a sentence that the trial judge gave to a pregnant defendant. The appeals court declared, "Since time immemorial the sins of parents have been visited on children."[304] At the Nuremberg Military Tribunal, such practices were described as "punitive double jeopardy" and were listed among crimes committed by Nazi prosecutors and judges.[305]

In the interest of increasing penalties, civic duty allows prosecutors to disregard the Fifth Amendment's protection against double jeopardy. Often local, state, and federal laws prohibit the same offense. Because a person is only supposed to be tried once for an offense, generally prosecutors in one jurisdiction will not file charges if a person has been tried for the offense in another jurisdiction. I listened once as a horrified prosecutor rejected a proposal that a person convicted of a municipal animal abuse crime should be tried again under state laws providing harsher punishment. In drug offenses, however, prosecutors find that civic duty requires evasion of the Fifth Amendment in order to extract the harshest possible punishment. Someone convicted on state charges of possessing cocaine with intent to distribute was subsequently convicted on federal charges of possessing cocaine with intent to distribute. The convict reported a statement from a federal agent: "He felt I did not get enough time in the state court."[306] A Florida man served one year in state prison for a 1985 marijuana cultivation offense and then returned to the community. In 1991, on the basis of the 1985 search warrant, he was charged with violating federal marijuana conspiracy law and received a mandatory life sentence.[307] That sort of technique is difficult to distinguish from the Nazi practice described by Minister of Justice Franz Gürtner: "The judge is now in a position to order that habitual criminals shall be kept in custody after they have served their sentence."[308] Another evasion of the Fifth Amendment occurs when one court dismisses charges against someone and prosecutors in another jurisdiction then file charges for the same offense. A Montana mountain man was convicted on marijuana charges, but the state judge dismissed firearms charges because many persons living in the woods possess guns for reasons other than protecting marijuana. Federal prosecutors thereupon filed gun charges and got an armed drug offender conviction, adding fifteen years to the sentence consecutively.[309] A Missouri man agreed to revocation of parole in return for state drug charges being dropped. Upon his subsequent release from prison, federal officials—instead of state officials—brought him to trial for the drug offense.[310]

These evasions of Fifth Amendment guarantees against double jeopardy follow the letter of the law. But following the letter of the law proved to be an inadequate defense for Nazi judges and prosecutors held accountable at Nuremberg. Their behavior was measured by effects on victims. Nuremberg Military Tribunal prosecutors noted that "discriminatory measures against Jews, Poles, 'gypsies,' and other designated 'asocials' resulted in harsh penal measures."[311] Those criminal penalties were characterized as out of proportion to any harm caused by prohibited acts. Nazi prosecutors and judges who perpetrated such penalties found themselves charged with crimes against humanity.[312]

We should not be surprised if ruthless attitudes encouraged by Nazi legal principles in America produce results reminiscent of Nazi jurisprudence. While a plumber worked on a kitchen drain, the homeowner was selling cocaine to undercover agents in the living room. The agents arrested both the owner and the plumber. Although both the plumber and the drug dealer insisted that the plumber had no connection with the drug transaction, he was charged with conspiracy and received a 15-year sentence. This was his first "offense."[313] A Michigan grandmother provided a ride to a friend of her sister-in-law. Although the grandmother knew nothing about the cocaine carried by the person, Michigan law defined her as a drug courier. She received a mandatory sentence of life imprisonment without parole.[314] A Texas grandmother received a 5-year sentence for using firearms in drug dealing. Undercover agents said she was present when they suggested a marijuana transaction to three other individuals. The secret agents agreed that she spoke with no one during the incident, that no one mentioned her name, and that she did not even observe the marijuana in question. For the past two decades, however, she had carried a registered pistol in her handbag, a handbag that was in her automobile during the incident. That was enough to cost 5 years of her life. This was her first "offense."[315] A Missouri farmer faced 6 months in jail for marijuana possession until federal prosecutors told him that he would be charged with using firearms in a drug offense because he kept registered firearms at his farm home. Unless he agreed to plead guilty to a crime carrying more than a 6-month penalty, he would face a 45-year mandatory sentence for using firearms to protect the marijuana (he readily admitted he kept the guns to protect his farm property, and federal authorities held that marijuana was part of his property). In addition, forfeiture proceedings would be used to seize the family farm and home unless he pleaded guilty to a crime more serious than marijuana possession. The farmer pleaded guilty to one count of being an armed drug offender, and began serving a 5-year sentence. This was his first offense.[316] A federal prosecutor bragged, "Over 5,700 armed criminals have been locked up for long federal sentences, all with no prospect of parole, in the last 18 months."[317] A Nazi prosecutor, too, boasted of convictions for "armed breach of the peace." Noted one student of such Nazi cases: "In most cases, the accused had not been armed at all. Still, the courts invented a link between . . . events that had taken place in entirely different locations at entirely different times."[318]

In 1991 U.S. Attorney General Richard Thornburgh declared that federal prosecutors were entitled to violate codes of professional ethics if such violations would promote convictions.[319] For example, federal prosecutors will now interview a defendant without notifying the defendant's attorney. One federal prosecutor declared he "is charged with the enforcement of Federal law and nobody—emphasize nobody—can interfere with that duty, whether it is the disciplinary committee or even the Federal District Court in disciplinary proceedings."[320]

Drug war attitudes have made Nazi legal principles so palatable that judicial officers now object to freeing innocent persons wrongly convicted. DNA tests granted to prisoners convicted of rape have exonerated so many that one legal observer has warned that continuation of such tests "could destroy our faith in the jury system."[321] An FBI official has warned of "potential for abuse" by convicts requesting DNA tests.[322] One Missouri judge has denied a convict's request for a DNA test.[323] Given the careful scientific analyses of evidence introduced at rape trials, along with "positive" identifications of defendants by witnesses under cross-examination, we can wonder if the percentage of wrongly convicted drug defendants is even higher than that of wrongly convicted rape defendants. In 1993 the U.S. Supreme Court carried Nazi legal principles to their ultimate conclusion in a ruling that new evidence demonstrating a condemned person's innocence was insufficient cause to stop an execution.[324] Justice Blackmun protested, "I believe it contrary to any standard of decency to execute someone who is actually innocent."[325] After someone was convicted of a capital offense in Missouri, key trial witnesses said their testimony had been coerced and their lies had convicted an innocent man. But the U.S. Supreme Court decision just noted was cited as preventing court action to stop the execution.[326] In another Missouri case, a prisoner was sentenced to death for murdering a fellow inmate. The court-appointed defense lawyer, however, did not present testimony from a guard who was talking to the condemned man when the murder occurred and who watched him stroll into the prison cafeteria, where a surveillance camera recorded the prisoner as guards suddenly rushed off in response to the disturbance where the murder occurred. Citing new federal rules restricting appeals, an appeals court refused to consider evidence that the court-appointed trial lawyer had not presented. "You may indeed be innocent, but you are not innocent enough early enough," said an appeals judge.[327] "Here were all these judges, and they just signed the death certificates which we turned in to them without a question. We had lost our sense of right!" exclaimed an SS concentration camp guard after the war. "Why did not the 15,000 judges of Germany rise as one man and say 'you can't do this!'"[328] At the end of the motion picture *Judgment at Nuremberg*, the convicted German judge says he had no idea that persecution of Jews would proceed to wholesale slaughter. The American jurist replies, "It came to that the first time you sentenced a man to death you knew to be innocent."

A striking element surrounding ruthless punishment is the admitted drug use of many drug warriors. After a friend of Missouri's anti-drug coordinator publicly spoke of how they frequently got high on marijuana together, the governor praised the coordinator: "Chuck's efforts have been tireless and his work has always been of the highest quality."[329] The number of legislators, judges, prosecutors, and police officers who freely admit past illicit substance use is staggering. Speaking in the state capitol, Missouri Senate Republican leader Thomas McCarthy declared, "This place would be pretty deserted" if former drug users could not hold office.[330] In one of Missouri's hottest county prosecutor elections of 1992, in which the drug war was a major issue, almost all candidates readily confessed to marijuana use. A marijuana user was elected state attorney general that November. Other users were elected vice president and president of the United States. Presidents Reagan and Bush each nominated marijuana users to the Supreme Court. In 1995 Republican members of Congress chose a marijuana user as speaker of the house. While enjoying a marijuana cigarette in the White House, President Kennedy joked about an upcoming drugs conference.[331] Yet government officials who approve marijuana use for themselves demand that other, "less dependable" citizens receive savage punishment for the same conduct.

Such savagery is being extended to foreign countries. In 1988 a federal grand jury indicted Panama's president Manuel Noriega for activity in Panama that violated U.S. drug control statutes. In 1989 the top federal law enforcement officer, George Bush, ordered U.S. military forces to invade Panama, abduct Noriega, and force him to stand trial in the United States. By U.S. government admission, 539 persons were killed in the arrest operation. The arrest also required violent overthrow of Panama's lawful government. Noriega's attorneys argued that a foreign citizen on foreign soil could not be held accountable by the United States for activity forbidden by U.S. law. The U.S. Supreme Court rejected that argument, holding that anyone anywhere in the world could be kidnapped (not extradited but kidnapped) and brought to trial in the United States for conduct that violated domestic U.S. law. In the case of Mexican citizen Humberto Alvarez-Machain, who was kidnapped from Mexico by U.S. drug agents, Chief Justice William H. Rehnquist ruled that if an extradition treaty with a nation does not prohibit kidnapping, kidnapping is legal.[332] A dissent by Justice

Stevens noted that such reasoning meant "if the United States . . . thought it more expedient to torture or simply to execute a person rather than to attempt extradition, these options would be equally available because they, too, were not explicitly prohibited by the Treaty."[333] Alvarez-Machain was held in a U.S. prison for almost three years without trial after being kidnapped from Mexico on orders of the DEA. He was finally released because insufficient evidence existed to bring him to trial.[334] In the name of drugs, federal officials can now kidnap and imprison persons for years without trial, just as Nazi kidnap squads did. These kidnappings could be done on a mass scale; during World War II the State Department and FBI kidnapped thousands of Japanese living in Latin America and shipped them to concentration camps in the United States.[335]

During the Civil War, a classic treatise on constitutional law declared:

> The law of nations is above the constitution of any government; and no people would be justified by its peculiar constitution in violating the rights of other nations. Thus, if it had been provided in the Articles of Confederation, or in the present constitution, that all citizens should . . . be lawfully empowered to make incursions into England, France, or other countries, and seize by force and bring home such men and women as they should select, and, if these privileges should be put in practice, England and France would be justified in treating us as a nest of pirates, or a band of marauders and outlaws. The whole civilized world would turn against us, and we should justly be exterminated.[336]

Application of domestic narcotics laws to foreigners in foreign jurisdictions was defined as a crime against humanity at Nuremberg.[337] And even Hitler never went so far as American drug warriors, citing drug laws as an excuse to invade other countries.

If courts say drug squads can operate in defiance of some jurisdictions' laws (such as Mexico's), the same legal principle can be applied to laws of other jurisdictions (such as the United States).

BOYCOTT

Having examined ways in which the American legal system works to destroy drug users, let us consider ways in which private boycott actions promote the same goal. Boycott actions may be promoted by government but are carried out by private individuals and groups. The strategy is to isolate victims from the rest of society and thereby separate them from means of surviving in society.

Current drug war strategy contrasts with the one used during alcohol Prohibition. Prohibition's target was commerce, the dealers. Users were left alone. At first the federal government claimed to pursue the same policy when enforcing laws against other drugs, but failure to eliminate commerce in illegal drugs led to a change in strategy. President Reagan targeted users, not dealers. The theory was that if the millions of illicit drug users were eliminated, dealers supplying them would automatically be eliminated, and the goal of eliminating illegal drug commerce would at last be achieved. In order to protect users from dealers, users would be destroyed. Just as villages in Vietnam were destroyed for their own good in order to protect them from communists. Just as was suggested in 1938 by an SS officer speaking to senior psychiatrists: "The solution of the problem of the mentally ill becomes easy if one eliminates these people."[338] Following Reagan's decision, a campaign of vituperative rhetoric was unleashed against drug users to prepare public opinion for the destruction process. Earlier we examined the organization and content of this campaign. Here we shall examine consequences.

Just as private German organizations expelled Jewish members, we also see private American organizations expelling members targeted as victims. Such organizations range from bar associations to athletic teams. As in the war on Jews, these private boycott actions are encouraged by government. In 1933 German education officials sought to end scholarships for Jewish students.[339] Almost sixty years later, Missouri drug war officials promoted legislation to terminate scholarships of student drug offenders and thereby prevent them from getting college educations. Moreover, students were to be required to pay back any scholarship money previously received.[340] Federal law not only revokes student loans from drug offenders[341] but penalizes colleges that fail to act against students and staff who use drugs. Under provisions of the Drug-Free Schools and Communities Act of 1989, colleges even require students to sign contracts that they will not be illicit drug users while enrolled at the school. Such a contract grants implicit permission for unannounced body fluid tests, and violation of the contract can terminate financial aid or even enrollment. Virginia Governor L. Douglas Wilder went further, suggesting that all Virginia college students be tested for drug use.[342]

Germans who resisted the anti-Jewish boycott were shunned. Americans who resist the drug war are shunned. Many employers will not hire anyone who declines to submit urine for testing. Refusal of employment is a powerful act of shunning and will be detailed later. Elected officials who privately believe the drug war is mistaken have told me they fear to say so publicly lest they be shunned and removed from office. I have been ridiculed and demeaned for asking that sick people be given access to marijuana upon their physician's request. Irate persons declare that if I think drug users should not be imprisoned, then I must be a drug user; such declaration is an implied threat of an anonymous phone call to instigate a drug squad raid on my house. (I also believe that citizens who vote for Republicans should not be imprisoned, but no one seems to conclude that I vote for Republicans.)

Just as Nazis pilloried anyone who resisted the war on Jews, drug warriors advocate that drug war resisters be pilloried. Speaking of users whose conduct is not impaired by drugs, federal drug czar William Bennett declared, "These are the users who should have their names published in local papers. They should be subject to . . . employer notification."[343] He also urged that their pictures be published in newspapers.[344] Because drug use does not harm such persons, Bennett wanted publicity of their drug use to harm them. In adopting *Der Stürmer*'s pillory tactic, Bennett hoped for the same result sought by Julius Streicher: ostracism by the user's neighbors, badgering of the user's children, loss of the user's job. Bennett sought government action (such as civil forfeiture and driver's license loss) to tighten private shunning, and in the meantime he wanted private shunning to accomplish what he did not yet have the power to decree. The U.S. Customs Service went further yet, releasing to news media a weekly list of "small-scale [drug] smugglers who were neither arrested nor prosecuted for their alleged crimes."[345] In the name of drugs, police now decide who should be ostracized as a criminal, regardless of whether the person is accused (let alone convicted) in court.

REVOCATION OF LEGAL RIGHTS

On top of private shunning, drug users suffer loss of legal rights. Such loss by drug users is in addition to constitutional rights lost by all citizens in the name of drugs. For example, although most citizens can keep firearms in their homes, drug users who do so become armed drug offenders subject to lengthy prison terms. Another example: Most residents of a college town are free to rent houses or apartments owned by the school or privately owned but near school property. Not so for a drug user. A "small-time junkie" who did not sell drugs received a ten-year sentence for living near a school.[346] A gainfully employed single mother who summons police after shooting at someone attempting to burglarize her school-owned rental house can be imprisoned for decades as an armed drug offender near a school if responding officers notice marijuana in the house. Such things can happen: A Missouri man summoned police to rescue a woman being attacked outside his residence. As police were en route, she broke free and ran to the Good Samaritan, who let her inside his residence. When police arrived, they noticed marijuana in the residence and arrested the Good Samaritan.[347]

Nuremberg Tribunal prosecutors highlighted with disgust a Gestapo man's recollection of law enforcement officers who "arrested those who sent their cries for help to the police."[348]

Even simple pleasures can become crimes. Maryland's governor demanded revocation of fishing licenses held by drug users.[349] Most citizens, including convicted murderers, are allowed to drive automobiles. In many states, however, someone convicted of smoking marijuana at home is thereafter forbidden to operate a motor vehicle. And just as Jews were banned from libraries, the Missouri legislature considered imprisoning citizens for life if they shared a marijuana cigarette within 1,000 feet of a library.[350] Drug users are considered unfit for community service as well. For instance, drug use is often used to discredit a witness in an American court, just as being Jewish discredited a witness in a German court.

In addition to losses of legal rights, drug users find special legal obligations forced upon them, as happened to Jews under Nazis. Some years ago, New Jersey introduced identity cards for drug offenders. Anyone who had paid a fine in California for marijuana possession ten years earlier could not remain in New Jersey for more than twenty-four hours without carrying a special registration card issued by police after they fingerprinted and photographed the former drug offender. In addition to carrying the identity card, the former offender had to register with local police when staying in any town for more than twenty-four hours.[351] At one time anyone diagnosed as a drug addict in Indiana could be arrested for appearing in public without "positive proof" that the affliction was being treated by a physician.[352] In contrast, anyone with a contagious disease was free to move among fellow citizens without seeking treatment. In the 1990s Seattle banned drug probationers from assorted districts of the city.[353] Although many states encourage citizens to gamble, a drug offender on probation can be imprisoned for placing a legal bet at racetrack. Likewise, employment can be a condition of probation for drug offenders, and those who lose their jobs can also lose their liberty. For such persons, unemployment is illegal. And of course drug offenders are required to urinate and defecate on surprise demand from government agents, an obligation designed to degrade and humiliate victims rather than simply obtain scientific data.

In addition to discriminating against victims, drug warriors have begun to follow the Nazi model of discriminating against relatives of victims.[354] William Bennett said that parents should be held legally responsible for drug violations by their children.[355] The U.S. Department of Housing and Urban Development developed a program to evict accused drug users from public housing even if they have not been convicted,[356] and the federal government has promoted state legislation evicting drug offenders from public housing. Missouri's Governor

John Ashcroft went further in the omnibus drug control measure he sought from the legislature in 1992. Under that legislation, if a teen were caught with a marijuana cigarette in a shopping mall, the teen's entire family would be evicted from public housing.[357] As in Nazi Germany, responsibility for the offense was determined by genealogy of victims rather than by their actions. Punishment was through civil penalty rather than criminal law, in order to evade criminal law restrictions on punishing innocent persons. The federal Anti-Drug Abuse Act of 1988 allows public housing tenants to be evicted if one of their guests is accused of a drug offense.[358] Not only are innocent persons punished, but they are punished when someone else is merely accused of an offense, not convicted of one.

Just as in the war on Jews, the war on drug users applies criminal penalties to friendship. A Massachusetts law made it illegal for a person to be in a house where a friend was using marijuana, even if the visitor refrained from using the drug. Indeed, friendship with the marijuana user was viewed as graver than marijuana use itself: The user faced imprisonment of 3½ years, but the visitor faced 5 years.[359] Federal authorities offered to reduce a marijuana distributor's penalty if he would turn in friends who had trusted him. He refused to betray his friends, and prosecutors adjusted the indictment so he was convicted on charges carrying a mandatory sentence of life imprisonment. Life imprisonment for marijuana, and for friendship.[360]

Aryans were persecuted for maintaining business relations with Jews. So, too, are Americans persecuted for non-drug business relationships with suspected drug offenders. We have already seen government searches of persons who buy garden equipment from sources that are allegedly "drug-tainted." The same can happen to persons who rent real estate from accused drug offenders. One such person arrived home to find a drug squad ransacking the house he rented. The landlord was a suspected drug dealer, and officers had a warrant to search all property owned by the landlord. Although the renter was accused of no crime, the drug squad confiscated his family pictures and financial records. "I don't even have access to my checking account," the bewildered victim said. Moreover, government agents seized ownership of the house and ordered the renter to either sign an agreement holding the government blameless for any actions or else vacate the premises by 9:00 the next morning. When a drug squad arrived at another renter's house, she told the news media that this was the second time her home had been searched because of the landlord's alleged drug offenses.[361]

Persons who retain any connection with a drug offender can find themselves targeted for more than harassment. They can be punished if they fail to stop others from using drugs. The punishment can be boycott, such as an employer firing a wife who failed to prevent her husband from using marijuana,[362] a throwback to the Nazi policy of firing the spouse of someone who offended the community.[363] Or punishment can involve civil sanctions, such as evicting a family from public housing if a family member is caught with a marijuana cigarette. Punishment can even include criminal sanctions, such as laws holding parents responsible if they fail to prevent crimes committed by their juvenile offspring. Such failures would have been termed "crimes of omission" in Nazi courts. Nazis believed that civic duty required citizens to be held accountable for the conduct of anyone they could influence. Germans lost their university jobs because their maids bought meat from Jewish butchers, and a German notary was held criminally responsible for his wife's purchase at a Jewish business. Another example was a hit-and-run auto accident, in which a Nazi court held a passenger criminally liable for not preventing the driver from leaving.[364] Crimes of omission emphasize civic duty owed to the community by all citizens. Being personally law-abiding is not enough. If citizens fail to halt crime around them, they become accomplices to perpetrators. Citizens who do not stop crime are part of the problem, traitors to the war effort (whether the war be against Jews or drug users). "Whoever stands on the sidelines while others risk life and limb for the glory of Germany and the liberty of future generations is a parasite. He incurs the contempt of the nation and the punishment he deserves from our courts."[365]

Similarities in the war on Jews and the war on drug users are obvious. An important difference in strategy can be seen, however, in efforts to produce Jew-free and drug user-free economies. The Nazi effort included businesses owned or operated by Jews. In contrast, drug warriors rarely urge boycott of products or services provided by drug-using business people. Drug warriors continually warn of threats posed to society by drug-using workers, but we hear nothing about threats posed by drug-using business managers or owners. We hear no calls to boycott a car dealership or grocery store run by someone identified as a drug user or who employs drug users. This silence is revealing. Nazis who made war on Jews and Americans who make war on drug users seek to transfer jobs and personal property to citizens who are more "pure" than others. Unlike Nazis, however, American drug warriors do not seek to alter management or ownership of the nation's business structure. Individual employers may become casualties of friendly fire, but the drug war bombards workers rather than employers. Such a dichotomy in effort suggests that the drug war is intended as a tool to give employers more power over employees' lives. "It is no longer enough to simply be a productive employee, but one has to be productive in a certain manner, while living a particular and accepted life style."[366] Because illicit drug use is incorrectly assumed to reflect rebellious attitudes that make an employee hard to discipline, through urine tests "many managers feel they can infer answers to questions about workers' personalities and beliefs that cannot be asked openly in interviews."[367] Moreover, if an employee can be ordered to give up an illicit drug in the name of productivity (regardless of whether off-duty drug use affects job performance), the same excuse allows an employer to forbid workers to use a licit drug such as alcohol. Employers can now fire workers if their body fluids indicate that tobacco has been smoked at home.[368] The same excuse allows an employer to use electronic monitoring to be sure employees are home after 10:00 P.M. and getting a good night's sleep. If private contracts can require citizens to give up civil liberties (such as the right to smoke tobacco at home), then private contracts can be used to extinguish other rights (such as complaining to a government official or giving birth to a child). If exercise of a "right" deprives a person of employment, food, and shelter, then fines or imprisonment are unnecessary to prevent conduct disliked by government officials. Private contracts accomplish what is forbidden to government. Job contracts allow authoritarians to implement a larger agenda of control over citizens' lives.

Drug war regulations target the same occupations targeted in the war on Jews. At a legislative hearing, I watched Missouri's director of public safety (the state's top police officer) urge that professional and occupational licenses be revoked upon conviction for marijuana use. "Once a few barbers lose their livelihoods, we'll be sending a powerful message." Under legislation promoted by Missouri drug warriors, marijuana users were to be banned from the following occupations: barber, cosmetologist, hairdresser, manicurist, dental hygienist, funeral director, embalmer, speech pathologist, real estate broker or salesperson, insurance agent, bail bond agent, investment adviser, cigarette wholesaler, salvage dealer, private employment agency manager, theatrical booking agency operator, hearing aid dealer, certified public accountant, architect, land surveyor, and engineer.

Driver's license revocation is intended to eliminate employment; often the ability to drive a car is crucial to holding a job. A Wyoming court considering the issue declared driving to be a "fundamental" right and crucial "in order to be a productive citizen and to maintain gainful employment."[369] In Massachusetts a truck driver convicted of possessing a marijuana cigarette lost his driver's license even though the offense was unrelated to driving. He thereupon lost his $400 weekly paycheck and eventually found part-time work at a grocery store for $100 a week. Another Massachusetts marijuana offender lost his license in similar circumstances, losing a day's wages whenever he was unable to get rides to his workplace 25 miles from his residence.[370] Persons using marijuana at home are banned from driving motor vehicles in many other states, even if the marijuana offense had nothing to do with a motor vehicle. Missouri Governor John Ashcroft demanded that driver's licenses be revoked if a person was simply arrested on suspicion of using marijuana. He said no trial should be necessary; accusation by a police officer should be sufficient grounds for punishment.[371] In evaluating driver's license revocation for conduct unrelated to driving, one judge found the punishment to be so arbitrary that it opened the way to "analogous laws"[372] (an American legal term equivalent to the Nazi educational nature of law).

Proponents of the driver's license ban do not argue that someone who unwinds with marijuana at bedtime is unfit to drive the next day. They argue that marijuana users reject civic duty (the duty not to use marijuana), and society must—for its own survival—reject persons having such an unpatriotic attitude. The same thinking and tactics were promoted by Nazis who made war on Jews: "He has deserted the inner front and, in a despicable manner, has thought only of himself and not of the community."[373] Civic duty even prohibits employment of persons using legal substances. A telephone company rejected job seekers whose bodies showed evidence of quinine use, on the grounds that illicit supplies of heroin may contain quinine, therefore the job seekers may have been heroin addicts.[374] An air force nurse was fired and jailed after a urine test revealed she had taken oxycodone. The jury agreed she had a legal prescription to use the drug to relieve pain from oral surgery, but she admitted using remnants of the prescription to relieve pain from a hip injury. Legally that unauthorized use made her a criminal drug abuser.[375] A truck driver who applied for a job failed the drug test because he took Tylenol 3 prescribed by his physician. Mindful of civic duty, the company said he was an opiate abuser and had to wait three years before applying for work again. That injustice contained irony: The applicant had served as a local law enforcement officer promoting the drug war. He was dumbfounded that he could be harmed by attitudes he had promoted.[376]

When people can lose employment upon mere accusation, even if they are later exonerated, Nazi legal principles are in force. For example, upon false Gestapo accusation of "communist" activity, an attorney was disbarred. A high court refused to hear his suit for damages, on grounds that the disbarment resulted from a political act of the Gestapo and courts could not intervene in such acts.[377] The truck driver applicant also learned that appeals to courts were fruitless. Moreover, the 1991 Workplace Drug Testing Act considered by the Missouri legislature said that employees fired on basis of false urine tests generally could not sue employers for damages, nor sue for defamation if the employer released false test results.[378] The EMIT urine test is known for its problems with false positives, yet courts often rule that a repeat EMIT test on the same sample confirms that the tested person is an illicit drug user.[379] But if EMIT yields a false positive the first time, chances are high that the same result will continue to occur no matter how many times the EMIT test is run on the sample. Many employers do not even bother with a second test; an initial positive result disqualifies a job applicant.[380] Likewise, employers who rely on the unproven technology of testing hair for evidence of illicit drug use often fail to confirm positive results with a more reliable test.[381]

Work performance of Jews was irrelevant to dismissal. Excellent Jewish employees were fired. The same is true of drug users. A truck driver lost the job he had held for nineteen years when the first urine test ever administered to him indicated he was a marijuana user. He also lost his pension benefits and had to sell his house. Another driver's personnel file bristled with commendations, and he had the company's top safety rating. He was fired for weekend marijuana use. One interesting use of workplace drug testing is to fire employees whose work is so outstanding that they are promoted to a position requiring a drug test.[382] In each case the point is to make it impossible for a victim to work. The point is to purify the workplace, not improve its output. Indeed the 1991 Workplace Drug Testing Act considered by the Missouri legislature explicitly declared that testing "need not be limited to circumstances where there are indications of individual, job-related impairment of an employee" and that competent employees could be fired if they failed the drug test.[383] The same reasoning was used in Nazi Germany in 1935 when a court held that employers could dismiss workers for listening to radio broadcasts from Moscow after working hours, even though such home life activity had no effect on job performance.[384] Another Nazi court ruling held that a worker could be fired for refusing to let his sons join the Hitler Youth even though that conduct did not harm job performance.[385] Still another Nazi court decision provided an intriguing argument adaptable to the drug-free workplace. In May 1935 a Jew who managed a store lost a lawsuit claiming breach of contract in his job termination. The court ruled the termination justified because having a Jewish employee would prevent an enterprise from advertising itself as a German business "at a time when this designation is a condition of business success."[386] Drug-free workplace agitation lends itself to the same sort of reasoning, that public disdain for a worker's status is a firing offense. Ostracism is itself grounds for deeper ostracism through job loss.

In addition, employers fulfilling government contracts can cite "drug-free workplace" clauses in those contracts as justifying job dismissals.[387] Such clauses have three effects. First, they force job dismissals in firms that might be otherwise inclined to retain excellent drug-using employees in defiance of government urgings. Second, firms can cite the clauses as a bureaucratic excuse for brutality. "Our hands are tied. We must follow the rules. Nothing personal about limiting your ability to survive." Lastly, drug testing clauses transform employers into law enforcement agencies, identifying and targeting drug users who cannot otherwise be detected by police. For example, we have seen a

Christian college pledge to report drug-using employees to police, and the Code of Federal Regulations authorized the Federal Railroad Administration to release employee body fluid samples to prosecutors.[388] An employer might even announce that employee records would be released to government agents upon demand; workers who stayed after such an announcement would thereby waive their Fifth Amendment right to withhold drug test results from police—another example of private contracts being used to extinguish rights disliked by authoritarians.

As early as 1934, an observer of Nazi Germany saw the connection between a policy of unemployment and a policy of annihilation: "Jews can survive pogroms. They cannot survive being robbed of all means of earning a livelihood."[389] The possibility of an illicit drug user finding and keeping any sort of employment in the United States is small if the person is subjected to unannounced drug tests. I have even seen signs at a convenience store and an office supply store warning any drug user who wanted to be a clerk to look for work elsewhere, just as signs in German stores used to tell Jews to go elsewhere. An economy can escape damage from a war on productive workers only if unemployment is high enough. That was the case in Nazi Germany. Waiting Aryans took over jobs of dismissed Jews, and no net loss of national productivity occurred. In addition, dismissed Jews disappeared from unemployment statistics because they stopped looking for work; Nazi agencies controlled hiring. American drug warriors have not only followed this model but avoided a key economic cost of the war on Jews. Because Jewish businesses were integrated with the rest of the German economy, actions taken against business owners disrupted the nation's economic well-being. Drug warriors, however, generally avoid actions against businesses owned or operated by drug users.

The ultimate Nazi argument for a Jew-free workplace was expressed by Minister of Economic Affairs Walther Funk in November 1938: "One cannot exclude the Jews from the political life, but let them live and work in the economic sphere."[390] A group that did not merit full political rights did not merit economic rights either. Although American drug war leaders have not vocalized that argument, their actions betray a similar attitude in which victims are denied both civil and economic rights, in hopes of removing victims from American society. Political conservatives who champion such dual sanctions are well aware of their devastating effect. "There can be no liberty unless there is economic liberty," declared British Prime Minister Margaret Thatcher,[391] whose views were rarely distinguishable from those of Presidents Reagan and Bush. A destruction process will encompass denial of both economic and civil rights. The two sanctions compliment and build upon each other. Notes one historian, "Once Jews had been eliminated from the economic life, it was possible to deprive them of all legal protection without adversely affecting the economic system."[392] After observing Nazi Germany firsthand, in 1938 (long before death camps were even considered, let alone established), Stephen Roberts wrote,

> At present, the German Jew has no civil rights. . . . He has no liberty of speech and cannot defend himself in print; he cannot become a civil servant or a judge; he cannot be a writer or a publisher or a journalist; he cannot speak over the radio; he cannot become a screen actor or an actor before Aryan audiences; he cannot teach in any educational institution; he cannot enter the service of the railway, the Reichsbank, and many other banks. . . . It is a campaign of annihilation—a pogrom of the crudest form, supported by every State instrument.[393]

DRUG USERS AS ZOMBIES

There are three ways to survive: gainful employment, welfare, or crime. By losing the possibility of employment, drug users must resort to welfare or crime. Yet drug warriors seek even to cut off welfare, as through evictions from public housing in Missouri. Drug warriors want to leave drug users with one option for survival: crime. The public will then accept merciless attacks on drug users, because there will be a high correlation between drug use and predatory criminality. But that correlation will have nothing to do with pharmaceutical chemistry. Instead it will be caused by the setting—the laws—in which drug use is forced to occur. In order to encourage destruction of drug users, drug warriors encourage an increase in predatory crime.

Loss of employment, loss of friendships, loss of family life. We saw all these techniques used by Nazis who went to war against Jews, turning Jews into zombies, the living dead who wander through a community but are not part of it. We see the same techniques used by Americans who go to war against drug users—not because the Americans consciously model themselves after Nazis, but because such techniques naturally arise if a policy leads to destruction of a defined group of people.

As in Nazi Germany, no central office in the United States directs the process of destruction. Those who fought Jews and those who fight drug users have each complained about duplications of effort, conflicting jurisdictions, and other impediments. Despite such complaints, both war efforts targeted and seized victims with alacrity. Bureaucratic disorganization does not limit the war's efficiency because every element of society cooperates in the war: public housing bureaucrats, state license bureaucrats, business owners, churches, schools, clubs. Missouri farmers adopt "policy statements" supporting drug squad tactics, and bicycle enthusiasts in the state have enlisted as "Anti-Drug Pedalers."[394] Even stamp collectors discuss philately's role in fighting the drug war.[395] Victims can find no sanctuary, no escape. They are relentlessly hunted. They exhibit characteristics of hunted animals: fear, bewilderment, depression, exhaustion, malaise, despair. Such conduct is often blamed on drugs, but Jews demonstrated the same conduct in Germany as formerly supportive elements of society—from police to physicians—turned against them.[396] When every good citizen is sworn to eliminate targeted persons, bureaucratic paper flow is superfluous to the effort.

Federal drug czar William Bennett declared:

> The addict is almost completely present-minded—preoccupied with finding and taking his drug; other planning and organizational skills have largely deserted him. He very often cannot maintain anything resembling a normal family or work life. Some addicts may attempt to become dealers to earn money, but most fail at this work, too, since they lack sufficient self-control to avoid consuming their own sales inventory. What's more, an addict's active enthusiasm for his drug's euphoric high or soothing low tends significantly to recede over time; for biochemical reasons, that high or low becomes increasingly difficult to reproduce (except at risk of a lethal overdose), and drug taking becomes a mostly defensive effort to head off the unpleasant psychological effects of a "crash"—or the intensely painful physical effects of actual withdrawal.[397]

According to Bennett's criteria, drug warriors are superior to any drug addict they master. The master race mercifully reduces suffering by accelerating the journey to doom that is biologically ordained for the inferior group. Without intervention, the inferiors might have to await their doom for decades before their casual drug use becomes a problem for them. More than once Bennett publicly praised vigilante murder of suspected drug dealers.[398] In Kansas City, Missouri, a group of Vietnam War veterans contacted a minister and made a vow of violence: "Give your methods a try but if they don't work, we're going to use the same tactics we used in 'Nam."[399] Groups such as Guardian Angels and the Nation of Islam have produced "anti-drug" vigilante patrols known for violence.[400] Vigilantes who burned a suspected drug house in Detroit were acquitted of arson charges.[401] In a two-week period, Miami vigilantes burned thirty-five suspected drug houses.[402] Governmental endorsement of ferocity, combined with refusal of legal redress to citizens whose property is destroyed or confiscated by government agents, encourages a climate of violence. The Nazi regime used such strategy and tactics in Germany. Can results in America be any different?

Although parallels between Nazi discriminatory actions against Jews and American actions against drug users are disquieting, a modern reader may be tempted to interpret the parallels as historical coincidence, a mere curiosity that poses no warning. Prosecutors at Nuremberg, however, believed that discriminatory legislation was linked to other horrors: "The terrorization, murder, and persecution of political opponents, the dissolution of all organizations affording opportunity for opposition, criticism or even free speech, the systematic perversion of youth and training for war would not, however, have sufficed without persecution of the Jews." The persecution provided an excuse for destroying democracy, an excuse embraced by a public filled with fear and hatred by propaganda about a nonexistent threat from Jews.[403]

Historian Raul Hilberg took a still longer view when arguing that discrimination against ordinary fellow citizens holds a deadly potential: "The missionaries of Christianity had said in effect: You have no right to live among us as Jews. The secular rulers who followed had proclaimed: You have no right to live among us. The German Nazis at last decreed: You have no right to live."[404]

When the present book was written in the 1990s, many Americans were skeptical that the war on drug users would ever proceed to state-sponsored killing. German anti-Semites of the 1890s shared similar skepticism. At that time *Reichstag* member Hermann Ahlwardt said, "We wouldn't think of going as far as have the Austrian anti-Semites in the Federal Council (*Reichsrat*) and to move that a bounty be paid for every Jew shot or to decree that he who kills a Jew shall inherit his property. We have no such intention. We shall not go as far as that."[405] But others, in later times, inspired by years of discriminations against ordinary people, did go farther.

3

CONFISCATION

Courts try cases, but cases also try courts.
Robert H. Jackson[1]

Confiscation of property is a major element in a destruction process aimed at ordinary people. Once victims are identified they can be ostracized. When ostracized they can be deprived of jobs. But as long as victims have assets convertible into cash, victims can still buy food, shelter, or health care. Confiscating such assets, however, guarantees that victims can no longer survive (unless they resort to crime, thereby opening new levels of sanctions against them). Property confiscation is a key element to removing a group of ordinary people from society.

Previous to the war on drug users, the United States had two experiences with mass confiscation of individuals' private property. The first was not a transfer of ownership but an elimination of ownership: the liberation of human slaves. Despite the tremendous financial blow to owners, Amendment Fourteen to the U.S. Constitution forbade compensation. That factor is not cited to suggest that restitution was justified, but merely to recall a national experience with separating large numbers of ordinary persons from large amounts of property, lawfully and without redress.

The second great experience involved property left behind when Americans were sent to concentration camps during World War II. As in Germany, victims were targeted by race and identified by their genealogy—selected not because of anything they did, but because of their biological status as persons of Japanese descent. Targeting victims on the basis of their physical bodies is directly applicable to the war on drug users, but property confiscations from drug users are based on legal principles differing from those used against Japanese-Americans (whose property losses depended upon regulations concentrating those

Americans into camps).

As we shall see, drug warriors are forthright about intentions to seize the property of all drug users in the United States. Such avowals may seem fantastic, but necessary legal mechanisms have been constructed and set in motion. Two great examples of mass property confiscation, in the 1860s and 1940s, are mentioned above to remind us that programs of mass confiscation have historical precedent. Historical experience suggests that drug warriors will face little resistance to their confiscation program.

PROPERTY SEIZURE TECHNIQUES

In contrast to previous programs of mass confiscation, the war on drug users has no laws confiscating property from large numbers of persons simultaneously and en masse. By running forfeitures against one person at a time, drug warriors can operate silently. Hindered by neither public outcry nor organized resistance, drug warriors bring the full power of the state against each individual victim.

Two basic types of forfeiture exist. One uses criminal law, the other civil law. Criminal forfeiture occurs when a defendant is convicted of a crime. Sometimes a jury determines that the property in question played an essential role in the crime, and sometimes no jury determination is needed. Either way, the forfeiture operates as punishment. In criminal forfeiture (also called in personam forfeiture) the government must follow all due process guarantees of criminal trials. By contrast, in civil forfeiture (also called in rem) government has much more latitude. For example, a property owner[2] is not necessarily entitled to attend the civil proceedings, nor is there always a right to jury trial.[3] If a civil forfeiture trial occurs, the government need not prove its case. Instead, the property owner must disprove the government's accusation. "This is an advantage of enormous consequence," said one Justice Department forfeiture expert.[4] Procedural rules further strengthen the government's advantage; for example, hearsay is accepted as evidence for the government's case but cannot be used in the property owner's defense.[5] Admissible hearsay, notes a Justice Department forfeiture manual, "includes . . . even tips from confidential informants."[6] Indeed, mere "probable cause" is sufficient grounds for a civil forfeiture.[7] This is the same legal standard required for a search warrant, a standard now met by an anonymous telephoned accusation. The DEA recommends that drug squads seek civil forfeitures instead of criminal forfeitures because "the drug agent is faced with the development of evidence on a probable cause level, as opposed to proof. . . . It gives us a fighting chance."[8] The fight, however, is rigged in the drug squad's favor, as a Justice Department forfeiture expert admits: "Probable cause is defined flexibly in this context."[9] Perhaps most important of all, civil proceedings operate against property regardless of who owns it. As we shall see, the owner can be a blameless law-abiding citizen and still lose the property. Such factors make the civil forfeiture route attractive to drug squads.

Although different rules govern criminal and civil forfeitures, both types are punitive. The difference is a matter of form, not of purpose. "Proceedings instituted for the purpose of declaring the forfeiture of a man's property by reason of offences committed by him, though they may be civil in form, are in their nature criminal." So said U.S. Supreme Court Justice Joseph P. Bradley in 1886.[10] Justice Arthur Goldberg agreed in 1965: "A forfeiture proceeding is quasi-criminal in character. Its object, like a criminal proceeding, is to penalize for the commission of an offense against the law."[11] Indeed, a pardon bars civil forfeiture based on conduct that led to the conviction,[12] although civil forfeiture can take property from someone never convicted of a crime—a distinction readily exploited by drug warriors.

In addition to factors noted above, a drug squad's choice between criminal or civil forfeiture also depends on whether the squad prefers to gain absolute title to limited amounts of an owner's property or challengeable title to an unlimited amount. Criminal forfeiture allows government to acquire a person's interest in all property owned by that person, but outsiders having a claim on the property can prevent the government from perfecting title of ownership. In contrast, civil forfeiture can take only specified individual pieces of property (rather than a person's entire estate), but all outsiders lose any claim to those individual items. The scope of civil proceedings is more limited than criminal proceedings, but the civil route guarantees the government's title to the property.

WHAT FORFEITURE LAWS WERE INTENDED TO DO

Civil forfeiture laws are as old as the Republic, but originally had nothing to do with drugs. At first, only property that was illegal or used to commit a crime was subject to forfeiture. The owner was required to prove that the property was legal, but this was reasonable in the context of the early laws because they were directed against smuggling and piracy. A person wrongly accused of storing smuggled contraband in a warehouse merely had to produce forms showing that import duties had been paid. Illegal contraband found in a warehouse could be forfeited, but the warehouse itself could not be forfeited because it was legal property that had not been used to commit the crime of smuggling (an immobile building could not be used to transport goods). In contrast, pirate ships could be forfeited; the vessels themselves were legal but were used to commit crimes.

Such forfeitures punished shipowners who resided safely outside the jurisdiction of American courts.

A change came during the Civil War, in which forfeiture became a weapon in the war against the Confederacy. Congress considered a bill to punish Confederate soldiers, civil officers, and sympathizers by seizing their property if these persons could not be reached by federal courts. Unlike past forfeitures, these would not be for illegal use of legal property but for actions of owners, actions irrelevant to use of their property. Congressional debate revealed deep concern about violating the Constitution's prohibition against "forfeiture of estate" (the taking of property having no involvement with a crime). The Constitution's framers saw that forfeiture could be abused to destroy people convicted of crimes,[13] and the first Congress not only implemented the ban on forfeiture of estate but also forbade forfeiture as punishment for any crime. During the Civil War, Senator Jacob Collamer declared:

> A considerable part of the projects before the two Houses propose to confiscate people's property, real and personal, either all of the people in the South, or classes of them. How are you to do it without trying and convicting the men . . . ? There has been a recent discovery that there is a certain term—a law phrase—which, perhaps, the people will not understand, that has a vast deal of *hocus pocus* in it by which we can get rid of all that sort of business. What is it? It is what is called proceedings *in rem*.

Collamer protested, "This word 'confiscate' literally means 'put into the Treasury.' . . . If we make laws by our power under the Constitution we must regard the prohibitions of the Constitution, else we are lawless. And it makes very little difference to what department of the Government all this usurpation goes."[14] Senator Orville Browning noted that forfeiture was punishment and that the proposed law punished Confederate sympathizers through legislative fiat without criminal trial—punishment through a bill of attainder.

> If this power of legislative punishment really exists, what is to prevent us in any individual case . . . where the offender has fled from justice and got beyond the reach of the process of law, what, I ask, is to prevent us . . . from proceeding to a legislative outlawry of the fugitive, and the absolute confiscation of all his estate . . . and the total impoverishment of his family?

Senator Browning asked, "Does not this newly-invented, India-rubber, *in rem* proceeding for the punishment of offenses committed by the person, and in which the property was not implicated, stretch itself over the entire category of crimes, and cover them all?"[15] Proponents nonetheless urged swift action in the face of national emergency. Representative Elijah Babbitt thundered, "The contest in which we are engaged is a terrible and bloody war, which requires the use of every means at our command. . . . The hot season is even now upon us."[16] In contrast, Senator Browning warned against the lure of perceived emergency:

> The prohibitions were inserted because it was foreseen that occasions would arise when Congress would think it necessary to exercise the forbidden powers; when the strongest temptation to their exercise would exist; when popular clamor might demand their exercise; and when the danger of their possession would be enhanced just in proportion to the intensity of popular feeling and resentments. These restrictions were not provided for periods of tranquility . . . but for times of turbulence and danger, when inflamed passion would override reason, and resentment dethrone discretion and justice.[17]

Senator Collamer concurred, "Limitations and prohibitions of power in the Constitution were put there on purpose to prevent our doing such things when we wanted to do them. They were not put in to prevent our doing things we never wanted to do."[18]

Collamer also astutely pointed out a major attraction in the forfeiture legislation, an attraction peculiar to the era but important to congressional support for the proposed law: "There is another purpose that is covered up by this pretense of forfeiture or confiscation and proceedings *in rem*. . . . The truth is, that there is a large provision in this bill for the liberation of slaves, and I am strongly apprehensive that the more particular friends of this bill regard that as *the* bill."[19] Congress proposed civil forfeiture as a subterfuge to free slaves. That desire was seldom spoken aloud in debate, but was an engine driving Civil War forfeiture proposals.

President Abraham Lincoln shared concerns expressed by Collamer and Browning, and threatened to veto any confiscation acts, but in the end he decided that military necessity required extreme measures and signed the acts into law.[20]

Accordingly, persons who assisted the Confederacy lost all their property. Critics feared the war measure would establish a principle allowing forfeiture to become a tool for punishing unpopular persons accused of crimes other than treason or even persons accused of no crime at all. In 1871, however, the U.S. Supreme Court forbade such abusive use of civil forfeiture, saying it could not punish criminal conduct because otherwise civil forfeiture could evade the necessity of criminal trials before punishment. The Court did uphold the newly expanded notion of civil forfeiture (allowing seizure of property having neither criminal use nor connection with militarily harmful conduct by Confederate sympathizers), but only as a military measure expressing the government's war power. The Court ruled that forfeiture could not be used simply to punish Confederate sympathizers (as that was not a military necessity); nor could it be used against anyone who was not a military enemy.[21] Although that ruling prevented peacetime confiscation of property from law-abiding citizens if the property had no involvement in a crime, the ruling established that government can run such forfeitures in wartime. That prospect should be considered when evaluating calls for Congress to activate war powers by declaring a national drug emergency.

In 1886 the U.S. Supreme Court further limited use of civil forfeiture, ruling that civil forfeitures resulting from criminal activity had to follow rules of criminal jurisprudence, giving much more protection to property owners than civil jurisprudence provides.[22] That decision was prompted by laws requiring civil forfeiture victims to produce evidence that the government needed in order to win the forfeiture. Justice Bradley said that writers of the Fourth and Fifth Amendments would never have written laws like those in this case. "The question cannot admit of a doubt. They never would have approved of them. The struggle against arbitrary power in which they had been engaged for more than twenty years, would have been too deeply engraved in their memories to have allowed them to approve of such insidious disguises of the old grievance which they had so deeply abhorred."[23]

HOW DRUG WARRIORS TWISTED FORFEITURE LAWS TO EVADE LIMITS ON POLICE POWER

Abuses feared by nineteenth-century skeptics of forfeiture became a reality in the twentieth century, but a constitutional amendment was required for abuses to begin. In 1919 the Constitution was amended to prevent commerce in beverage alcohol. Public attitudes were aflame against demon rum. Prosecutors argued that any vehicle transporting beverage alcohol was being used for a criminal purpose and was subject to civil forfeiture, even if a passenger merely carried a small quantity for personal use without telling the driver. In 1920 a Colorado judge ridiculed that argument,[24] but the next year the U.S. Supreme Court ruled that the war on alcohol justified exactly that kind of forfeiture.[25] The principle that property could be forfeited by a person innocent of any crime was eagerly promoted by drug warriors long after Prohibition ended. They also pushed a natural expansion of that principle. If property of an innocent person could be seized, then so could property not involved in a crime. For example, an entire ranch could be forfeited if a small patch of cultivated marijuana were found somewhere in the hundreds of acres. Laws enacting those two principles (seizure of property from innocent people and seizure of property not involved in a crime) have been steadfastly supported by the U.S. Supreme Court in the name of drugs. Those principles are hard to distinguish from the forfeiture of estate that had been ruled impermissible except in wartime as a military necessity. One court decision illustrates the passion driving such brutality:

> Even for an infraction of the narcotics laws far smaller in magnitude than that of the appellants, forfeiture of the entire tract of land upon which the drugs were produced or possessed with intent to distribute is justifiable as a means of remedying the government's injury and loss. The ravages of drugs upon our nation and the billions the government is being forced to spend upon investigation and enforcement—not to mention the costs of drug-related crime and drug abuse treatment, rehabilitation, and prevention—easily justify a recovery in excess of the strict value of the property actually devoted to growing the illegal substance, in this case marijuana.[26]

Nazi judges felt no less righteous when blaming an individual Jew for society's ills. Justice Thurgood Marshall protested such thinking. "To rationalize sentences by invoking all evils attendant on or attributable to widespread drug trafficking is simply not compatible with a fundamental premise of the criminal justice system, that individuals are accountable only for their own criminal acts."[27]

It is compatible, however, with drug warrior desires to hold innocent persons responsible for drug use by spouses, relatives, and friends. American judges are glad to blame institutional litigants as well. In disallowing a bank's claim against forfeiture of a "drug-tainted" house on which the bank held a mortgage, a judge declared, "Congress has determined that the financial community must bear some of the costs, because narcotics inflict a much greater cost on society. . . . This opinion merely follows that clear message. We do so with little reluctance."[28] Such little reluctance that a higher court granted the bank's claim after discovering nearly all the district judge's findings of fact to be erroneous or irrelevant.[29]

Although hundreds of civil forfeiture laws exist, most have been used sparingly. Two innovative statutes, however, made forfeiture a crucial element of the drug war: the Racketeer Influenced and Corrupt Organizations Act (RICO)[30] and the Continuing Criminal Enterprise Act (CCE).[31] RICO and CCE included the first criminal forfeiture provisions in American legal history. These were so innovative that for several years the Justice Department hesitated to use them, fearing the provisions would be declared unconstitutional, thus invalidating forfeitures won under them.[32] CCE is also called the "kingpin" law because supposedly it is directed at the biggest drug traffickers. Federal prosecutors, however, have used CCE to forfeit cars driven by drug users.[33]

RICO is portrayed as a measure to combat organized crime; indeed, the original statutory language described that as its purpose.[34] Under RICO, however, marijuana possession can be racketeering.[35] RICO also covers violations of state drug laws. President Bush urged Congress to pass a law declaring any felony racketeering offense (such as drug possession) to be a crime of violence. Not only would this expanded definition of violent crime increase the severity of sentences received by offenders, it would also broaden the scope of forfeiture provisions available to the government.[36] Drug warriors use RICO to subject otherwise law-abiding citizens to harsh penalties originally designed to break the Mafia's leadership. Victims have protested that RICO's forfeiture provisions specifically say they are directed against organized crime, but courts have no qualms about other uses for RICO. Declared one federal judge, "While addressed to organized crime, the [RICO] Act is not limited in application to members of that undertaking."[37] Prosecutors point out that RICO explicitly instructs courts to make broad interpretations of RICO's powers.[38] The U.S. Supreme Court has supported such broad readings even though they conflict with the previous tradition of construing criminal statutes narrowly. Justice White declared that Congress intended RICO to provide "novel remedies . . . attacking crime on all fronts" and "it is in this spirit that all of the Act's provisions should be read."[39] Courts consistently behave as if every house forfeited by a resident growing a few marijuana plants is a gain against the Mafia. One commentator notes that RICO is such a big money machine for the government that interest in "RICO supports its own set of newsletters and reporters, its own American Bar Association Committee, its own special review unit within the Department of Justice, and its own set of guidelines and 'blue sheets' that bind all federal prosecutors. . . . There are probably more RICO seminars conducted around the country at any time than for any other single federal statute."[40] The statute itself refers to dozens of other laws, interlocking its operations with them.

State courts follow the federal example by expanding the coverage of state "drug asset forfeiture" laws. Over a three-year period in one Missouri jurisdiction, not a single forfeiture using laws directed against drug dealers came from a conviction for drug dealing.[41] A Crawford County, Missouri, judge approved forfeiture of a 23-acre homestead, three Honda all-terrain vehicles, and an ATV trailer because the owner conceded that enough evidence existed to convict him on one count of training pit bull fighters. This happened even though Missouri's forfeiture laws exempted dog fighting offenses as grounds for seizures.[42] In 1984 Justice Department experts noted emergence of circumstances in which "property may be forfeited or permanently retained by the government in the absence of a specific statute subjecting the property to forfeiture."[43] Such are some effects produced by the Nazi "educational nature of law" principle.

REMEDIAL VERSUS PUNITIVE

Courts have long recognized that civil forfeiture can be either remedial or punitive. Remedial action is designed to make the government whole, to compensate the public for any loss caused by conduct leading to the forfeiture. Punitive action is motivated by vengeance and is designed to hurt the victim. Either type of civil forfeiture is permissible. Legal fiction aside, forfeiture's purpose is punitive. A Justice Department drug war manual declared that "forfeiture of otherwise legitimate property is a punishment" and that forfeiture's "purpose is to impose a punishment."[44] The chairman of a Missouri drug squad described forfeiture as "a good punishment."[45] A county prosecutor agreed, saying "loss of property often hurts a drug user . . . more than a short jail sentence or fine."[46] Modern courts, however, are extending the definition of "remedial," holding that any forfeiture promoting a government activity is remedial.[47] By that definition, all forfeitures are remedial, since the income promotes government operations. If civil forfeiture is thereby defined as remedial no matter how disproportionate it may be to criminal use of the property, owners lose any protection from the Eighth Amendment's ban on excessive fines and cruel punishments. The Eighth Amendment applies to punitive actions by government, not remedial ones.

Distinguishing between remedial and punitive aspects of civil forfeiture becomes important when a victim has been convicted of a criminal offense involving the same conduct for which a civil sanction is sought. A remedial civil sanction is then permissible, but a punitive one is forbidden: Under the Fifth Amendment government cannot keep punishing a person over and over for the same offense. As with other civil liberties written into the Constitution, the writing did not express mere noble ideals but expressed determination to avoid abuses inflicted on ordinary people by English prosecutors. Before the war on drug users, this principle had been long settled. In a classic nineteenth-century case a defendant was convicted and punished for failing to pay a whiskey tax. That punishment was followed by a civil action in which the government sought to collect a sum that was twice as much as the tax revenue in question. Sitting as a circuit justice, U.S. Supreme Court Justice Samuel F. Miller forbade any civil sanction based on the same act for which a defendant was convicted. Miller added that even civil sanctions based on acts *similar* to those in the criminal conviction, rather than the same acts, would probably be double jeopardy; but the facts of this case did not require a ruling on that latter question.[48]

Nonetheless, abuses feared by patriots who enacted the Bill of Rights have reappeared in the name of drugs. In theory, punitive civil sanctions are still forbidden as double jeopardy, but in practice drug prosecutors have persuaded courts to keep expanding the perimeters of remedial sanctions. In 1974 a judge indignantly rejected a drug squad's forfeiture action against a $10,000 car in which one ounce of marijuana had been found, calling the sanction so punitive as to be "unconscionable" and "absurd."[49] Fourteen years later, after President Reagan unleashed the war on drug users, federal prosecutors in New York readily persuaded a court to permit forfeiture of a $25,000 car in which the remains of a marijuana cigarette had been found. The quantity was so small that possession had been decriminalized in state law.[50] When police in Kansas City, Missouri, inspected a car at a sobriety checkpoint, they discovered enough marijuana to make two cigarettes. The car owner denied using marijuana and was never charged. Police, however, turned over the car to federal authorities. In approving forfeiture, the federal judge solemnly intoned, "Forfeiture is not limited to property that is used by drug couriers or traffickers."[51] In another case, a man in Georgia received a $45 fine in municipal court for marijuana possession. No other charges, state or federal, were filed, but a federal drug squad ran a forfeiture against the car he was driving while possessing marijuana.[52] Local police in Illinois arrested someone for smoking marijuana in a parked car, and the car was thereupon forfeited to a federal drug squad.[53]

The principle holds in forfeiture of houses as well. A U.S. court of appeals approved forfeiture of a $94,810 house where the owner had cultivated marijuana seedlings worth less than $1,000. "Because this is a civil forfeiture," the court said, "proportionality analysis was not necessary. We hold that there was no eighth amendment violation."[54] "We find," said another federal appeals court, "the proportionality between the value of the forfeitable property and the severity of the injury inflicted [on society] by its [illegal] use to be irrelevant."[55] In the name of drugs, prosecutors have used civil forfeiture to inflict tens of thousands of dollars in loss upon drug users found guilty of misdemeanor conduct so minor that it carried a trivial fine. Into the 1990s, courts sustained civil forfeitures against any property owned by someone convicted of a drug offense, regardless of whether the property was associated with offense. A federal appeals court hypothetically noted that "the Empire State Building . . . can be seized by the government because the owner, regardless of his or her past criminal record, engages in a single drug transaction."[56] The same principle has expanded to cover activities beyond drug cases. The Justice Department declared the federal government could now "seize the King Ranch, a legendary Texas spread covering hundreds of square miles, were it to detect an illegal crap game in one stable."[57]

With the principle that brutal forfeitures are merely remedial in drug cases, we see what a jurist of an earlier era called "the tendency of a principle to expand itself to the limit of its logic,"[58] expanding the perimeters of remedial sanctions. Having spent $16,000 to investigate and convict someone for a $585 Medicare fraud, prosecutors filed a civil suit to collect $130,000 in "remedial" civil fines from the person. After a lower court balked at such a definition of remedial, prosecutors took the case to the U.S. Supreme Court. That tribunal also found the prosecutors' definition of remedial to be too broad,[59] but drug cases helped create the climate in which those prosecutors acted. For example, federal case law has long permitted forfeiture of cars used for commuting to drug deals, and the logic of that principle has expanded beyond drug cases. In Missouri homosexual conduct is illegal, and the police chief in a St. Louis suburb sought forfeitures against cars that men drove to a spot where homosexual activity occurred (the cars having facilitated the crime by bringing occupants to the site).[60] The same principle would work for apartments or houses in which homosexual activity occurred. Police seized a pickup truck when the driver reached through an open window to hit someone; the vehicle had been used to facilitate a criminal assault because the defendant was sitting in it when he committed the crime.[61] After owners of a multimillion dollar bookstore and video rental business were convicted of selling and renting out $105.30 of obscene materials, the multimillion dollar business was forfeited.[62] A U.S. attorney in Ohio announced, "The seizure of assets is a common tactic in the war on drugs. It will now become one of our major weapons in the war on health care fraud."[63] New Jersey authorities charged a medical student with practicing psychiatry without a license. The student reported that police seized his "diplomas, paintings, carpets, a coffee maker, household furniture, beds, antiques, personal photographs, and his antique pen collection."[64] Seized health care fraud assets have included patients' medical records. Through precedents established by the drug war, an anonymous phone call alleging that a physician ordered unnecessary hospitalization of a patient is grounds for police seizure and examination all medical records in the doctor's office as health fraud assets.[65] Although drug squads theoretically may not be able to use patient records seized in a fraud investigation as formal evidence of illicit drug use, the information can be used informally to target patients for surveillance to detect a chargeable drug offense.

And drug warriors do not always accept theoretical limits on their power. Warriors sometimes evade the spirit of court rulings, such as by convicting a drug offender in state proceedings and running a subsequent forfeiture in federal proceedings, a variation on a double jeopardy abuse examined in the previous chapter. Sometimes court rulings are outright defied. In many states people convicted of possessing a marijuana cigarette at home can then lose their driver's licenses in subsequent civil action. Despite court rulings that such civil action is punitive and therefore unconstitutional,[66] numerous persons continue to lose their driver's licenses after conviction for misdemeanor drug possession having no relation to driving. Such administrative action at variance with court findings is a textbook example of the Nazi principle of civic duty, whereby "right" police actions are not only permitted but required in defiance of statutory or court language prohibiting them.

One argument defending driver's license revocation is sinister. Drug warriors argue that activity licensed by the state is a privilege, not a right, so the state can withdraw that privilege for any reason. Because states require persons to obtain a license before marrying, the implication here is that the state can forbid drug users to marry. As we shall see in a later chapter, that principle has already expanded into the most intimate of human relations: Not only are ordinary middle-class drug users losing custody of their children, pregnant drug users are being forbidden to carry pregnancies to term. Expansion will continue unless the underlying principle is rejected, unless we insist that punitive civil sanctions no longer be called remedial in the name of drugs.

PUNISHMENT VERSUS REVENUE

Police frankly confess that forfeiture inspires them to target property rather than criminals. In the 1980s a Kansas City police chief replaced his official automobile with a Lincoln Town Car seized from a drug dealer, and said that forfeitures were a motivation for moving against drug offenders. In a story headlined "KC Police Are Getting a Free Ride," a reporter said, "The [police] department has directed all district officers to watch for seizure opportunities." The assignment was not to be observant of crime per se, but of crime that would pay the police.[67] (That order was reminiscent of one from the head of Nazi Germany's criminal police, Reinhard Heydrich, who directed police to make rich Jews a priority when doing arrests.)[68] The Kansas City chief said he hoped the public would get a message as more and more police were seen driving cars confiscated from drug offenders. Police elsewhere in Missouri followed the same practice, driving cars seized when small quantities of marijuana were found in them.[69] A small town drug user recalled being brought into headquarters, where a police officer cried out in triumph, "Oh boy, the chief's got himself a new convertible!"[70] The same happens across the country. A New Jersey prosecutor began driving a forfeited Corvette.[71] The Suffolk County, New York, prosecutor drove a forfeited BMW, spending almost $3,500 from the county's forfeiture fund to do maintenance and cosmetic work (such as pin striping).[72] Assorted members of one Missouri county prosecutor's staff were seen "routinely driving confiscated vehicles, including on weekends, for trips to convenience stores, softball games and banks and to move furniture." The prosecutor "considers such use 'perks' or part of their compensation."[73] The wife of Washington's mayor used a forfeited Lincoln Town Car.[74]

Official use aside, police are known to acquire personal ownership of forfeited cars. A detective who ordered seizure of a Chevrolet Camaro Z28-IROC sports car wound up with title to the vehicle. Officials claim he bought it at a public auction, but records of the alleged auction were withheld from newspaper reporters who asked about it. The federal government appraised the car at $11,500, and the detective's winning bid was $5,000.[75] Similar incidents happen on the federal level. Property can be forfeited to the U.S. Customs Service, which hires a contractor to auction off cars and other property, and the contractor in turn hires subcontractors. The General Accounting Office (GAO) found instances of Customs or subcontractor employees or relatives apparently winning auction bids, but GAO was unable to determine if the abuse was widespread because over one-fourth of auction records did not name the winning bidder.[76]

Sometimes police are selective in their choice of merchandise. Irked by a businesswoman's advocacy of marijuana legalization, Maryland police disguised in United Parcel Service uniforms delivered an unordered package with a fake return address to the businesswoman's house. (A drug dealer had used the package to send marijuana to the businesswoman's teenage son.) When the package was taken inside, officers obtained a warrant to search the house—where they found the UPS package which they knew to contain one-half ounce of marijuana. They also found a few grams in a plastic bag by her bedside table. Police then confiscated all the woman's business computers as drug-tainted assets.[77] Even if such a package is not delivered, property at the address or return address can be forfeited.[78] The Justice Department has told local drug squads that entrapment is no defense, giving the following example: Police send a notice to someone saying that a package is at the post office. Police know the package contains drugs. The addressee gets the package, puts it in a vehicle, and is arrested while driving off. The vehicle can then be forfeited for illicit drug transport even though police set up the situation.[79] The Justice Department has also informed local drug squads that they can illegally seize property for forfeiture: "The fact that the property is illegally seized is no defense."[80]

Forfeiture seizures by police can be comprehensive. When federal drug agents seized a Custom Sport Fisherman Vessel, they confiscated the following "drug assets" found on board:

Various and all power tools

One large red tool box
One small gray tool box
One 12 volt battery charger
One 32 volt battery charger
Two large hunting knives
    Buck and Hunter
Two pairs of binoculars
    (1) German Steiner
    (2) American Swift
Two diving regulators
Two diving masks
One set of diving fins
One Shortic wet suit
Three sets of foul weather gear
One portable FM stereo
Two Igloo ice chests
One pair of Rayband [*sic*] sunglasses
One blue leather Bummer [*sic*] jacket
One leather money belt
One Homelite generator
One small leather attache case
Personal fishing tackle: 5 reels and 5 rods
Sixteen life preservers
Miscellaneous kitchen utensils
One tan ultra suede jacket
One green sleeping bag
One spear gun
One ten-power scope target (Lyman)
One box of jewelry with these contents:
    2 gold tie tacks, high school ring,
    bracelet, gold wedding band, chains
One duffel bag[81]

In Crawford County, Missouri, police confiscated the entire contents of accused persons' homes. In Clay County, Missouri, an amazed victim noted, "It was like Home Shopping or something. They even took my desk stapler."[82] In Columbia, Missouri, I listened to a man describe a marijuana raid on his residence in which a drug squad seized his cameras, microwave oven, and other property, with a total value of $5,000. Police gave him no receipts, and he was unable to get his possessions back. "Drug assets" seized from a home by a New Mexico drug squad included a child's Mickey Mouse fishing pole.[83] One prosecutor admitted "problems in proving an armchair was used in a crime,"[84] but such forfeitures are not unusual. Indeed the Justice Department's *Drug Agents' Guide to*

Forfeiture of Assets, issued to educate state drug squads, has cover illustrations of cash, a car, boat, wristwatch, sofa, coffee table, and a house.[85]

In 1938 Hitler put seizure of houses at the bottom of Aryanization priorities,[86] but American drug warriors have treated dwellings as prime targets. In one case the victim was vice president of a Fortune 500 company. He thought a federal drug squad invading his house was a robber gang, got into a firefight with them, and spent six weeks in an intensive care unit. He emerged with permanent lung damage, diaphragm paralysis, and limited use of the right side of his body. No drugs were found in the house. Subsequent inquiry revealed that the drug squad had paid for a tip they knew to be unreliable and became interested in seizing the executive's home as a drug asset. Officials responded to the revelations by indicting the tipster for providing false information.[87] Zealotry for house forfeitures can cool, however, if the property owner is a law enforcement official. The Hartford, Connecticut, prosecutor earned a national reputation for seizing houses allegedly used in drug offenses. She boasted, "We have never lost a real estate forfeiture case." No case was run against her own house, however, after her son was arrested for selling marijuana from it. After her son's arrest, the Department of Justice invited her to speak at a closed meeting in Washington, where she explained how to expedite forfeitures.[88]

In 1938 Hitler specified that Jewish-owned rural land such as farms and forests should be priorities for confiscations.[89] A similar attitude can be found among American officials directing forfeitures against drug users. Eyeing an improved 60-acre rural property, a police officer gloated, "Osburn's place—we already have that; it's just a matter of waiting for the formalities before it becomes our law enforcement recreation and training center."[90] Regarding a forfeiture against 80 Pennsylvania acres, "FBI and drug agents openly boasted that they 'couldn't wait to use the defendant's property for deer hunting and other social activities.'"[91] In another case, the owner of a $5 million California ranch refused to negotiate with officials who wanted to merge the property into a park system. Subsequently a search warrant was obtained for a drug squad raid on the rancher's home. When applying for the warrant, police said an informant had reported thousands of marijuana plants on the property. Police did not tell the judge that they were skeptical of the informant's credibility. In the application, one officer swore to what he was told by another officer, but the other officer's statement was false (by using this technique neither officer could be accused of perjury). Nor was the judge told that more than one secret warrantless search had recently been made of the ranch land without finding a single marijuana plant. Maps handed to all members of the strike team included handwritten notations saying "200 acres" and "80 acres sold for $800,000 in 1991 in same area." When the drug squad burst into the ranch couple's home, the wife started screaming, "Don't shoot me! Don't kill me!" as team members manhandled her. The commotion apparently roused her sleeping husband who ran downstairs with a pistol. Squad members told him to lower the firearm, and as he obeyed they shot him to death. They ejected the woman from the house when she ran to her stricken husband. When a neighbor phoned during the raid, a squad member said the rancher could not come to the phone because he was busy. No marijuana was found in the house or anywhere on the 250 acres. The squad did, however, find and seize maps and historical documents showing the land's place in California's scenic heritage. The county prosecutor admitted the raid "was motivated, at least in part, by a desire to seize and forfeit the ranch for the government." Governmental desire to merge the ranch into parkland may explain the otherwise curious presence of U.S. Park Service agents in the drug raid team.[92]

Small amounts of drugs are sufficient cause to seize enormous amounts of property. To get the entire 60-acre "Osburn place" mentioned above, authorities merely charged the owners with germinating marijuana seedlings in the house on the property. This was sufficient to run a forfeiture against not only the dwelling but a barn, shop, and 60 acres of fenced rural land.[93] A marijuana seed under a floor mat transforms an expensive automobile into a drug transport vehicle. A drug squad took the oceanographic vessel "Atlantis" after one marijuana cigarette was found on board, in crew quarters.[94] A federal squad seized a commercial fishing craft when marijuana totaling under 0.1 ounce was recovered from a crew member's coat. This was off the coast of Alaska, a state where such marijuana possession was legal under state law. In addition to the seizure, a $10,000 civil fine was slapped on the owner—who was innocent of any involvement with the crew member's conduct, an innocence freely conceded by the federal government. In fact, no criminal charges were filed against anyone. The boat owner eventually got the fine lowered but did not recover his vessel before losing a season's fishing income.[95] Presence of drugs is not even required for forfeiture. In Missouri authorities seized cash found near drug paraphernalia. In court the owner proved the cash had nothing to do with drugs. Nonetheless, the court ordered the cash forfeited on grounds that the victim might have intended to buy drugs with the money someday, even though the government produced no evidence of such intention.[96] Such legal thinking not only demonstrates the Nazi principle of civic duty but also adopts the Nazi principle of basing punishment on someone's "criminal nature" rather than on a specific act committed by the person.

After property is targeted, courts are generous in accepting government reasons used to justify forfeiture. DEA agents seized a man's house and its entire contents as drug assets. Noted one judge who considered the case, "Petitioner has not even been indicted, yet . . . at oral argument, the government kept referring to petitioner as 'the defendant' and 'a drug violator.' Furthermore, the government purports to indefinitely divest petitioner of everything he owns even though there is no question that the seized 'contents' of petitioner's residence include . . . possessions totally unrelated to narcotics activity."[97] Noted a higher judge, "The Magistrate who issued the warrant stated that he knew he had authorized the seizure of items not subject to forfeiture."[98] Nonetheless, a U.S. court of appeals authorized the forfeiture to proceed.[99] In another case, an undercover agent claimed to have phoned a defendant with a request to buy drugs. The government argued that the building to which the defendant's telephone was attached should be forfeited, and a court ordered the home forfeited.[100] Because a driveway abutted a house, the house was forfeited when a single drug deal was conducted in a car sitting on the driveway.[101] In still another case, a federal prosecutor argued that being able to remain in bed helped a defendant make a drug sale, and therefore the house in which the bed was located should be forfeited.[102] Commenting on cases involving house forfeitures, Virginia Governor L. Douglas Wilder said the technique "clearly shows that in Virginia there are no havens for drug users."[103]

Such reasoning shows how forfeiture can be used to ostracize drug users. Forfeiture constricts the ability of drug users to function in normal society. Under American law drug users cannot be forbidden to own a car or home, but such possessions can be forfeited no matter how remote their involvement with drug use. We have just seen a case where possession of a telephone was grounds to forfeit a house. A few publicized instances would motivate drug users to give up telephones rather than risk loss of their residences, depriving them of telephones just as effectively as Nazi decrees that forbade Jews to have telephones. Citizens would tighten the boycott by refusing to carpool with drug-using friends lest the car be seized. Forfeiture can cut off drug users from society just as Jews were ostracized. Drug squads thereby have limitless power to ostracize drug users. Implementing this aspect of anti-drug-user law is hindered because forfeiture must be directed against one individual at a time. In contrast, Nazi confiscation decrees covered everyone who was defined as a Jew. Because American courts have accepted the forfeiture principles demanded by prosecutors, however, those principles can now be codified. A law could declare that drug users shall forfeit the following items of property: a car involved with their drug use, a telephone, a house, and any number of other items. Because courts have agreed that such items are inherently involved with an offender's drug use, individual forfeiture actions would no longer be needed. To get such property, the government would merely have to prove the owner is a drug user, no harder than proving someone is a Jew. Some drug warriors argue that a single unconfirmed urine test is proof enough. It can all be done scientifically.

PUNISHING THE INNOCENT

If government can seize property having no link with drug use, why must seizures be limited to drug users? Why not take property from persons who abstain from illicit drug use? In fact, drug warriors have established legal principles allowing government to do exactly that. Often victims are astounded to learn we have lost what was once an elemental civil right, the quiet enjoyment of lawful property. "The Audrain County prosecutor doesn't believe for a minute that 64-year-old Sherwood Craghead planted and cultivated the high-grade marijuana found on the Craghead farm last fall. Nevertheless, he is trying to seize Craghead's 112-acre farm—double-wide trailer, new shed and all." No charges were filed against anyone in this matter.[104]

The war on drug users is sucking away the property of innocents. A top Justice Department official stated that eighty percent of federal forfeitures are taken from persons whose innocence is so obvious that they are never even indicted, let alone brought to trial.[105] Said another Justice Department forfeiture specialist, "Whether innocence can ever be a legal defense to forfeiture is unclear."[106] (In contrast, even property possessed by Nazi war criminals (including stolen property) could not be taken from them unless they were first convicted).[107] Drug warrior attacks on innocent persons come from several directions.

One is the use of probable cause to establish grounds for forfeiture. As noted earlier, probable cause is the standard used to obtain a search warrant and can be satisfied by an anonymous accusation. Customers of a New Mexico chemical company included the New Mexico Fish and Game Commission, the U.S. Department of Forestry, and other government agencies. One of the company's products has thousands of legitimate uses, but unfortunately for the company's owner, its product containers were found in a laboratory manufacturing illicit drugs. Several years later, drug agents purchased the legal product from the company. They also obtained a tip that the company's owner led a motorcycle gang in Las Vegas, and another tip that the owner instead led a motorcycle gang in Albuquerque. The company's willingness to sell its legitimate product, the product's presence in an illegitimate laboratory, and contradictory tips alleging ties between the owner and a motorcycle gang became grounds for searching the home of the company's owner. No evidence of illegal activity was found (and the owner did not even possess a motorcycle, let alone lead a gang), but the information on which the search was based became grounds to begin a forfeiture of the company, its entire inventory, the proprietor's house, two cars, and all his personal possessions.[108] An informant reported 200 pounds of marijuana stored in the home of a Connecticut couple. Later the informant said the amount was 100 pounds. Still later the tipster said the amount was 16 ounces. No matter; the contradictory and uncorroborated stories were sufficient grounds to seize the house without even searching it.[109] A secret informant told federal drug agents that a man accepted $10,000 from drug dealers (whose names the informant could not remember) who unloaded cocaine from a boat (whose name the informant could not remember) to a dock on the man's residential property (on a date the informant could not remember). After the accused man died and could not defend himself, the feds asked a judge to approve forfeiture of the house. The judge agreed. The man's heir was evicted from the house, which the federal government then rented out for $2,200 a month.[110]

Another angle of attack comes from abuse of the Fifth Amendment. If a criminal trial finds an accused person innocent, the Fifth Amendment forbids our government to bring the person to trial on the same offense again. In that regard, over a century ago the U.S. Supreme Court was asked whether civil forfeiture proceedings could be initiated against the property of someone found innocent of allegations on which the forfeiture suit was based. The Court said no, that running a civil forfeiture on the same issues previously decided in a defendant's favor would force the person to defend against the same accusations again:

> Acquittal in the criminal case may have taken place because of the rule requiring guilt to be proved beyond a reasonable doubt, and . . . on the same evidence, on the question of preponderance of proof, there might be a verdict for the United States, in the suit *in rem*. Nevertheless, the fact or act has been put in issue and determined against the United States; and all that is imposed by the statute, as a consequence of guilt, is a punishment therefor. There could be no new trial of the criminal prosecution after the acquittal in it; and a subsequent trial of the civil suit amounts to substantially the same thing.

After all, parties in the criminal and civil actions are the same.[111] In the name of drugs, however, this long-settled legal principle was overturned in order to give drug warriors another "tool." In 1986 a U.S. court of appeals ruled that a civil forfeiture trial could be held on the same issues settled in the defendant's favor by an earlier criminal trial.[112] This goes even further than the Nazi legal principle of "balance" that permitted prosecutors to appeal acquittals because defendants could appeal convictions. Now the same question can actually be brought to trial again. Moreover, in the first trial (criminal), the government must prove itself right. In the second trial (forfeiture), the victim must prove the government wrong; acquittal on underlying criminal charges is evidence but not proof. Keep in mind, too, that although in forfeiture proceedings victims are held to higher legal standards than in criminal proceedings, their access to legal counsel is more limited. The chance of victims prevailing under such circumstances is illustrated by records of state forfeitures in ten Missouri jurisdictions, where over half of all seizures were made from persons never convicted of an offense.[113]

A legal principle expands to the limit of its logic; if property can be forfeited without conviction, so can liberty and life. That principle is particularly ominous because, as we shall now see, prosecutors can attack innocent bystanders never accused of involvement with crime.

For example, when seizing an automobile under civil forfeiture statutes, prosecutors need only demonstrate its use in transporting an illicit drug. The amount of drug is irrelevant, as is an innocent owner's lack of knowledge that the car was used in this way. Although some civil forfeiture statutes include an "innocent owner" defense, allowing victims to retrieve seized property if they were innocent of knowledge about its illegal use, in practice owners are held to such high standards of vigilance that proving their innocence can be impossible. In cases where innocent owners do leap the hurdles, prosecutors can cancel the legal owner's interest in the property by arguing that whoever used the property illegally was the "actual" owner. For example, a parent who takes out a loan and holds title to a car used solely by offspring is the legal owner, but an offspring involved in a drug violation is deemed the car's "actual" owner in order to avoid consideration of the parent's innocence.[114] Cases do exist in which innocent owners prevail,[115] but those experiences are not typical. When Congress passed the Comprehensive Forfeiture Act of 1984, drug warriors made sure that it omitted an innocent owner defense. That omission made it the "statute of choice" for drug squads.

Assorted cases hold that innocent owners must not only prove innocence but demonstrate that "reasonable steps" were taken to avoid illegal use of the property.[116] Failure to search employees is failure to take reasonable steps to prevent business premises from being used for illegal purposes. A worker at a Michigan record store was accused of selling a small quantity of marijuana on the premises, and a police raid at the store recovered a small amount in the employee's possession. No evidence emerged that the business owners knew of illegal conduct by the employee at work; moreover, charges against the employee were dropped. Nonetheless, a drug asset forfeiture was run on all magazines, compact discs, tapes, phonograph records, and cash register receipts.[117] Failure to search passengers and luggage on a boat is failure to take reasonable steps to prevent the vessel from being used to transport drugs. The U.S. Supreme Court upheld forfeiture of a rented yacht where one marijuana cigarette had been discovered. The Court said the rental company had failed its civic duty to enforce federal drug laws and must pay the consequences.[118] The Justice Department applies the same principle to cars: Rental companies "can be expected to protect themselves by following careful business practices and investigating suspicious borrowers."[119] Department policy is harsher still toward family cars: "Friends and family members who lend out their conveyances are in a better position to suspect criminality and to make reasonable inquiry."[120] Despite a mother's attempts to keep her son from using her car for drug transactions, he defeated her efforts, and a federal drug squad took the car.[121] A laundromat manager used a company car for travel to a drug deal. The laundromat company contested the forfeiture because the manager made unauthorized use of the car for private business. A judge approved forfeiture, however, because the company failed to demonstrate any attempt to prevent the manager from using the car for illegal activity if ever he made unauthorized use of the car.[122]

Moreover, for an innocent owner to defeat a forfeiture on the basis of facts, the owner must prove that the person making illegal use of the property not only had unauthorized custody but had acquired custody through an illegal act.[123] Otherwise the property is gone, no matter how innocuous the situation. Forfeiture took a family car when the son gave a ride to someone who, unknown to the son, possessed a small amount of marijuana; prosecutors argued the car had been used to transport drugs and was thereby a criminal vehicle. The judge agreed, saying the driver had the option of searching the rider and refusing to carry someone who possessed drugs.[124] In another case, a judge sternly warned, "Courts are closed to innocent vehicle owners, who must suffer the consequences even of the surreptitious transmission of contraband by passengers."[125] When prosecutors won a forfeiture against a car driven by a man arrested for drugs, his wife protested that she owned the vehicle and was innocent of any offense. A court ruled that she was not really innocent because she failed to explain why she would let her husband drive the car.[126] One of the earliest automobile cases stated the principle that has been followed ever since: "It is the illegal use that is the material consideration, the guilt or innocence of its owner being accidental."[127]

That principle applies to real estate as well. The mentally disturbed son of a couple in Hawaii threatened to commit suicide if they damaged a marijuana patch he was growing in their yard. The son had been under psychiatric care, and his parents took the threat seriously. A police helicopter spotted the marijuana. The son pleaded guilty, resumed psychiatric care, and never grew marijuana again. Because the parents had knowledge of the cultivation, however, they were not deemed to be innocent owners of the real estate. Four years later federal forfeiture proceedings began against the family home; federal agents inventoried all household furniture and ordered the parents to dispose of none. "There was a violation of the law, and that makes this appropriate," explained an assistant U.S. attorney. "The other way to look at this, you know, is that the Lopeses could be happy we let them live there as long as we did."[128] In a Connecticut case, a judge noted the parents had tried assorted means of stopping their children's drug involvement: "The children, despite the intervention of their parents, continued to use narcotics, hid the narcotics from Mr. and Mrs. Gonzalez and repeatedly lied to them regarding their narcotics-related activity." Saying the parents should have either evicted their drug-involved adult children or turned them over to police, the judged approved forfeiture of the family home.[129] In order to save their home from forfeiture a California couple evicted their drug-using son.[130]

The federal trend is to forfeit if real estate owners are not performing a police function regarding fellow residents, tenants, or customers. A retired couple owned a three-unit apartment house in Inglewood, California. A neighbor accused a tenant of drug dealing, but the couple found a private citizen's accusation to be insufficient grounds for eviction and feared a lawsuit if they made the attempt. Police then provided sufficient grounds by making drug arrests there, but rather than permit eviction the drug squad seized the building. A judge approved forfeiture, citing the retirees' "willful dereliction of social responsibility" in failing to accomplish a law enforcement goal that had eluded armed police backed by the full power of the government.[131] A real estate company was judged to have failed its civic duty to stop drug activity in a six-story Manhattan apartment complex containing forty-one units. The structure was forfeited.[132] When drug violations were reported in another New York apartment building, the owner helped police gain easy access to the structure and filed criminal trespass charges when requested by police even though a court found that he had reason to fear violent retaliation. The Queens County District Attorney's office praised the owner's cooperation and said his help demonstrated good citizenship. A drug squad deemed such cooperation insufficient and ran a forfeiture against the building.[133] Expanding the principle, the DEA told a landlord that his building would be forfeited unless he evicted the lawn and garden business operating there. Although the garden store had refused to sell products to undercover agents who indicated the products would be used to cultivate marijuana, the DEA noted the store nonetheless sold grow lights that could be used by marijuana cultivators. Fearful of losing his building, the landlord complied with the DEA's desires and evicted a tenant engaged in lawful business.[134] Tolerating sale of legal products that could be put to illegal use is now grounds for forfeiture of store buildings. Not many merchants or landlords can meet that standard.

The federal trend of requiring property owners to perform police duty is duplicated on the state level. An elderly pool hall owner in Maryland told police he was concerned about drug dealers using his property and asked for assistance. A detective responded, "We're overworked as it is. There's really nothing we can do about it." On the basis of the owner's plea for help, however, police sent undercover agents to the property and confirmed the presence of drug dealers. Authorities then ran a forfeiture against billiard parlor.[135] California police warned a landlord's association that their real estate could be seized if they failed to report tenants who might be using drugs. This warning was a clever ploy. By reporting such tenants, landlords would document their belief that their property was being used for criminal purposes, eliminating their ability to claim ignorance of such criminal use if drug squads seize the property.[136] This actually happens. Landlords received a letter from a New York City councilman alleging that tenants were involved with drugs. The councilman said the landlords should contact an attorney to take action. They did so, but the lawyer said allegations were insufficient grounds for eviction, and attempting such an eviction would make the landlords liable for damages to the tenants. The landlords then met personally with the tenants, who told them that a family member had merely been busted for possessing a small amount of marijuana. The landlords sternly told them that such conduct was absolutely forbidden on the property. A drug squad then got the property through forfeiture, on grounds that the landlords knew marijuana possession had occurred on the property and therefore were not innocent owners.[137] The same tactic was used by police in the university town of Charlottesville, Virginia. In August 1991 the police chief sent form letters to fraternity house owners saying,

> As the school year approaches, we are reminded that a number of University fraternity houses have traditionally become centers for both on-campus and off-campus related alcohol violations and drug trafficking activity. . . . Federal law provides that real estate that facilitates the unlawful distribution of drugs may be seized and forfeited to the government. If your property was seized, you would have the burden to prove that you had no knowledge of drug dealing on the property and that you had done all in your power to prevent the illegal activity. . . . Please take whatever actions you may deem appropriate to address the situation.[138]

Chances are that few recipients of the form letters paid attention to a lecture on federal law from a local police chief, but his letters removed an innocent owner defense when he orchestrated a drug squad raid to forfeit these properties to the feds, who agreed to split their take with Charlottesville police. In Milwaukee the owner of an apartment building evicted tenants suspected of drug use, gave police free access to the building, and hired two security patrol companies. Despite the owner's cooperation, the city ran a forfeiture against the building. Municipal authorities explained they lacked enough police resources to build a case against drug offenders in the building, so civil forfeiture was the best way to fight drug offenses there.[139]

Merely being inside an apartment or house while talking about a drug sale may subject the residence to forfeiture; a long string of cases holds that discussing a drug sale in a car is grounds for forfeiture.[140] Extension of that principle's logic is illustrated by forfeiture of a restaurant where criminals discussed their activity; prosecutors successfully argued that the restaurant facilitated crime because persons later convicted of a crime had conversed there.[141] Here the restaurant owners were found guilty under RICO, but the principle of holding an innocent restaurant owner responsible for conversations by customers was nonetheless established. In defending forfeiture of another restaurant where a customer had discussed drug deals, an assistant U.S. attorney explained, "It's a deterrent for the future so people who operate businesses have an incentive not to permit known violators of drug laws on their premises."[142] How restaurants are supposed to determine the past and future criminal records of customers is unclear.

In addition to case law, statutory authority now exists to seize restaurants if undercover agents conduct drug deals in them.[143] Police ran a civil forfeiture against one restaurant because they believed the owner knew that betting occurred on the premises; no charges were filed against the owner, however, because no evidence existed to support charges. This forfeiture was dropped when the owner agreed to pay the prosecutor's office $10,000.[144] Will waitresses one day lose their cars because they drove them to work where they served food to criminals, thereby helping give those customers the necessary energy to facilitate their crime? Already jobs can be forfeited.[145] A clear record of court rulings holds jobs to be property for the purpose of forfeiture (though not for the purpose of getting compensation when workers are laid off). A disquieting element of job forfeiture is that government receives no income from it; it is purely a punitive action. The legal logic of government ordering persons dismissed from their jobs is thereby in place, with job forfeiture providing yet another means to ostracize drug users, just as Nazis ostracized Jews through job dismissals. Employers can lose their property if they knowingly hire a drug offender who later makes unauthorized illegal use of the property.[146] The message from drug warriors to employers is: You will be punished if you let drug users earn a living.

In addition to attacking employers, drug squads use the "relation back" doctrine to attack property owners and lienholders innocent of any drug involvement. This doctrine holds that government title to forfeited property relates back to the time criminal use of the property occurred. That means no one can purchase the property from the old owner. A purchase contract can be signed and money can be paid, but the payer buys only a worthless quitclaim because the government holds title to the property. For example, if a drug offense occurs in an apartment complex in 1986, and you pay the owner for the complex in 1989, the government can seize it from you in 1990 because the old owner lost title to the government in 1986 even though no one knew it at the time. In the early days of the Republic, the U.S. Supreme Court rejected relation back, saying that invalidating someone's title to property because of actions by the previous title holder "would have the effect of an *ex post facto* law. It forfeits the estate of Fletcher for a crime not committed by himself, but by those from whom he purchased."[147] Although a later court accepted relation back,[148] Congress did not insert it into RICO until 1984. Attorney General Richard Thornburgh called that action the key to drug war forfeiture.[149] In the entire decade from 1970 to 1980, only ninety-eight RICO and CCE indictments sought criminal forfeitures, involving $2 million in assets. From 1976 to 1979 civil forfeitures totaled $29.9 million. In FY 1985 alone, $27.2 million in assets were forfeited to federal drug squads. In FY 1989, the total was $580 million.[150]

In addition to relation back, drug squads use the "taint doctrine" to prevent creditors from receiving compensation for claims on seized property. This policy discourages loans to drug users, denying them credit vital to survival in modern society. Even Nazis recognized the legitimacy of claims that non-Jewish creditors had on forfeited Jewish property,[151] but American drug warriors find the old Nazi policy too constricting. The taint doctrine is similar to relation back and holds that drug-tainted money cannot be used to purchase anything (because the government holds title to the money). Under the taint doctrine a lien or mortgage on property purchased with tainted money has no validity, and the government can seize the property as a drug asset (due to involvement of tainted money in the sale). Government has it both ways here: Sale to the drug offender is invalid, but instead of the property going back to the seller, the government gets it as a drug asset. The loan to the drug offender becomes unsecured. If the offender defaults on the now unsecured loan, the creditor cannot foreclose.[152] The government can even seize tainted payments received by lien or mortgage holders, leaving them without the money and without the collateral, making the loan transaction a 100 percent loss for lenders.[153] When federal prosecutors in Florida seized a drug defendant's mortgaged house, they decided to deny the bank any compensation, keeping the house and declining to pay off the mortgage.[154] In effect, the drug squad achieved two forfeitures for the price of one: The defendant lost the property and the creditor lost the loan. This is similar to the Crystal Night technique by which Jewish property owners were required to repair damaged property and then turn it over to Aryans. Through "double billing," drug squads punitively double the loss to society.

On rare occasions, creditors or lienholders preserve a claim to forfeited property, but they are still not protected against loss: Government can sell the property at auction. If bargain-hunting bidders fail to reach a price that covers the creditor's interest, the government does not make up the difference when turning over the proceeds. The creditor loses the difference.[155] This is vexing enough to banks, but can be ruinous to ordinary individuals who choose to sell their real estate on a contract basis without going through a bank. A confidential informant told authorities that the buyer of an apartment and feed store was a drug dealer. In order to protect the informant's identity, authorities did not charge the buyer and instead ran a forfeiture against the drug-tainted property. The couple who sold the real estate on a contract basis faced losing not only the property but a $70,000 loan they had made as part of the deal.[156] A retired Texas couple sold their farm via contract when they could no longer keep up with operating the property. A few months later a drug squad accused the buyer of a drug offense, seized the farm, and not only refused to make mortgage payments but rented out the seized farm and kept the rental income.[157]

Principles established by drug squads have expanded the practice of seizing property while denying compensation to innocent lienholders. Security Pacific Business Credit made a multimillion dollar loan agreement with Delco, under which assorted monies were loaned over a period of years and backed by changing items of collateral. Delco was indicted for bribery. Prosecutors agreed that Delco could continue pledging its assets to back loans, and Security continued to finance Delco. When Delco pleaded guilty, however, prosecutors ran a RICO forfeiture seeking not only assets backing the loan but all the $7.8 million that Delco had repaid to Security. Prosecutors argued that they did not have to abide by their previous agreement approving continuation of the loan arrangement; moreover, they argued that Security was not an innocent third party because it was aware of Delco's indictment and thereby Security should have suspected it was funding a criminal enterprise. Prosecutors put Security in an impossible situation. Had Security broken off the loan arrangement after government approval of its continuation, Delco could have sued Security for damages far exceeding the amount of the loan agreement[158] (damages that the government would then have collected from Delco as a forfeitable asset). In the end, Security was able to keep the loan repayments,[159] but as this case progressed through the courts, one commentator noted its potential sweeping impact: If the prosecution prevailed, every lender and retailer in the country would forfeit money that convicted criminals had used to pay their bills.[160] Observing this trend in forfeiture, another commentator warned, "The pervasiveness of the penalty, combined with the breadth and flexibility of the statutory definitions and the severe impact of the relation back or 'taint' doctrine, make it extremely difficult to predict what property will be forfeited to the government in any particular case. Innocent persons . . . may ultimately lose the benefit of normal commercial transaction."[161]

In the 1980s, some courts, but not all, mildly tempered relation back. Sometimes, but not always, lienholders were allowed to retain the principal and interest collected before the date of the illegal act or the date of seizure, and sometimes they were allowed to retain principal paid on a loan after the illegal act. But interest received by the lienholder after the illegal act was forfeited,[162] a substantial loss because in self-amortizing mortgages, interest payments can be the bulk of loan installments. In addition, some courts treated innocent owners with more generosity if the forfeiture statute used by prosecutors gave the judge power to decide whether illegally used property should be taken from innocent owners.[163] Ordinarily, of course, prosecutors prefer to use a statute denying such discretion to a judge.

Drug squad attacks on innocent bystanders can be random. An entire business checking account was forfeited after drug dogs indicated that some cash deposited by the firm had a drug odor. Numerous persons held checks written by the firm, checks that could not be cashed due to the forfeiture. A U.S. court of appeals ruled that none of these innocent check holders had any claim on the funds.[164]

Avoiding forfeiture of cash with a drug scent is difficult. If police dogs indicate a drug odor on money, the cash can be turned over to the DEA without a laboratory analysis to verify the canine analysis.[165] The lab work would probably prove nothing anyway: U.S. Attorney General Richard Thornburgh declared that over ninety percent of U.S. paper money contains illegal drug residue.[166] Scientists agree. Over a seven-year period, one group of researchers found that ninety-six percent of paper money circulating in ten American cities contained traces of cocaine. Another group of scientists found that eighty percent of bank currency had cocaine. Levels of contamination were high enough for a dog to smell.[167] Cocaine has been found in the currency sorting equipment used by the Federal Reserve System, contaminating all paper money that passes through.[168] Such findings are supported by the experience of drug squads. Detroit police had a dog sniff money in a food market cash register. The dog reported that three of the one dollar bills smelled like cocaine. Police confiscated the store's receipts as a drug asset.[169] When a man was jailed, his family and friends raised $5,000 bail. His attorney noted that over half the cash came straight from a bank. Police confiscated the bail money, saying a dog indicated a drug odor on it. The cash went to the DEA as a drug asset instead of to the court as bail money.[170] Drug agents confronted a woman when she stepped off a bus in New York. She had $4,750 to get her husband out of jail. Although she documented that all the money came from legitimate sources, the drug squad confiscated it on the claim that a dog had reported a drug odor on the cash.[171] In Nashville drug agents halted a landscape businessman who paid cash for a ticket at the airport. Nurserymen with whom he dealt preferred cash transactions, and he was carrying $9,600 to buy shrubs from Houston growers. The agents claimed he intended to use the money to purchase drugs, took the cash, and then reported that a dog they refused to exhibit had confirmed that it was drug-tainted. They gave him a receipt for the cash reading, "undetermined amount of U.S. currency." He sought return of the money, but the DEA rejected his request on grounds that it was "deficient" for unspecified reasons. Only his ability to mount a two-year court battle allowed him to get a judge's order for return of the money.[172]

Drug officers halted a woman at a Houston airport. They claimed a dog had indicated her luggage was drug-tainted, but refused to verify that a dog had actually examined the luggage. (Such examination would prove nothing anyway; a dog trainer has found that odor from a suitcase filled with marijuana will permeate dozens of luggage pieces in the same baggage compartment, causing dogs to indicate that all of those pieces are drug-tainted.)[173] No drugs were found in her belongings. No drugs were found on her person despite a strip search. Authorities did find $39,110 in her purse. Later examination of her financial records supported her contention that the money represented her savings and an insurance settlement that she was using to buy a house. Nonetheless, at the airport the DEA seized $39,100 of the cash as drug-tainted, and the woman was unable to get it back.[174] When drug squads confiscate drug-tainted cash they do not destroy it. Typically they deposit it in squad bank accounts, and banks then put the smelly cash back in circulation, ready to be confiscated again from unwary recipients.[175]

Avoiding forfeiture of money desired by a drug squad is difficult, regardless of its odor. A man attending a sheriff's sale brought a large sum of cash because personal checks were not accepted. Afterward he and the remaining $13,000 were at a relative's house when a drug raid occurred. No drugs were found and no charges were filed, but the local drug squad confiscated the $13,000. When a state court ordered return of the money, the man discovered that it had already been given to the DEA as a drug asset. And state courts have no jurisdiction over the DEA.[176] A Florida family driving through Georgia was luckier. Police stopped them for an improper traffic turn and asked permission to search the vehicle. Six hours later the family was allowed to leave, albeit without their $2,300 traveling cash, confiscated as a drug and gambling asset. The gambling taint occurred because police found ten state lottery tickets in the family's possession. The drug taint occurred because police claimed they found a "stick of cocaine." A laboratory test later showed the stick to be bubble gum. After an eleven-month legal battle, the family finally got their money back.[177] Victims who lack the resources to mount such legal actions, however, usually fail to retrieve their money from drug squads.

EFFECT OF FREE ENTERPRISE ON LAW ENFORCEMENT

The U.S. Justice Department has directed prosecutors to transfer resources from criminal prosecutions if necessary to increase forfeitures.[178] The attorney general reiterated those instructions: "We must significantly increase production to reach our budget target. . . . Failure to achieve the $470 million projection would expose the Department's forfeiture program to criticism and undermine public confidence in our budget projections. Every effort must be made to increase forfeiture income during the remaining three months of 1990."[179] A former Justice Department official reflected, "The desire to deposit money into the asset forfeiture fund became the reason for being of forfeiture, eclipsing in certain measure the desire to effect fair enforcement of the laws."[180] Law officers who put a priority on how much money they can make from an offense, rather than how much public danger is involved with an offense, exhibit robber ethics. When two Kansas City drug squad members wearing ski masks "to protect their identity" served forfeiture papers on the owner of a Corvette charged with no offense and drove off with the car,[181] the ability to distinguish police from robbers diminished.

The distorting effect of robber ethics in law enforcement can even be seen in judicial consideration of civil liberties, such as a citizen's Sixth Amendment right to have an attorney in a criminal case. The U.S. Supreme Court has declared that the value of forfeiture income going to law enforcement agencies outweighs the value of a defendant being able to hire an attorney with those lost assets.[182] Government's need for a defendant's assets is allegedly greater than the defendant's need; revenue is more important than civil liberties. That argument was familiar to authors of the Sixth Amendment, some of whom had risked their lives by rejecting that argument when made by the British.

In an article entitled "Civil Forfeiture of Assets: A Final Solution to International Drug Trafficking?" a commentator praised forfeiture because it "provides a significant source of revenue to financially-strapped drug law enforcement agencies. This income allows the DEA and other agencies to continue the costly and time-consuming investigations . . . as well as creates new incentives for undertaking these actions. As a result of the increasing use of the civil forfeiture statute, the drug law enforcement program has a weapon that will . . . pay for the continued operation of the enforcement agencies themselves."[183]

The police chief of Prairie Village, Kansas, agreed. "Drug investigations are very expensive," he said when noting the importance of $107,000 in forfeiture income received from July 1988 to July 1989.[184] The police chief of Kansas City, Missouri, said the department's undercover work in 1991 depended on $450,000 in forfeiture income.[185] A police reporter agreed that undercover work was horrendously expensive:

> To cultivate informants, the drug officers hang around bars and restaurants, eating and drinking—wearing suitable clothes and driving suitable cars, and then, having cultivated the secret "informants" they have to pay them handsomely; all told about 25-percent of the drug funds being used for these hard-to-document purposes. (While undercover, of course, you can't ask for receipts, since that would blow your cover. And, if you have a secret informant named "Ramon Salazar," who is to say different? And, if it comes time for him to make a case, and he blows town, who is to say different?)[186]

Referring to drug war cases, one Missouri police chief declared, "If we didn't have that [forfeiture] money, there's no way we could do it."[187] "It comes in handy when your budget is cut," said one Missouri sheriff. "It is a big windfall for us—these forfeiture funds, as with other departments."[188] A Missoula County, Montana, detective proclaimed that drug cases are "just about the only type of law enforcement where you get a return on your dollar."[189] A Justice Department official told budget-conscious senators that "adequate forfeiture laws" would enable the department to start "running a profitmaking operation at DEA."[190] The larger police agencies grow, the more forfeitures they can run. Indeed, police in Kansas City, Missouri, used forfeiture proceeds to hire two persons to run more forfeitures.[191] Forfeitures funded Florida's Law Enforcement Trust Fund, which in turn paid local police to promote forfeitures. Ft. Lauderdale police used fund money to hire three forfeiture specialists plus a lawyer and secretary to serve them.[192] In 1989 the U.S. Attorney for Southern Florida had a dozen assistants working on forfeitures.[193] The Justice Department's Executive Office for Asset Forfeiture noted in a May 1990 report, "Forfeitures begat more forfeitures like a snowball rolling downhill."[194]

The "Final Solution" article noted "forfeitable assets often result in 'bonuses' to the DEA in the form of functional equipment."[195] Visitors to the DEA's Dallas field office found "curio cabinets, end and coffee tables, paintings, figurines, and decorative plates were used to enhance the appearance of the Special Agent-In-Charge's office." Those items were all forfeiture booty, as were the stereo system, VCR, and television.[196] Police in Little Compton, Rhode Island, used forfeitures to fund law enforcement equipment such as an animal control van, a twenty-three foot boat, and a $17,000 wood chipper.[197] A Missouri drug squad used forfeiture money to buy a vacuum cleaner, an oak dining table, a sofa and love seat, a stereo receiver, a 100-watt amplifier, an equalizer, and speakers.[198] In Lakewood, Colorado, forfeiture money allowed police to hold holiday parties, buy amusement park tickets, and purchase a police aquarium.[199] Forfeitures bought $6,000 in tennis club memberships for the Somerset County, New Jersey, prosecutor's staff.[200] The Shawnee, Kansas, police department used forfeiture income to throw dances for local students. "The money's free," explained Shawnee's police chief.[201] Officials say it is only right that seized property be used for law enforcement purposes, only right that an agency keep property it seizes. Drug warriors even sought to finance prison construction with the Justice Department Forfeiture Fund,[202] giving prison administrators a stake in seeking victims who could be stripped of both their liberty and property.

Similar reasoning was used by Nazis, who used seized inmate property to fund concentration camp operations.[203] When property was not formally seized from inmates, Nazis sometimes persuaded inmates to sell it and donate proceeds to the Gestapo.[204] Nazis also used such property, whether confiscated before or after arrival at camps, to fund expenses involved in rounding up and transporting victims.[205] The Third Reich saw justice in making Jews pay for enforcement of anti-Jewish laws, but the moral corruption in such practices was obvious to Nuremberg Military Tribunal prosecutors.

The corruption is illustrated by the worsening lack of interest in crimes that cannot make money for police. I once asked a county prosecutor, "Why not run forfeitures on cars of drunk drivers, who use their vehicles as weapons?" The reply was, "Most habitual drunks have such old clunkers that we couldn't get enough money from those forfeitures to make them worthwhile." For me, that was an exquisite explanation of what the zero tolerance policy is all about. Not about protecting the public, but about finding victims with assets coveted by drug squads. "Value is always important," said the U.S. Attorney for Eastern Missouri. "We don't do stupid stuff; we don't waste our time."[206] A reader who examines the legal case citations in this chapter will find no forfeitures run against clunker cars. Perhaps "riding in a fancy automobile" should be added to the drug offender profile described in the previous chapter.

Law officers' dedication to the drug war cools if drug users are not a source of cash for police. When controversy arose in Missouri about whether police should obey the state constitution and turn over forfeiture proceeds to schools, one police chief announced, "We have just about stopped doing seizures until we know where the money is going to go."[207] When the Missouri Supreme Court directed police to obey the law and deliver forfeiture proceeds to schools, the Lafayette County prosecutor complained, "It's a pretty sad day in the state of

Missouri for those committed to law enforcement."[208] A Cass County deputy sheriff agreed, "I think this is wrong."[209] "As a practical matter," declared the Clay County prosecutor, "law enforcement has more incentive to seize money . . . if they know they will get the proceeds to fight crime."[210] Jackson County's Drug Task Force head put it bluntly: "We can't afford to put that time and effort in it and have someone else get the proceeds."[211] The police chief of Kansas City, Missouri, agreed: "It's not worth doing the horrendous amount of paperwork."[212] The Grain Valley, Missouri, police chief also concurred, "Why put in that work and get nothing out of it?"[213] Federal cops take the same attitude. When Senator John Glenn (D-OH) asked whether forfeiture proceeds should go to the treasury rather than to agencies making seizures, a GAO official explained that letting agencies keep the proceeds "can provide some incentive for the people who are running the program to take more of an interest in it and be more enthusiastic about it, because they have a stake."[214] Paychecks and oaths of office are no longer sufficient to motivate law officers; the drug war has given us "law enforcement" that depends on how much money police and prosecutors make from enforcing particular laws. Perhaps this is why authorities are now far more successful at apprehending and convicting drug users than in clearing thefts, rapes, and murders: There is no gain in making neighborhoods safe.

If local drug squads cannot make enough money at home, they can expand operations beyond their normal jurisdictions. Deputies of the Broward County, Florida, sheriff are simultaneously deputy U.S. marshals. They use that status to operate across the country; after finding marijuana growing on a Michigan farm, the Florida deputies seized sixty-four horses plus the farmer's automobiles. When Detroit police arrived at a farm in Tennessee, they seized the farm itself.[215]

A top U.S. Customs Service official admitted, "If the locals (police) have a guy with a ton of marijuana and no assets versus a guy with two joints and a Lear jet, I guarantee you they'll bust the guy with the Lear jet."[216] A criminologist working with drug squads reported, "Efficiency is measured by the amount of money seized rather than impact on drug trafficking."[217] The criminologist watched as a drug squad let a suspect sell large quantities of cocaine so the proceeds could be seized instead of the cocaine. In another instance a detective explained why a suspected dealer was not arrested: "Because that would just give us a bunch of dope and the hassle of having to book him. We've got all the dope we need in the property room, just stick to rounding up cases with big money."[218] An undercover agent agreed: "You want to seize the big money for your department. For our unit, that was a sign of whether you were doing good or poorly was how much money you seized. . . . My supervisor made it extremely clear that big money cases were a lot more favorable for your overall evaluation than big dope cases."[219] At one point California repealed its state laws permitting forfeiture of cars carrying trivial amounts of drugs because the income received by police was distorting law enforcement priorities, directing drug investigations away from trafficking conspiracies because police could not make enough money with such investigations.[220] Distortion of drug squad priorities was illustrated by Arizona state troopers who provided almost 13 tons of marijuana to dealers and users in Tucson over an eighteen-month period. The director of the operation praised it as successful law enforcement because it produced a minimum of $3 million in forfeiture income.[221]

The income that police receive through forfeiture is staggering. When drugs were found in raids of fraternity houses in Charlottesville, Virginia, police seized all the houses. Proceeds from sales of the houses "will produce a windfall for the local police department which its chief predicts will be 'awesome.'"[222] Police in Little Compton, Rhode Island, (population 3,339) have received about $4 million in forfeiture money; Lakewood, Colorado, police received $1.5 million in 1989.[223] Over a three-year period, police in one Missouri county collected over $1 million in forfeitures against persons accused of small-time law infractions.[224] Authorities in Louisiana's Jefferson Davis Parish matched that total in just one year.[225] In 1991 the Somerset County, New Jersey, prosecutor seized over $1 million in cash alone.[226] In 1988 Los Angeles police seized $1.5 million in cash just from guests at area motels and hotels.[227] In the same year, Los Angeles sheriff's deputies seized $33.9 million in cash, and almost as much the next year.[228]

When the Missouri Supreme Court ordered police to obey the state constitution and deliver drug forfeiture proceeds to school districts, police across the state began "adopting out" local cases to federal authorities, who shared the income with police, cutting out schools entirely.[229] In 1989 Congress explicitly authorized local drug squads to keep their entire share of adopted forfeitures in defiance of any state constitutional provisions.[230] This practice was lauded by a top North Carolina law enforcement official, who noted that otherwise drug squads would have to obey North Carolina's constitution and give forfeiture income to schools. The official noted that without an economic stake in the outcome of cases, police would not enforce drug laws:

> In 1986 the Regional Director of DEA came to my office and asked us to start Operation Pipeline, which is using patrols to interdict drugs going north and money going south on Interstate 95 and other inter-states. At that time the leadership of the [state highway] patrol did not really want to get involved because it was not a traditional function of their department, . . . and they really saw no interest in it until he started mentioning [forfeiture] asset sharing. And then everybody's eyes lit up.[231]

After dropping marijuana charges against a rural Missouri couple for lack of evidence, county officials adopted out a forfeiture against the couple's house and entire acreage. The prosecutor explained, "There is marijuana use here [in the rural county] and we had to get somebody. We don't get big enough cases to get the state police here to do an investigation up right." He admitted, "The federal sharing plan is what affected how the case was brought, sure." He added, "Seizures are kind of like bounties, so why shouldn't you take it to the feds so it comes back to the local law enforcement effort?"[232] An assistant U.S. Attorney for Eastern Missouri said, "Nothing has contributed more to cooperation between state and federal authorities than working together on forfeitures."[233] A sheriff agreed, saying that sharing forfeiture income between federal and state drug squads "is the glue that holds it all together," because otherwise local law enforcers would get no reward for cooperating in enforcement of federal drug laws.[234] Bush administration policy gave eighty-five percent of adoption proceeds to the locals if victims could be prevented from contesting the forfeiture; if victims went to court the local drug squad share fell to eighty percent.[235]

One criminologist who observed competition among assorted law enforcement entities disagreed that forfeiture builds cooperation: "Operations often disintegrated due to a general lack of interagency cooperation, leaving numerous suspects at large."[236] In what was described as a "dash for cash," local law enforcement agencies received $200 million from adopted out forfeitures in fiscal year 1989.[237] From 1988 to 1990, local police in the St. Louis area received almost $6 million from adopting out forfeitures to federal authorities.[238] In the same period, forfeitures under state law, without involvement from federal authorities, brought in $33,159 for police in the St. Louis suburb of Calverton Park, population 1,404. Police in the suburb Pine Lawn (population 5,092) received $12,032; Frontenac police (population 3,374) received $11,565. Those are incomplete totals from fragmentary records and include only cash income; assets such as cars converted to police use are not included.[239] From July 1988 to July 1989 law enforcement agencies in Johnson County, Kansas, obtained $800,000 through forfeitures under state law.[240] From 1986 through 1989, annual seizure income for police agencies in the metropolitan Houston, Texas, area was $38 million.[241] In 1990 Jackson County, Missouri, drug authorities received about $1.5 million in forfeitures.[242] From 1989 to 1991, the Volusia County, Florida, sheriff's department acquired over $6.5 million in cash alone from drug suspects.[243] In 1990 the Wayne County, Michigan, sheriff's department forfeiture income exceeded $4 million.[244] Detroit's 1991 forfeiture receipts exceeded $3.5 million, and Flint, Michigan, police took in over $1 million.[245] In Lenexa, Kansas, (population 29,000) a drug squad member bragged in 1991, "We've got about $250,000 moving in court right now."[246] Every police department in the country has a vested interest in forfeiture laws.

At the federal level, in 1991 a senior Justice Department official told Congress that the attorney general "has made forfeiture a top priority."[247] The department was holding forfeiture seminars for federal, state, and local law officers across the country.[248] In 1991 the GAO found the Federal Marshals Service was "mismanaging more than $1.4 billion in commercial property seized from drug dealers."[249] From 1985 to 1990, federal forfeitures exceeded $2 billion. In 1991 the Justice Department estimated the year's forfeiture income at $500 million.[250] The fiscal 1992 total was put at $641 million.[251] Those figures appear deceptively low, representing only Justice Department proceeds; in fiscal year 1989, Justice and Treasury had a combined forfeiture income of $675 million.[252] In 1988 a federal judge predicted, "The amount of property seized in the next three years will make the present amount look very, very small."[253] An FBI agent agreed, "We're only scratching the surface."[254] Senator John Glenn declared, "When we passed [drug war forfeiture] legislation several years back I don't think any of us had any idea that we were going to have this much money."[255] Said the Justice Department, "Forfeitures produce vast amounts of revenue. Law enforcement has the potential, through forfeiture, of producing more income than it spends."[256] The transcript of a congressional hearing summarizes the situation with an excited exchange between two amazed officials. Deputy Associate Attorney General Jeffrey Harris said, "The potential in this area is really unlimited. My guess is that, with adequate forfeiture laws, we could—" Senator Jeremiah Denton interrupted, "We could balance the budget."[257]

Government officials are no longer the only persons with a stake in promoting forfeiture. Private citizens are paid for tips leading to forfeitures. Drug squads routinely get motel employees to provide guest lists that are then matched against a drug offender profile.[258] Employees may do preliminary matching themselves to save drug squads the bother.[259] Speaking of the squad's "ongoing relationship" with innkeepers, a Missouri deputy sheriff said, "the Narcotics Unit has set up hotlines with all the hotels in Clay County."[260] In some jurisdictions motel proprietors get cold cash for their cooperation.[261] Nashville airline clerks received ten percent of any money confiscated from passengers.[262] One Denver Continental Airlines clerk received $5,800 in finder's fees from federal drug agents.[263] When contacted by reporters, the clerk said, "What do you want to know about the rewards? I can't talk about any of it. It's not something I'm supposed to talk about."[264] DEA agents revealed the drug offender profile to Detroit airline employees, who would notify the DEA whenever a passenger fit the profile.[265] A federal judge noted, "Agents have taught the employees of the airlines serving Los Angeles, San Diego, Miami, and New York to be alert for persons who match the [drug offender] profile and to notify agents when they spot such travelers."[266] A report from an airline clerk becomes grounds for stopping a passenger, and as we have seen, innocent travelers can then lose huge sums to drug squads. So offering finder's fees pays off for drug squads. One South Carolina sheriff erected billboards saying, "Need cash? Turn in a drug dealer." The sheriff said citizens would get a percentage of property forfeited by the dealer.[267] Each year the Justice Department's forfeiture branch pays tens of millions of dollars to forfeiture informants, based on a percentage of property targeted by informants.[268] Such informants are not always of sterling character, and may be willing to plant drugs in a car, house, or farm, or conduct an undercover drug deal there unbeknownst to the property owner, in order to get twenty-five percent of the income from subsequent forfeiture.

Finder's fees allow police to evade the Fourth Amendment. Knowing the potential income, employees of airline and parcel companies routinely open packages for "security inspection" in hopes of finding either drugs or items that match the drug offender profile. Police have no right to make such inspections, but they can act upon information received from company employees who do have such a right. A "security inspection" can even be done by X-ray without physically disturbing an item. X-ray guards at an airport reported an object that might have been cash. DEA agents confronted the air traveller. When the gemologist refused permission to search his belongings, the DEA seized his luggage and the $190,000 it contained. Lengthy litigation to reclaim the cash ensued.[269] Without a percentage of the forfeiture action, it is doubtful that company employees would be so zealous about opening parcels passing through their hands. After all, their employers pay them to expedite parcel shipments, not delay them. "These (X-ray) guards are getting paid less than burger flippers at McDonald's and the promise of 10 percent of $50,000 or whatever is attractive," said a Nashville police official. "It's hard to keep them watching when they have to wait for those rewards. We can't lose that incentive."[270] The Nashville drug squad avoids paying finder's fees to airport employees until a case is disposed of in court, so defense attorneys cannot force them to testify about why they thought a parcel or person was suspicious.

Ironically, although law officers claim forfeitures are designed to attack major drug offenders, such offenders can profit handsomely from finder's fees.[271] Such payment transforms those citizens into police agents, making the police legally responsible for acts committed by those informants;[272] but unlike most employers, drug squads are not held accountable for actions of their agents. Between 1985 and 1988, a member of Hell's Angels made $250,000 by alerting authorities to forfeiture opportunities. Sometimes police have informants arrange for a crime to involve a particular piece of property coveted by police.[273] An international drug smuggler *got a contract* from federal drug agents promising him twenty-five percent of proceeds from forfeitures he steered to them.[274] In 1990 one informant received $780,000. "We're paying them," said a top federal forfeiture official, "because they put money in the [forfeiture] pot."[275] A Missouri drug squad even bought a life insurance policy for an informant.[276]

Another type of payoff to informants is absent from government records. That payoff is revenge. Hatred motivates some informants to contact authorities in hopes of hurting someone. The Gestapo was overwhelmed by such unfounded "tips." Unlike the Gestapo, American forfeiture squads leave the percentage of malicious informants undocumented. They do exist, however. A California drug squad used a confidential tip to seize all property owned by a beauty salon operator. For two years prosecutors refused to reveal the informant's name lest the "investigation" be harmed. When the informant's identity was finally revealed as a disgruntled former salon employee who fabricated the tip, the case collapsed. The forfeiture was cancelled and the innocent employer recovered her property, but she had suffered two years of deprivation because a disgruntled former employee exploited the drug war.[277] Federal agents descended on a Lear Jet sold by a Texas aviation company, on a tip it would transport a large amount of currency to Brazil. They found neither cash nor any other evidence to support the allegation, but nonetheless confiscated the plane for nine months. No forfeiture was completed, but the aviation company was thrown into turmoil. One of the firm's competitors later bragged about having supplied the feds with the tip.[278] A scholar who studied Gestapo informant files found that they, too, showed business competitors reporting one another to authorities.[279] Even more common may be the practice of one drug dealer planting evidence in another's residence and making an anonymous phone call to police:[280] at one stroke eliminating a competitor, boosting drug squad arrest statistics, and subjecting property to forfeiture. Cops and criminals both benefit from such corruption. Perhaps the most enterprising use of drug squad power, however, comes from burglars who anonymously report a "drug violator" and then hit a residence once the victim is removed by police (who have also obliged the burglar by breaking locks and doors).[281]

USING CIVIL FORFEITURE TO PROMOTE CRIMINAL CONVICTIONS

Just as forfeiture can be used to encourage plea bargains, forfeiture can be used to evade plea bargains once they are agreed to. A defendant pleaded guilty in order to get work release, allowing him an income to retain his home. Prosecutors then used the guilty plea as grounds to start a forfeiture against his house. The defendant said he would never have accepted the plea bargain if prosecutors had said it would cost him his house.[282] That forfeiture allowed prosecutors to increase the punishment approved by a court. The principle of police enhancement of judicial punishment was declared a crime against humanity at the Nuremberg Military Tribunal.[283]

Forfeiture can also be used as a tool to harass persons disliked by drug squads. California police claimed that three men were drug dealers. They did not live with their parents, but the drug squad told the parents' landlord that the rental property might be seized unless the parents were evicted. The landlord complied with police wishes. In this way authorities were able to harass the sons by hurting the parents. None of the sons was charged with a drug offense.[284] One police department said it rarely seized a car if only a small amount of marijuana was found in it, but they made an exception and took a late model Ford Mustang driven by someone they characterized as "a constant troublemaker."[285] Drug squads can use property seizure to torment someone even if a court dismisses forfeiture proceedings. One federal squad seized a car allegedly involved in misdemeanor drug possession. Federal rules require car forfeitures to be filed within sixty days of seizure, but for eighteen months prosecutors in this case refused to act. When the forfeiture was finally filed, the court dismissed it.[286] Yet for eighteen months the owner had to get along without the vehicle. In the name of drugs, such police harassment is tolerated.

A destructive form of harassment uses civil forfeiture to strip defendants of assets to hire an attorney. In this way prosecutors can veto skilled advocates chosen by a defendant, thereby improving chances for conviction. Using the "relation back" doctrine, the U.S. Supreme Court has held that forfeited assets are not a defendant's money in the first place, so the defendant is deprived of nothing. Quoting an earlier lower court decision, Justice White thundered at defense attorneys, "The privilege to practice law is not a license to steal," that is, steal what becomes U.S. government funds through relation back.[287] Such judicial conduct and rhetoric approach that of Nazi judges who cooperated with prosecutors in determining the outcome of trials before they were held, a practice promoted by the war on drug users but condemned as a crime against humanity at Nuremberg. Analysis by one commentator suggests that the drug war practice goes further than the Nazi one: "Disabling a defendant's ability to choose counsel . . . seeks to punish him *before* trial."[288] Dissenting from that practice, four members of the U.S. Supreme Court declared, "It is unseemly and unjust for the Government to beggar those it prosecutes in order to disable their defense at trial."[289] Prosecutors have also used forfeiture to prevent payment for defense work already done[290] and to take assets a client paid to an attorney long before indictment.[291] Officials have even refused to let defendants examine seized records needed for their case, instead offering copies if exorbitant photocopying fees are paid—knowing that defendants have no access to frozen financial assets for payment.[292] Even before these forfeiture abuses started, from 1976 to 1981 eighty-two percent of federal drug defendants were being convicted.[293] Nonetheless, a prosecutor who worries about facing a top-quality defense team can discourage such representation by hinting that a forfeiture will be run at some point during the trial. Prosecutors can thereby use forfeiture to constrict the Sixth Amendment's guarantee of counsel in criminal cases. The U.S. Supreme Court has linked the Sixth Amendment's guarantee of counsel to the First Amendment's guarantee that citizens may petition government,[294] thereby linking forfeiture abuses to attacks on the First Amendment. A handful of American judges have warned against the trend. "The government must prove that an accused is guilty beyond a reasonable doubt. It must do this by obtaining convincing evidence of the defendant's guilt, not by preventing the defendant from retaining counsel of choice."[295] "Due process cannot tolerate even the opportunity for such abuse of the adversary system."[296] "If society merely wants automatic convictions then a hamstrung defense will facilitate achievement of that shabby end."[297] In the name of drugs, however, that is exactly what society is demanding. In order to achieve convictions, forfeiture is now used to evade the Sixth Amendment so that prosecutors' cases need not be as strong as before. That is the real purpose of such forfeitures.

Attorney fee forfeiture can even be used to strengthen a prosecutor's case. In order to forfeit the fee, prosecutors can force a defense attorney to reveal information harmful to clients.[298] Defense attorneys who incriminated their clients were a common element of Nazi jurisprudence. Forfeiture has added that element to America's, in the name of drugs. Plea bargains offer a more insidious opportunity to prosecutors, allowing them to guarantee no forfeiture of fee if the defendant pleads guilty to a lesser charge.[299] Such a guarantee gives the defense attorney incentive to persuade a client to plead guilty.

THE PUBLIC BE DAMNED

An important reason why so many forfeiture abuses occur is that government agents enjoy a lack of accountability in their actions. Not only does widespread hate propaganda create public support for taking property of drug users, but public support is backed up by laws giving government every advantage while crippling victims with numerous disadvantages as they try to defend themselves.

Normally when a plaintiff files a civil suit, the plaintiff must prove the case in order to win. Not so in civil forfeiture. In these cases, courts require the victim to prove the property was not involved with a crime. As noted earlier, this burden of proof is a holdover from the earliest civil forfeiture statutes, directed against smuggling and piracy. Expecting an importer or sea captain to have papers demonstrating that goods were neither smuggled nor stolen was reasonable. Drug warriors, however, have changed the context of that expectation. Now property owners are expected to prove a negative, that a piece of property was never involved with a drug law violation. If, for example, the owner of a seized car allowed a friend to ride in it and the friend is accused of selling marijuana, it may be hard to prove that giving the friend a ride did not in some way eventually help the friend reach a customer's house. Indeed, a drug squad ran a forfeiture against a Corvette Sting Ray on those grounds, admitting that neither the driver nor the vehicle had transported marijuana.[300]

Abuses also occur because civil forfeiture victims have no right to counsel. Even middle-class victims can be suddenly without means to hire an attorney if their bank accounts are seized, and seized property (such as a house) cannot be used as collateral for a loan. If victims cannot pay a lawyer, they probably cannot find one to take the case for free. The contingency fee arrangement that provides counsel in many civil litigations is seldom available in civil forfeiture; lawyers know that government advantages in forfeiture cases virtually guarantee loss of victims' property. Thus at the end of a case there are no assets from which counsel can obtain a contingent fee. Without an attorney, victims have little chance against arcane legal system rules. One county prosecutor staff member told me that almost all state forfeitures in her jurisdiction are won by default; victims are unable to mount a defense. In 1992 the U.S. Attorney's office for Western Missouri boasted that it had never lost a civil forfeiture.[301] Nationwide, in 1992 federal prosecutors won more than eighty percent of civil forfeitures by default, often because victims could not afford to hire a lawyer.[302]

Federal drug warriors found a slick way to achieve default victories in Hawaii. After jailing someone on drug charges, notice of forfeiture would be mailed to the defendant's vacant residence and published in a newspaper inaccessible to the jailed defendant. That way victims would not know of a forfeiture action until they had missed the last date to file an objection.[303] The U.S. attorney approved this practice even though the U.S. Supreme Court had ruled it unconstitutional.[304] Defendants without lawyers were unlikely to know they could challenge the practice on constitutional grounds. If they filed no protest, the property was forfeited by default.

Even victims who mount a defense can be defeated by repeated trials. Because a unanimous jury verdict is required in federal forfeiture trials, a single juror who accepts the government case can cause a mistrial. As long as the government can convince one juror, the case can be tried again and again until victims' defense resources are exhausted, allowing the forfeiture to succeed by default when victims can no longer exercise their rights.[305] Another tactic is to stall proceedings after seizing property, thereby depriving the victim of the property as a punishment even though forfeiture has not been approved. Appeals can be just as exhausting. In 1975 a woman entering the United States after a trip to Canada told U.S. Customs officials that she had no cash to declare. She later said she understood the Customs question as referring to cash she obtained in Canada rather than cash she carried from the United States into Canada and back again. Customs agents seized $8,850 in U.S. currency from her. After protracted investigation, officials found no evidence connecting the money with drugs. In 1976 prosecutors charged her with Customs cash transportation violations and sought criminal forfeiture of the cash, but although convicted of one offense she was acquitted of charges involving forfeiture. She repeatedly asked for return of her money. In 1977 prosecutors sought a civil forfeiture, but a U.S. court of appeals ruled that the government had unduly delayed the whole proceeding and ordered the money returned. Prosecutors appealed to the U.S. Supreme Court, which did not rule until 1983. The Court noted the undue hardship that deprivation of property can cause, a hardship requiring prompt action by the legal system lest proceedings become so unjust as to be unconstitutional. The Court then held that this case had been moving promptly enough and approved the civil forfeiture.[306] Even had the woman prevailed, we may be sure that the cost for eight years of litigation all the way to the U.S. Supreme Court would have exhausted the $8,850 at issue. Few civil forfeiture litigants are able to duplicate the feat and, given the outcome, fewer even try.

Many victims do not get as far as a jury trial. Unless a victim has followed the arcane rules governing a request for a jury trial, that right is deemed to have been waived.[307] One rule can require posting $5,000 as a bond before a forfeiture can be contested on property valued under $100,000. If there is no bond money, there is no trial, and the drug squad wins by default.[308] Another rule requires paperwork contesting a forfeiture to be filed within twenty days after seizure. If someone accused of a crime becomes distracted by efforts to mount a defense against criminal charges and the twenty days elapse without filing of the paperwork, the property goes to the drug squad. For that reason, civil forfeiture proceedings can be attractive if drug charges are filed against someone, especially if charges are later dropped for lack of evidence.

Often forfeiture cases are filed simultaneously with criminal charges against victims. Different sets of rules govern the two types of litigation, and drug warriors can exploit the differences to hammer victims. For example, providing information needed to protect property against forfeiture can waive certain legal defenses in criminal litigation, putting the victim at higher risk of conviction. Conversely, preserving defenses against criminal charges can endanger defenses against forfeiture.[309] The Justice Department has advised prosecutors to promote convictions through civil forfeiture:

> The claimant may be deposed and disclosure of his records compelled. Perjury and contempt sanctions are potentially available against untruthful or recalcitrant witnesses. And, while the Fifth Amendment may still be asserted, a civil claimant risks an adverse factual finding by doing so. This possibility places the claimant in a particular bind if criminal charges against him are still pending. Asserting the Fifth Amendment may result in an adverse factual determination, while answering questions may have incriminating consequences in the criminal proceedings. And, regardless of whether criminal charges are pending, discovery is likely to provide useful information for impeachment if the claimant testifies at the forfeiture proceeding.[310]

Battering a citizen between civil forfeiture and criminal charges is the sort of abuse forbidden by Justice Bradley a century earlier, before authoritarians found they could camouflage their intentions with a war on drug users.

Innocent owners who appeal forfeitures normally obtain no relief from courts, as courts tend to follow the lead of drug squads in interpreting forfeiture statutes. In federal forfeitures, normally the only course of action available to innocent owners is to petition the U.S. attorney general for return of the property. "By law," says the Justice Department, "the authority to grant relief from a drug-related forfeiture is given exclusively to the United States Attorney General. Federal courts have no authority to remit or mitigate a drug-related forfeiture. And, they have no power to review the Attorney General's decision on a petition."[311] After the attorney general's agents have targeted property and gone through the necessary procedures to obtain it by forfeiture, generally the Justice Department does not change its mind and give the property back. The form of a legal appeal to the attorney general exists, but the form has little more substance than did legal appeals for mitigation of Gestapo actions, a police agency that (like the U.S. Justice Department) asserted that courts had no jurisdiction over its actions.

One of the most interesting forfeiture abuses is to file criminal charges and then drop them if the defendant will turn over property to whomever filed the charge. A federal drug squad seized a 208-acre ranch after fifty-two live marijuana plants and one pound of dead marijuana were found on the property. Prosecutors told the owners they faced thirty years in prison but that charges would be dropped if the owners agreed not to oppose forfeiture. They agreed, and the U.S. government gained a large agricultural property without the owners ever being found guilty of an offense.[312]

Still, drug warriors complain of too many restrictions on their forfeiture power. Senator William Cohen attended a drug war hearing in Maine: "There was one complaint from law enforcement officials, and that was that the Federal asset forfeiture program was too slow, too cumbersome, with too many unnecessary delays."[313] Impatient authorities sold a seized Miami residence before forfeiture proceedings were completed.[314] Fearing that court proceedings put too much burden on drug squads wishing to sell or use property, Congress has authorized administrative forfeitures: If the desired property is worth less than $100,000, drug squads can take it unless the owner posts a bond of up to $5,000 to dispute the forfeiture in court. A convenient way for drug squads to discourage a court challenge is to seize items separately, running one forfeiture on someone's house, another on property in the house, another on the car, another on the bank account. No single action involves property exceeding $100,000, so the victim is not entitled to a court review without posting a bond. But each of those actions requires a bond to challenge it in court. In one instance, the victim had to post a $25,000 bond in order to get a court review.[315] The bond requirement can be waived if someone lacks sufficient assets to pay, but proving lack of funds can be difficult. In one case, the DEA said it had confidential information that the victim could afford a bond. Application denied. The DEA has also rejected applications on grounds that the value of seized property showed the victim could afford a bond (even though seized property cannot be used as collateral for a loan).[316] Moreover, an application for waiver can simply be rejected as "deficient" without explaining the deficiency.[317] Like the Gestapo, the DEA has argued that its denial of application cannot be reviewed by any court.[318]

In the unlikely event that a drug squad fails in a forfeiture attempt, the squad can still keep the property if the victim cannot pay storage fees. A man on horseback was arrested on a marijuana charge by a rural drug squad. His spouse recalled that the "horse spent three days in jail and was never charged with a crime. It took us several days chasing paper and $300 to bail her out of the cinder block cell at animal control."[319] After authorities held a $7,600 boat for over three months, the owner had to pay $4,000 in storage fees to get it back.[320]

Those victims were luckier than a St. Louis driver stopped by police who found a container of white powder in the car trunk. The driver said it was flour; police suspected it was an illicit drug and seized the car until the substance could be analyzed. Whenever the owner asked for return of the car over the next three months, police told him the powder had not been analyzed yet. The owner lost his job when he lost his transportation to work and was evicted from his trailer when he ran out of rent money. He began living in the streets and asked police to arrest him for something so he would have a place to live. Finally police reported that no charges would be filed against him and that he could have the car back as soon as he paid them over $900 for towing and storage costs, money he did not have. Eventually the storage fee was waived and law officers told him he could have the car back upon paying the $33 towing fee. He tried panhandling to get the money, but police cited him for begging and confiscated the $22 he had obtained. The man wept as he told his story to a reporter.[321]

Drug squads are not responsible for damage to seized property while it is stored pending forfeiture proceedings.[322] After police decided that a confiscated vehicle had not been used in a drug offense, they allowed the owner to reclaim it. He found a dead battery, a flat tire, no oil in the engine, an empty radiator, and a cracked engine block. Repairs were his responsibility.[323] Highway Patrol records showed that a confiscated pickup truck contained tools valued at $3,000 by the owner. When he tried to get the tools back from the prosecutor, they had disappeared without a trace.[324] Asserting that a Lear Jet pilot knowingly flew a cocaine trafficker to a drug deal, federal authorities seized his plane. After a jury exonerated him of charges, the pilot discovered the aircraft had been torn apart by DEA agents hoping to find drugs on it. He mused, "That plane's going to need about $50,000 worth of work to bring it up to FAA standards again."[325] Instead of going through a bank, a man bought a house by giving a deed of trust to the couple who sold it to him for $289,000, obligating himself to giving them periodic payments on the mortgage. After he was convicted of a RICO violation, the house was forfeited. The couple could not foreclose against the federal government nor collect payments from the convict's family, who arranged to live in the house without paying any rent to the government. When the federal "tenants" finally left, the house had suffered so much damage from neglected maintenance and repairs it was worth only $115,000. Ten years after the ordeal began, a federal appeals court ruled that the couple was entitled to compensation for the original forfeiture but set no amount.[326] While an accused marijuana offender awaited trial, a county drug squad seized his late model Pontiac Firebird and put 5,000 miles on it.[327] A victim may be able to get a court order for immediate sale of property that is declining in value under government storage, but bargain prices bid at auctions normally fail to realize the market value.[328] Victims have a difficult choice: Ask for sale of seized property now in hopes of collecting a fraction of its value if the government does not prevail in forfeiture proceedings, or watch the value decline as time passes and get back property worth only a fraction of the value it had when seized. This is yet another way for government to punish victims even if they manage to stop the forfeiture.

Although a victim can get no compensation if drug squads harm the value of property before returning it, drug squads can get compensation if a victim either reduces the value of property before it is seized or arranges to put it out of the squad's reach. Such action by a victim is uncommon because government has such broad power to impound assets before a victim can do anything to them. Nonetheless, if a victim succeeds in thwarting a seizure in this way and the forfeiture is sustained in court, drug squads can take other assets from the victim to compensate squads for the loss even though the substitute assets have no connection with an offense. The legal term for this is "forfeiture of estate," a practice outlawed from the early days of the Republic until drug warriors repealed the prohibition in 1984 with an amendment to RICO—even though in 1980 a federal court had warned that such a repeal would be unconstitutional (a finding that has not affected subsequent RICO forfeitures, which have been construed as constitutional actions against property rather than unconstitutional actions against owners).[329] The previous remedy if victims reduced the value of assets was a court fine, but drug warriors deemed that inadequate because it gave judges a chance to rule in favor of victims. The Justice Department demanded forfeiture of estate because it could be imposed by prosecutors without judicial permission.[330] It is a punishment authorized and administered by police. Punishment power wielded by police was condemned by Nuremberg Tribunal prosecutors.

An even more ominous abuse emerged when forfeiture of estate was legalized through RICO prosecutions. A person convicted of a RICO offense can be ordered to forfeit all interests in a "racketeering enterprise" regardless of whether those interests have anything to do with criminal activity. If someone begins building a multimillion dollar enterprise from scratch in 1960 and is convicted of submitting a fraudulent bill for $500 in 1988, the person can lose everything acquired before 1988. Keep in mind that under RICO marijuana possession can be racketeering. Although the legal principle has not yet been carried to the limit of its logic, the necessary structure is emerging to confiscate all property owned by a drug user—especially since (as one commentator has noted)[331] courts feel such a civic duty to promote RICO forfeiture that they are known to disregard RICO's limits.

THE PRICE OF JUSTICE

Rather than bother with forfeitures, drug squads often simply return property if the victim will pay a "settlement fee." Given the expense and complexity of forfeiture litigation, such an arrangement appeals to many victims. And it appeals to drug squads because they get money without ever having to show the property was forfeitable. Those private fee arrangements are not covered by forfeiture law, so income need not be shared with any other government agency. Such fee arrangements often require the victim to refrain from objecting to the drug squad's action in court or even in the news media.

Police responding to a disturbance complaint discovered marijuana that a guest had brought into an apartment. They seized the tenant's computer, stereo, and music collection as drug-related assets but offered to return them if the tenant would pay $600.[332] Police seized a car and $460 in cash from a woman arrested for prostitution; the car was returned when she agreed to pay $460 in settlement.[333] Police seized a woman's car when her son was stopped for a traffic violation and marijuana was discovered in the ash tray. Police said they would return the car and drop charges against her son if she paid a $200 settlement fee.[334] Police seized a man's late model Cadillac, alleging he had used it to facilitate shoplifting a $31 electric razor. They said he could have it back for a $1,000 settlement fee. The man refused. Even though he was never convicted of the shoplifting charge, police ran a civil forfeiture on the car using a state drug asset law. After seven months of litigation (including an appeal by police after a court ruled in favor of the innocent man), he finally prevailed, but throughout that time he was unable to use his automobile.[335] Police confiscated a Harley Davidson motorcycle from a drug suspect who was buying it from another person. The lienholder paid a $2,500 settlement fee for police to release the cycle.[336] Police seized a father's late model Oldsmobile Cutlass when remains of a marijuana cigarette were found in the back seat while the son had the car. Officers told the father he could have the car back upon paying a settlement fee of $1,250.[337] Police stopped a young man driving his mother's late model Mercury Marquis and seized the car when they found a pipe in it. The police chief told the mother that for $200 she could have her car back and that the chief would intervene with a judge to stop drug charges from being filed against her son.[338] All incidents described earlier in this paragraph occurred in one Missouri county, but there is no reason to believe conditions there differed from conditions elsewhere. Examination of official records in ten Missouri jurisdictions found that over half of threatened forfeitures were dropped after informal fee payments to police.[339] One police chief said settlement fees of $200 to $500 were "very reasonable" for return of automobiles in which tiny quantities of drugs had been found.[340]

Upon receipt of $250 settlement fees, Broward County, Florida, authorities returned cars having a book value under $1,000.[341] If a seized vehicle was owned by a car rental company, Ft. Lauderdale returned the auto if the company paid a $250 "service charge."[342] After fifty cultivated marijuana plants were discovered on a farm in Audrain County, Missouri, a drug squad arrested the elderly farm couple—holding them handcuffed on the ground. Later the squad admitted that the couple had not grown the marijuana and no charges were filed. Nonetheless, a forfeiture was filed against the entire 155 acres as a criminal operation, on grounds that the couple probably knew who cultivated the marijuana. Forfeiture proceedings were dropped when the couple paid a $5,000 settlement fee to the drug squad.[343] When a heavy equipment buyer's truck broke down in Jefferson Davis Parish, Louisiana, he gratefully accepted road assistance from sheriff's deputies. They asked to search his truck, and he had no objection. At the same time, he freely admitted that he was carrying $23,000 cash because heavy equipment auctions rarely accepted personal checks. Deputies removed a door panel and announced that although no drugs were hidden behind it, such a space could be used to conceal drugs. He was not arrested, but his truck and cash were seized as drug assets. A two-year legal battle yielded no progress in getting his property returned. The sheriff then offered to drop forfeiture proceedings against the cash and truck for an $11,500 settlement fee. The man agreed.[344] A newspaper investigation found many of these "settlement" fees to be private arrangements between police and victims, done without knowledge of prosecutors, let alone courts.[345] Said one attorney whose client paid a settlement fee, "Police shouldn't act as judge and prosecutor. They should not decide what penalty people should have to pay, or who should be charged."[346] It is challenging to distinguish settlement fees from extortion and bribery.

The challenge is even greater when drug suspects are released without criminal charge if they agree to forfeit enough cash to police. When Florissant, Missouri, police found $50,000 in a motel room, they persuaded the room occupant to give all the cash to them. Because this was an informal donation, it did not appear in forfeiture records kept by prosecutors or courts. Police allowed the guest to depart without criminal charges being filed. Department records listed the money as a drug asset even though no drugs were found in the room.[347]

The propriety of forfeiture settlement fees becomes even murkier when intertwined with settlement of filed criminal charges. A detective for the prosecutor's office in Somerset County, New Jersey, offered to refrain both from pressing felony charges and from running a forfeiture against an accused person's home if he would convey two vacant lots to the prosecutor's office. The victim, who had paid $174,000 for the lots, turned them over. A few months later the prosecutor sold them for $20,000, and the buyer then conveyed them to two acquaintances of the detective.[348] Crawford County, Missouri, authorities found barely more than 35 grams of marijuana in a Ford van. That exceeded the cutoff point for misdemeanor possession, so the driver was charged as a felony drug offender and the vehicle was confiscated. Authorities offered to return the van and reduce charges to a misdemeanor upon receipt of a $3,000 settlement fee plus $400 storage costs.[349] (Much seized property awaiting forfeiture in that county was stored on land owned by a sheriff's deputy.)[350] In the same county, the driver of a late model Corvette was arrested when an unstated amount of cocaine was allegedly discovered in the car. Felony charges were reduced to a misdemeanor and forfeiture against the sports car was dropped when the sheriff's department received an $18,000 settlement fee.[351] An Ohio man was accused of cultivating six marijuana plants on his farm. Authorities said they would seek a five-year prison sentence for this felony, but offered to reduce their demand to a thirty-day jail sentence if he would convey half interest in the farm to law enforcement authorities. He took the deal.[352] The Audrain County, Missouri, prosecutor agreed to recommend a two-week jail sentence and probation for someone who pleaded guilty to growing marijuana at home, while at the same time dropping a civil forfeiture against the home. This was in exchange for a $10,000 fee. The prosecutor frankly admitted he was "unsure whether he would have recommended probation had Hicks not agreed to pay the $10,000."[353] The prosecutor in Clay County, Missouri, denied making such deals, but a newspaper investigation found evidence to the contrary. One defendant and attorney contended, with supporting correspondence, that drug charges carrying a twenty-year prison term were dropped when the defendant conveyed his high performance, late model pickup truck to the prosecutor's office. Court records documented another defendant's conveyance of a Peterbilt eighteen-wheeler "in consideration of a plea bargain being entered."[354] A U.S. Justice Department forfeiture expert noted, "A carefully drafted plea arrangement in which a defendant agrees to . . . surrender . . . assets under his or her control can accomplish much more in less time and with less expense than a criminal trial or forfeiture proceeding."[355]

Like settlement fees, the conveyances noted above are useful in evading state laws requiring police to transfer forfeiture proceeds to schools or other agencies. Cautious drug squads may require barter; if no cash changes hands, it cannot be shared. The Broward County, Florida, sheriff's department returned a seized truck when the owner upgraded department radios so they would work on more channels.[356]

When innocent forfeiture victims are able to prevail, before getting return of their property they may be forced to agree they will not sue authorities for wrongful conduct. An assistant U.S. attorney described such agreements as routine.[357] In one case the FBI seized a Mercury Grand Marquis from a Roman Catholic priest. The priest was not accused of wrongdoing, but had bought the auto from a car dealer who was revealed to be a drug dealer, and the FBI reasoned that the dealership's cars were drug-tainted assets. Only after agreeing not to sue the FBI did the priest get his car back.[358] Missouri authorities charged a couple with processing marijuana and adopted out forfeiture of their 60-acre homestead to the federal government. No marijuana was ever found on their property; the charge was based on an undercover informant who was found to have fabricated evidence in other cases. State officials dropped the drug charge, but the U.S. attorney pressed forward with a civil forfeiture: "I don't know if they're innocent or not," an assistant said. The county prosecutor, whose drug squad stood to gain eighty percent of proceeds from the federal forfeiture, refused to ask for a halt, saying he was too busy to make even one phone call. Ten months after proceedings began, the U.S. attorney's office agreed to drop the forfeiture if the couple agreed not to sue for compensation.[359]

Sometimes victims must even agree they will not discuss what happened to them. A man found innocent of marijuana possession spent eleven months fighting a forfeiture against his late model Pontiac Trans Am. Eventually prosecutors agreed to drop proceedings in exchange for a $700 settlement fee and a promise that the victim would not comment about what happened. When the victim told an inquiring reporter that he was forbidden to comment, an enraged prosecutor accused the victim of violating the agreement by revealing that he could not comment upon it.[360] Requiring silence from victims was a characteristic of Nazi law enforcement; victims were threatened with further measures if they filed official complaints, and revelation of experiences in a concentration camp was legal grounds for renewed incarceration.[361]

Even at the federal level, learning facts about civil forfeiture cases can be impossible. The U.S. Attorney for Western Pennsylvania explained why he routinely sealed records of civil forfeitures: "There are just some things I don't want to publicize. The person whose assets we seize will eventually know, and who else has to?"[362]

AND SO IT GOES

In 1991 a senior Justice Department official told Congress that forfeiture has three goals: "to immobilize crime syndicates," "to enhance intergovernmental cooperation," and "to produce revenue."[363] We have seen forfeiture accomplish two of those goals. Admittedly, crime syndicates continue to thrive under this "law enforcement" policy, but government is not perfect.

We have seen federal laws that are directed against Mafia drug lords used against a bookstore owner who sold magazines deemed to be obscene. We have seen state laws that are directed against major drug dealers used to run a forfeiture against someone accused (but never convicted) of a municipal shoplifting offense. Such abuses are in addition to actions taken against drug users minding their own business. Drug warriors are using civil forfeiture to hammer ordinary people for trivial or even legally blameless conduct that displeases members of drug squads. Police are using civil proceedings to wreck lives of citizens who commit crimes carrying a $25 fine, enhancing criminal punishments that police deem inadequate.

In 1993 the U.S. Supreme Court handed down two decisions hindering those practices. Austin v. United States[364] allowed victims to challenge forfeitures that seem disproportionate punishment for a criminal offense, although police can retain custody of disputed property throughout the years of challenge. Under the Austin decision, police can also maintain income simply by increasing the number of forfeitures, taking smaller amounts of property from many more victims. The other case (United States v. 92 Buena Vista Avenue)[365] limited the relation-back doctrine, allowing some third parties to retain title to property purchased from a person who committed a crime. That limitation had troublesome implications for drug squads. As two forfeiture specialists noted earlier, "Ultimate effectiveness of the whole forfeiture scheme depends upon the development and acceptance of a legal theory that will allow the government to forfeit criminal assets that have been transferred to third parties."[366] After an initial flurry of concern among drug squads, an official from the Justice Department's Asset Forfeiture Office urged law enforcement colleagues not to worry. He noted that U.S. Supreme Court rulings had once appeared to limit the ability of prosecutors to bring charges of bribery and corruption against state officials.

> These decisions were as devastating to prosecutors and investigators in that field as *Buena Vista* and *Austin* have been to us. And yet, when I last checked, there has been no decrease in the number of Federal investigations and prosecutions of state and local Officials since these cases were decided.
>
> How is it that something that appears so devastating turns out to be a minor blip, the most serious effect of which is the nuisance of retrying a few cases? It is not that the precedent is misunderstood, but rather it is the incredible adaptability of the Federal law enforcement community that finds new ways to solve the problem.
>
> Maybe it's our confidence in the validity of our mission, but we seem to overcome obstacles and problems that might be insurmountable to others.[367]

After World War I the Versailles Peace Conference declared certain types of conduct to be war crimes. That conduct included "confiscation of property" and "exaction of illegitimate or of exorbitant contributions and requisitions."[368] After World War II prosecutors at the Nuremberg Military Tribunal used the term "crimes against humanity" when describing "deprivation of rights to file private suits and rights of appeal" along with "denial of right of counsel," "repeated trials on the same charges, criminal abuse of discretion," "prearrangement of sentences between judges and prosecutors," and "discriminatory trial processes . . . all of which resulted in . . . plunder of private property."[369] Drug warriors running forfeitures characterize the same tactics as law enforcement tools.

Just as the consequence of civil liberties violations demonstrate why the Founding Fathers cherished civil liberties, abuses in drug war forfeitures demonstrate why the Founding Fathers put such strict limits on forfeiture. Indeed, U.S. Supreme Court Justice Potter Stewart warned that any distinction between human rights and property rights is artificial:

> The dichotomy between personal liberties and property rights is a false one. Property does not have rights. People have rights. The right to enjoy property without unlawful deprivation, no less than the right to speak or the right to travel, is in truth a "personal" right, whether the "property" in question be a welfare check, a home, or a savings account. In fact, a fundamental interdependence exists between the personal right to liberty and the personal right in property. Neither could have meaning without the other.[370]

After property confiscations eliminate an ostracized group's ability to survive in normal society, the way is clear for implementing the concentration element of the destruction process. The internment of drug users is our next chapter's topic.

4

CONCENTRATION

> The Germans could not stand the idea of living in a world where one was not protected by law and order. They just would not believe that the prisoners in the camps had not committed outrageous crimes since the way they were punished permitted only this conclusion.
>
> Bruno Bettelheim[1]

The penultimate stage of the destruction process is concentration. Victims are not only physically removed from society but are gathered together to make further brutalities easier. Concentration also promotes the destruction process by removing both victims and brutalities from public view. As victims disappear, their normal conduct in society no longer challenges hate propaganda stereotypes, so resistance to the war on ordinary people declines. And paradoxically, disappearance of victims does not serve to warn "good citizens" about consequences of the destruction process. Instead, good citizens are no longer troubled by seeing their neighbors harmed and are reassured that victims are receiving whatever treatment has been decreed by authorities. Out of sight, out of mind.

PENAL SERVITUDE

Many Germans classified Jewish concentration camp inmates as criminals. And indeed, many Jewish inmates were incarcerated for criminal activity. But their crimes may well have been regarded as ordinary conduct in many societies—inviting a girl to the movies, complaining about the government. Such conduct could be illegal in Nazi Germany, and Jews paid the price for such "criminality." So-called ordinary criminals could be indistinguishable from ordinary people. Likewise, many "criminal drug users" in the American penal system are indistinguishable from ordinary people.

Despite declining drug use, twice as many drug arrests were made in 1990 as in 1980. Two-thirds of the one million drug arrests in 1991 were for simple possession;[2] victims were merely accused of being drug users. Moreover, punishment became more severe. In 1980 about 100,000 drug offenders were sent to prison; in 1990 the number was 300,000.[3] Those figures are not the total prison population but simply the number of drug offenders added to the prison population in one year. In 1980 about six percent of new state prisoners were drug offenders; in 1990 the total was thirty percent.[4] By 1992 the number of incarcerated federal drug offenders exceeded the total of *all* federal prisoners when President Reagan declared war on drug users.[5] Federal authorities expected two-thirds of all their prisoners to be serving drug time midway through President Clinton's term.[6] William Bennett not only supported use of U.S. Army troops to enforce drug laws, he urged that military prosecutors and judges handle the growing number of cases threatening to swamp the civilian legal system.[7] (Already the drug war had given Presidents Reagan and Bush an excuse to double the number of federal civilian judges, packing the federal judiciary with authoritarian jurists.)

The population explosion of drug offenders in the penal system was caused by politics. Not partisan politics, but a political decision to make war on drug users. Although few drug users turn themselves in to police, such criminals are easy to detect through means discussed earlier in this book. Generally a person's drug use is far easier to detect than a person's gun use. Take the ease of detection, add lengthy mandatory sentences that do not apply to non-drug criminals, and we get a penal system filling up with drug users.

Another political decision contributing to expansion of prison populations is the decision to include escalator clauses in drug laws. Because of hate propaganda promoted by politicians, the public became dissatisfied with fining a marijuana user $25 for misdemeanor possession. Such a penalty seemed insufficient for someone ostensibly threatening American society. Yet a harsh increase in penalty is difficult to achieve: If a $25 fine was sufficient penalty yesterday, how can the same offense carry a $10,000 fine plus ten years mandatory imprisonment today without lawmakers appearing to violate the ban on cruel and unusual punishment? The answer is to invent new offenses so that a single act can violate multiple laws. Through escalator clauses, a drug violation that starts as a misdemeanor can be transformed into a felony with lengthy mandatory imprisonment.

For example, Missouri law says that possessing less than 35 grams of marijuana is a misdemeanor, but under a bill considered by the legislature in 1994, anyone possessing more than 28 grams was defined as a dealer (a felony) if the person had failed to report such misdemeanor possession to state revenue authorities. Failure to pay a state tax on the misdemeanor amount was also classified as a felony.[8] Laws of other states had similar provisions. Authorities in Kansas bragged that $500,000 in annual revenue was generated by prosecuting drug offenders for tax fraud.[9] Less publicized is the fact that converting a misdemeanor offense into multiple felonies can imprison a harmless marijuana user for years. We have seen how "armed drug offender" clauses apply to drug users never accused of violence and how President Bush sought to define all drug offenses (such as marijuana possession) as crimes of violence. "Violent offender" status implements sentences far longer than those for "nonviolent" crimes (such as illegal arms sales by White House aides), and "violent offender" sentences are also mandatory and without parole.

Another escalator is dealer status. Drug dealing is always a felony, but typical "dealers" are users who share supplies with friends, sometimes for small reimbursement, sometimes for free. These felons are "drug dealers" in the sense that a tobacco smoker who hands a cigarette to someone is a tobacco dealer, or a beer drinker who shares a six-pack is a liquor dealer. Another escalator clause boosts penalties for repeat offenses. Police can depend on marijuana consumers to possess the product time and again, just as some sexually active persons routinely possess condoms or birth control pills. Escalating prison terms are unlikely to discourage marijuana use or contraceptive use, but such sanctions are guaranteed to sweep targeted persons off the streets. Legislation promoted by Missouri Governor John Ashcroft in 1992 would have converted a third misdemeanor marijuana possession offense into a felony.[10] That particular drug warrior effort failed, but laws already on the books escalated prison terms for repeated possession of felony amounts of marijuana (an amount equivalent to little more than one pack of tobacco cigarettes).

In addition to escalator clauses, double jeopardy helps concentrate drug users in prison by reincarcerating victims who have already served one sentence.

Civil commitment is another means of concentration. Victims can be removed from their homes without being convicted of any crime. Imprisonment under civil commitment can be indeterminate, for however long is needed to cure a victim of drug addiction. Because many medical authorities maintain that addiction cannot be cured and because no proof of criminal conduct is required for civil imprisonment, drug warriors like to promote the notion that drug use is a disease. That concept allows drug users to be imprisoned for as long as bureaucrats wish. As we have seen, participants in a drug conference endorsed by the Reagan administration advocated that a single unconfirmed urine test be considered sufficient grounds for civil commitment and urged that civil commitment proceedings be streamlined further. Through civil commitment, people can be imprisoned if they are merely certified as at risk of becoming drug addicts, and drug warrior rhetoric portrays everyone as a potential addict.

Concentrating drug users in prison allows them to become a source of slave labor for public and private employers. This slave labor pool has not escaped notice from drug warriors. In discussing what to do with drug users, authorities in Jackson County, Missouri proposed "confining convicts in a new minimum security jail or halfway houses at night and making them work during the day . . . to repair housing."[11] U.S. Senator Jeremiah Denton agreed, "I do not know what happened to the Georgia chain gang concept. You could put those guys to work on the highways and so forth and really do a lot on the budget."[12] Unlike burglars, rapists, and other social dregs that once predominated in prison populations, drug users may be highly skilled blue and white collar workers. A French videocassette informed companies that prison labor was suitable for "types of activity that range from the most repetitive tasks to the installation of computer equipment," without absenteeism or strikes. One French employer found the lack of paid holidays to be appealing.[13] Persons considered unsuitable for employment in "drug-free companies" can be transformed into desirable workers once the little matter of normal paychecks is eliminated. The Thirteenth Amendment to the U.S. Constitution permits slavery as punishment for criminal activity, with the potential of substantially diminished labor costs for employers who support the drug war.

Concentrating drug users in prison also allows them to be brutalized out of public sight. Although hard-liners continually complain about "country club prisons" providing resort-style vacations to criminals, in reality prison environments are generally unsavory, and local jails are worse. Inmates live amidst disease and violence. Citizens shrug off prison incidents that would evoke emergency rescue calls to police if witnessed on a public street. (Violent conditions in prisons, incidentally, make one wonder just how many police patrols would be needed to make dangerous neighborhoods safe.)

So-called boot camp prisons, adding military discipline to other oppressions, enjoyed growing public popularity when this book was written. Verbal and physical abuse administered by staffs were portrayed as nurturing inmates' self-esteem to help them function as good citizens upon release. Given that some inmates grew up under the same sort of abuse as children, it is unclear why more of the same would benefit them as adults. "Boot camps" were nonetheless portrayed as compassionate suppliers of "tough love" to inmates, helping them rather than punishing them. Imprisonment was transformed into psychological therapy, unquestioning obedience into self-reliance, mistreatment into kindness. Such transformations permitted citizens to feel complacent about concentrating more and more drug users ("who, after all, need therapy") in prisons. When the Bush administration popularized "boot camps," one criminologist described the policy as "a massive program of basically putting young black urban males in concentration camps."[14] Such "shock time" was nothing new. Nazis used the same technique for dealing with rebellious youth, who were sent to special labor camps. At first the maximum sentence was four weeks, but as the rebellious youth problem continued, "the 'shock' was made 'longer' and 'sharper.'"[15] Eventually Nazis established youth concentration camps, where members could graduate to adult concentration camps upon reaching age eighteen.[16]

FREE SOCIETY

Thus far we have considered ways of concentrating drug users who run afoul of the criminal or civil legal system. Victims can also be concentrated through government regulations and private ostracism. In Nazi Germany such measures were used to concentrate Jews in particular residential buildings. Such a policy reduced the need to construct new housing; Aryans could simply take over residences vacated by Jews. Concentrating victims also freed police from the need to patrol entire neighborhoods to supervise Jews; watchful Aryan neighbors now summoned authorities whenever proscribed Jewish behavior was noted in a Jewish apartment building or house.

Concentration can be incidental to other elements of the destruction process or can be promoted deliberately. An incidental aspect is illustrated by ostracism excluding drug users from gainful employment. As earnings decline, so do housing options. Ostracized drug users will tend to congregate in low-rent districts, typically ill kept and crime ridden (allowing drug users to be vilified for ruining neighborhoods). As we have seen, such degradation is regarded as insufficient by drug warriors, who seek to evict drug users from public housing. Whether these unemployed homeless victims are then arrested for vagrancy or for committing petty crimes to survive, the result is to concentrate those drug users in jail. To concentrate victims in free society, they need to be excluded from certain areas. Drug users lose federal home loan mortgage guarantees,[17] which can result in loss of their middle-class houses. Leases for private rental housing can exclude drug users;[18] a tenant who fails an employer's urine test can be evicted, leaving the victim not only jobless but homeless. Drug warriors promote provisions evicting all tenants of a housing unit if a guest uses marijuana on the premises or if a resident family member possesses a marijuana cigarette off the premises. That has the incidental effect of encouraging residents to ostracize drug users by expelling family members from the home or telling friends to keep out. "Keep out" restrictions are no longer applied solely to users of illicit drugs. Tobacco smokers are banned from common carriers, from inns, and from other buildings open to the public. The rationale goes beyond health claims about secondhand smoke. Entrances to the state veterinary school building at Kansas State University warn that tobacco chewers cannot enter. As drug users are banned from more and more places, they naturally concentrate in others.

Perhaps the most notorious way of concentrating ordinary people is to put them in concentration camps. In the 1970s, New York Governor Nelson Rockefeller made wildly exaggerated claims about a "drug menace" to demagogue votes. He pushed a law mandating life imprisonment for assorted crimes if the perpetrator ingested an illicit drug within twenty-four hours of the crime. The assumption was that an addict offender would invariably fall under those provisions, allowing life imprisonment of addicts who committed a minor offense normally resulting in no incarceration at all.[19] Although Rockefeller pushed for life imprisonment of drug users convicted of a crime, he also advocated five-year civil commitments of drug users who committed no crime. His staff asked the federal government to provide camps necessary for such a program.[20] More than once under Rockefeller's governorship the New York legislature considered establishing concentration camps for drug users. Said one legislative witness, "If we can draft our young men who are good and send them to camps in Vietnam, we can draft our addicts and send them to therapeutic communities in health camps for 10 years, 20 years—as long as it takes to cure them."[21]

Although a large number of drug users have been concentrated together through criminal or civil proceedings, those proceedings required each person's circumstances to be examined individually. In the war on drug users, we have not yet seen sweeps of neighborhoods such as were conducted by Nazis who made war on Jews, sweeps in which large numbers of persons were apprehended en masse and shipped off to camps. In such operations, authorities apprehend people first and consider individual circumstances later, if ever. By declaring a state of national emergency, the president of the United States has personal power to authorize neighborhood sweeps of innocent persons accused of no crime. That power should be remembered when zealots call for use of federal war powers in the struggle against drug users; war powers can be exercised without a formal declaration of war, even when no military attack has been made against the United States.[22] Large-scale internments could be conducted on short notice, as was demonstrated with Japanese-Americans during World War II. Legalities and rhetoric surrounding their internment are relevant to evaluating the potential for similar action against drug users.

GATHERING OF INNOCENTS

In the first four decades of the twentieth century, incessant hate propaganda was directed against Japanese-Americans living on America's West Coast. Despite harassment from private ostracism and petty regulation, they obtained jobs, businesses, and homes promised by the American dream. But regardless of the contributions these persons made to community prosperity, they were never fully accepted by their neighbors. Such lack of acceptance always puts a group at risk of destruction, however remote the possibility may seem in times of tranquility, however small the number of extremists. Widespread public hatred of a targeted group is unnecessary for its destruction. Public indifference toward extremist activity is sufficient. Those truths became self-evident after the Japanese military attack on Pearl Harbor in December 1941.

> If you would know how 110,000 innocent people could be robbed of their liberty and property, robbed by a nation proffering notions like "liberty," "freedom," "justice," and "innocent until proven guilty," you would understand the role of the mass media. . . . Political and publishing leaders on the west coast deliberately stoked the fires of popular distrust and racism toward Japanese-Americans. . . . The goal of this deceptive campaign was to panic public opinion.[23]

That retrospective analysis echoed contemporary observers: "The public is not showing hate or spite. But the reactionary press and the politicians are out for blood and wholesale internment. Jingoes are endeavoring, under the cover of war-time flag-waving patriotism, to do what they always wanted to do in peace time: get rid of the Japanese."[24] Some calls for internment of Japanese-Americans spoke of enemy aliens on American soil. Those calls conveniently ignored the fact that U.S. law prohibited persons born in Japan from becoming naturalized U.S. citizens.[25] This prohibition automatically classified most Japanese immigrants as enemy aliens, unlike Germans and Italians, who had been able to become naturalized citizens.[26] Zealots made no distinction between these Japanese-Americans and their children, who were U.S. citizens. "Many were held for days by local law-enforcement officers, no charges being filed against them. Many Japanese Americans were dismissed from private employment; others were evicted from their residences. Grocery stores and other business firms refused to sell them goods, and extensive economic and social boycotts developed against them."[27] For example, California revoked liquor trade licenses held by Japanese-Americans and fired all employed by the state civil service.[28] Nazis had taken similar measures against Jews in the 1930s, and the impact on Japanese-Americans was similar.

A presidential proclamation forbade Japanese-Americans from possessing specified items deemed threatening to national security. Banned items included drawings of any firearm.[29] John K. Burling, assistant chief of the Alien Enemy Control Unit, noted how the proclamation was enforced: "People were detained for having flashlights, Red Cross medals, rusty pistols, etc."[30] Although detentions were numerous, they were not of the sweeping nature desired by some federal officials. A young army major named Karl R. Bendetsen developed a plan to incarcerate all law-abiding Japanese-Americans. The plan was elegant. Drawing upon war powers, the president would issue an executive order written by Bendetsen[31] allowing the United States to be divided into military districts, each headed by a military commander. In a ten-day period, Bendetsen was promoted from major to lieutenant colonel and then full colonel, and was put in charge of many details of his plan.[32] Congress then passed a law requiring civilians to obey orders of their military district commander, making civilians subject to military rule without a declaration of martial law.[33] Commanders had authority to decide who would be permitted to reside within the districts, and in order to promote the goal of a "Jap-Free West Coast," law-abiding citizens would be removed from the West Coast district and put in concentration camps. Apologists sometimes note that conditions in these American concentration camps were superior to Nazi concentration camps, but surely we cannot excuse anyone's action on grounds that Nazis acted worse.

Credible accounts indicate that Census Bureau records were used to locate all Japanese-Americans.[34] A series of federal orders was directed against these U.S. residents. The sweeping nature of these directives was indicated by Supreme Court Justice Frank Murphy in his commentary on Civilian Exclusion Order No. 34:

> The order deprives all those within its scope of the equal protection of the laws as guaranteed by the Fifth Amendment. It further deprives these individuals of their constitutional rights to live and work where they will, to establish a home where they choose and to move about freely. In excommunicating them without benefit of hearings, this order also deprives them of all their constitutional rights to procedural due process. . . . One of the most sweeping and complete deprivations of constitutional rights in the history of this nation in the absence of martial law.[35]

The West Coast military district commander was Lieutenant General John L. DeWitt. He declared that Japanese-Americans should be "offered an opportunity to accept voluntary internment, under guard." Any who refused the offer would be transported to the east and held in concentration camps until they were "someday" resettled where they would not threaten other Americans.[36] Not only did Japanese-Americans suffer the trauma of losing their homes, jobs, and businesses, followed by incarceration; they could not know what fate authorities planned for them. Authorities themselves did not know.

Conflicting regulations whipsawed victims. Recalled one victim, "Every time we went anywhere more than five miles away, we were supposed to go to the WCCA [Wartime Civil Control Administration] office in Sacramento, nine miles away, to get a permit."[37] While considering the dilemma of another victim, U.S. Supreme Court Justice Owen Roberts noted that Proclamation No. 4[38] required the person to stay in a military zone but Exclusion Order No. 34[39] required him to leave.

> The two conflicting orders, one which commanded him to stay and the other which commanded him to go, were nothing but a cleverly devised trap to accomplish the real purpose of the military authority, which was to lock him up in a concentration camp. The only course by which the petitioner could avoid arrest and prosecution was to go to that camp according to instructions to be given him when he reported at a Civil Control Center. We know that is the fact.[40]

Because of failure to comply with the contradictory orders, the petitioner was convicted of violating the federal law requiring obedience to the executive order which both established military zones across the country and authorized military authorities to exclude anyone from those zones. Justice Jackson commented, however, that the victim

> has been convicted of an act not commonly a crime. It consists merely of being present in the state whereof he is a citizen, near the place where he was born, and where all his life he has lived. . . .
>
> But the "law" which this prisoner is convicted of disregarding is not found in an act of Congress, but in a military order. Neither the Act of Congress nor the Executive Order of the President, nor both together, would afford a basis for this conviction. It rests on the orders of General DeWitt.[41]

In other words, civil courts were trying people for violating military decrees. In this case, even though the victim was given probation and a suspended sentence, military authorities then used a technique familiar to students of Nazi jurisprudence: the U.S. Army immediately arrested the victim upon release by the court, thereafter holding him in an "Assembly Center" (a minimum-security civilian prison established by the military, from which inmates were transferred to concentration camps).[42] In another case, Justice William O. Douglas puzzled over such conduct by authorities: "The legislative history of the Act of March 21, 1942,[43] is silent on detention. And that silence may have special significance in view of the fact that detention in Relocation Centers was no part of the original program of evacuation but developed later."[44] In this case the Supreme Court found that the law's silence on putting citizens in concentration camps did not mean that authorities lacked such power under the statute.[45] In an associated case, an anguished Justice Jackson declared:

> A military commander may overstep the bounds of constitutionality, and it is an incident. But if we review and approve, that passing incident becomes the doctrine of the Constitution. There it has a generative power of its own, and all that it creates will be in its own image. Nothing better illustrates this danger than does the Court's opinion in this case.
>
> It argues that we are bound to uphold the conviction of Korematsu because we upheld one in *Hirabayashi* v. *United States*, 320 U.S. 81, when we sustained these orders in so far as they applied a curfew. . . .
>
> In that case we were urged to consider only the curfew feature, that being all that technically was involved, because it was the only count necessary to sustain Hirabayashi's conviction and sentence. We yielded, and the Chief Justice guarded the opinion as carefully as language will do. He said: "Our investigation here does not go beyond the inquiry whether . . . the challenged orders and statute *afforded a reasonable basis for the action taken in imposing the curfew.*" . . . However, in spite of our limiting words we did validate a . . . mild and temporary deprivation of liberty. Now . . . because we said that these citizens could be made to stay in their homes during the hours of dark, it is said we must require them to leave home entirely; and if that, we are told they may also be taken into custody for deportation; and if that, it is argued that they may also be held for some undetermined time in detention camps. How far the principle of this case would be extended before plausible reasons would play out, I do not know.[46]

Some victims held public protests; protestors were placed in mental hospitals under civil commitment for the war's duration.[47] Other victims appealed to courts as mass arrests were underway. Attorneys described

> forcible ejection of American citizens from their homes and places of employment at short notice, under penalty of law, by military force, and without accusations, hearings or trials. In the upheaval much of the personal property of these American citizens has been lost. In their absence, among other things, their names have been erased from civil service rolls and legislation (such as the Lowrey Act of California) has

been passed which authorizes seizure of their property. As a result of their prolonged exclusion, interests and possessions have had to be abandoned or sacrificed because they have not been able to properly safeguard or care for them.[48]

Camp inmates were considered a source of slave labor. Even before issuance of Executive Order 9066, which started the concentration of Japanese-Americans, federal officials discussed plans to use victims as low-cost labor.[49] Milton Eisenhower (brother of the famed general) was the civilian heading the apprehension and resettlement of Japanese-Americans. As mass roundups began in 1942, he told Congress of projects to exploit this labor supply. "Each project will be as productive as possible, and it will be the policy to encourage the evacuees themselves to develop the highest degree of community services consistent with the situation." Eisenhower anticipated that camp inmates would be used for "land subjugation, flood control, and development of natural resources," along with farm labor and "manufacturing—the production of articles requiring a good deal of hand labor directly useful to the military establishment." Eisenhower noted that "for the time being," inmates would not be allowed to build self-sustaining communities; inmate labor would be diverted for other purposes.[50] Inmate physicians and other professionals working inside camps were paid $19 a month; unskilled laborers received less.[51] Milton Eisenhower acknowledged the arrangements to be inconsistent with the Geneva Convention.[52] A congressional committee reported, "Some witnesses believed that Japanese under armed guard either in California agriculture or in the beet-sugar work in the Mountain States would be a reliable source of cheap labor."[53] California Governor Culbert Olsen and other western public officials saw camp inmates as cheap agricultural labor, an idea endorsed by Acting Secretary of War Robert Patterson.[54] Private employers clamored to exploit this labor pool. One Monterey County farmer suggested, "They might be put under restraint of one kind or another with the proper supervision of the military. . . . They might be taken out to work, if they desired to work, in the morning, and be brought back at night."[55] Said one federal official, "Many of these large growers have indicated that they would be glad to appear before the Army and present definite detailed propositions for employment and housing of the Japanese labor."[56] Impatient growers urged that Japanese-Americans be put into fields immediately under military guard. Senator James Murray (D-MT) found delays exasperating: "We have got all these Jap evacuees, but the Employment Service under McNutt has failed to get them out on the farms."[57] After the system began operating, one victim remembered, "We ended up in Blackfoot, Idaho, and they lined us up. And the farmer got to choose us. . . . It was traumatic, lining us up like slaves at the market. They did everything but open your mouth and look at your teeth and feel your muscles."[58] In theory victims who labored outside camps were supposed to get the prevailing wage for their work, but victims sent "harrowing tales" back to camps about ruthless exploitation by bosses who knew their workers could not resist.[59] Long afterward, a former camp inmate remembered: "My family was recruited from the relocation camp with the promise of a good life in a place called Seabrook Farms, in southern New Jersey, to work in a factory. At this factory, it was not unusual for a worker to work 16 hours a day. . . . Overtime pay was determined at the whim of the company, and it was not unusual to consider overtime payable only after 60 hours or more."[60]

Victims were identified by genealogy. Having a Japanese great-great grandparent made a person subject to concentration camp internment. Caucasians married to American citizens of Japanese descent found their spouses being sent to the camps, although the couples could stay together if the Caucasian accepted internment. Some couples endured separation so the Caucasian could hold a job and provide for the couple's needs. Eventually such policies were moderated: If the husband was Caucasian, the couple could remain free on the West Coast as long as they were not residing in a Japanese neighborhood, but if the wife was Caucasian, the couple could remain free only by leaving the West Coast.[61]

A thirty-year-old husband and father was forced from the thriving farm operated by his family. The family patriarch "now aged, and suffering from heart disease, despaired of rebuilding what they had lost at the time of evacuation, and was thinking of retiring to Japan with his meagre savings."[62] In August 1943 a victim said, "I've lost all hope of a future in America. I can't make money here any more. I've lost everything. My wife feels worse than I do about the whole thing. She wants to send the younger children back so that they can get a Japanese education over there."[63] Another victim asked, "What about the draft? If I and my brother get killed what happens to my family? My brother and I are the only ones old enough to help support the family. . . . They put us in here [in a concentration camp] and then they expect us to fight for this country. It's one thing for a son to go off to war when the father still has his job and the family still has its possessions; its [sic] another thing to expect it after people have been through what we have and have lost everything."[64] Still another victim agreed:

> I said I'd die for this country in the event of war. That's the way I felt. But since I lost my business when I was young and just starting up I've changed my mind. You Caucasian Americans should realize that I got a raw deal. . . . What did a war with Japan have to do with evacuating me? You've got to realize that I am an American citizen just as much as you. Maybe my dad is not, because of Congress. He couldn't naturalize. But my associates in school and college were Caucasians. It's been a hard road to take.[65]

The experience of victims was eloquently expressed by a young camp inmate who begged his mother to "take him back to America."[66]

Through use of war powers, "for the first time in the nation's history, race alone become a criterion for protracted mass incarceration of American citizens."[67] Incarcerated not because of their conduct, but because of their physical bodies.

Although war powers under the Constitution may supercede all other elements of the document, until the West Coast action against Japanese-Americans, war powers had been exercised only in military combat zones, particularly those in which federal courts no longer functioned (such as areas of the Confederate states during the Civil War). Supreme Court approval of Japanese-American internments allowed war powers to be applied where no military combat was underway and where all civil institutions functioned normally. That was the Roosevelt administration's desire; Attorney General Francis Biddle reminded the president in 1943, "You signed the original Executive Order permitting the exclusions so the Army could handle the Japs."[68] This was the president's personal decision; he never consulted his cabinet about the mass internment.[69]

Just as German officials interning Jews used rhetorical euphemisms to describe their work, so do did American officials interning Japanese-Americans. General DeWitt's Proclamation No. 4 spoke of a need "to provide for the welfare and to insure the orderly evacuation and resettlement of Japanese voluntarily migrating from Military Area No. 1."[70] We have seen how targets of that welfare program felt about its benefits. And contending that someone makes a choice "voluntarily" if the alternative is imprisonment is a contention ridiculed by Nuremberg Tribunal prosecutors.[71] General DeWitt also proclaimed, "The very fact that no sabotage [by Japanese-Americans] has taken place to date is a disturbing and confirming indication that such action will be taken."[72] Lacking evidence that Japanese-Americans posed any threat, authorities declared that the lack of evidence proved the case for internment.

They simultaneously argued that victims were not actually imprisoned but rather put into protective custody for their own safety. Attorney General Biddle, Secretary of War Henry Stimson, and General DeWitt all contended that Japanese-Americans were apprehended to protect them from mob violence.[73] If authorities can respond to mob violence by suppressing victims instead of violence, that response means that any group of citizens can be rounded up once enough hatred is directed against it. In the case of Japanese-Americans, however, no mob violence was happening. As the roundup of Japanese-Americans began, California's Commissioner of Immigration and Housing reported that only two attacks against Japanese-Americans had occurred since Pearl Harbor.[74] None were killed in Washington, Oregon, or Arizona during 1942. Seven died in

California that year, mainly in incidents related to internment. Although violence against Japanese-Americans was virtually unknown, their suicide rate increased when authorities implemented the concentration camp program.[75]

Some of the most chilling rhetoric from government officials came from the U.S. Supreme Court. Said Justice Felix Frankfurter, "To find that the Constitution does not forbid the military measures now complained of does not carry with it approval of that which Congress and the Executive did. That is their business, not ours."[76] While one would not expect judges to rule contrary to their understanding of law, one might expect judges to accept moral responsibility for actions they authorize (particularly when other members of a divided court are adamant that law forbids those actions). Similar rhetoric of denial is found in statements given by German officials when explaining away their roles in the Holocaust. Attorney General Biddle became familiar with such rhetoric when he sat in judgment at Nuremberg.

Soon after World War II, Congress passed the Emergency Detention Act.[77] Under its provisions, during an internal security emergency proclaimed by the president anyone believed to be at future risk of committing or conspiring to commit espionage or sabotage could be incarcerated. If a targeted victim asked a friend for advice and the friend suggested that the victim avoid detention, such advice would subject the friend to incarceration.[78] The president was authorized to activate Emergency Detention if a low-intensity war broke out on the other side of the planet, even though it posed no threat to the United States.[79] President Truman was appalled by the Emergency Detention Act's vast powers and the loose restrictions on their use. He vetoed the bill, but Congress passed the law over his veto. Empty concentration camps were established and kept in readiness. Over twenty years later, the Emergency Detention Act was repealed without the camps ever being used.

Truman's fear that unscrupulous authorities could abuse a national emergency proclamation received confirmation. Several months after the Korean War broke out, Truman declared a national emergency.[80] He left office before the war ended, and no subsequent president rescinded Truman's proclamation. Powers authorized by the Korean War emergency lay dormant until the Nixon administration began using Truman's proclamation to prosecute Vietnam War protestors.[81]

Nixon, of course, was interested in suppressing anyone who worked against his policies, though such suppression was hindered by constitutional guarantees of civil rights. Edward Jay Epstein found that Nixon and his aides decided to promote public hysteria about illicit drugs in order to justify a declaration of national emergency, while simultaneously establishing a secret police network that would be used to suppress Nixon's opponents on the excuse of investigating drug law violations. Several Nixon drug control advisers were later found to be involved with Watergate. Egil Krogh not only headed White House drug control efforts but was chief of Nixon's Special Investigative Unit, also known as the Plumbers, which took secret actions against the president's opponents. The CIA agreed to supply "narcotics work" funding for the Plumbers.[82] Watergate investigations named White House drug control liaison John Caufield as a wiretapper.[83] E. Howard Hunt, who ostensibly was a drug control consultant for Nixon's Domestic Council, was a key figure in the Plumbers.[84] Watergate burglar Frank Sturgis said he did anti-drug work on Hunt's behalf.[85]

The leader of the Watergate burglary, G. Gordon Liddy, proposed creation of an organization eventually called Office of Drug Abuse Law Enforcement (ODALE).[86] The nature of drug law enforcement strengthened Liddy's proposal because "drug investigations" gave Nixon's men an ostensible mission, providing cover stories that could not be disproved if Nixon's operatives were discovered to be harassing his opponents.[87] (A judge later noted a federal drug agent's claim that the drug courier profile "consists of anything that arouses his suspicions.")[88] Krogh recalled the president telling him that Liddy's memo proposing a White House–controlled police force supposedly fighting drugs was "the most brilliant memorandum he had received in a long time."[89] Nixon established a multimillion dollar fund funneled through the Bureau of Narcotics and Dangerous Drugs (BNDD) but not controlled by BNDD. BNDD director John Ingersoll was skeptical that the special money flowing through his agency was ever used for drug law enforcement, and he speculated that it was used for secret purposes. Any such purposes remains undocumented in public records; when Epstein tried to follow the money, its trail petered out and disappeared.[90] "The ODALE thing is one of the weirdest things going," said one local law enforcement official. "It's never been clear to me who the hell these people are responsible to. Supposedly they all work for the U.S. Attorney, but they really didn't work for the U.S. Attorney."[91]

In 1971 Nixon began promoting drug crisis rhetoric in order to grease establishment of his personal police force. His plan, Epstein found, was to declare a national emergency to "fight drugs," thereby silencing congressional opponents who would fear to be called traitors against the "drug war." An aide to Krogh told Epstein, "If we hyped the drug problem into a national crisis, we knew that Congress would give us anything we asked for." At that key psychological moment, Epstein reported, Nixon would call for drastic changes in the government's structure.[92] Under laws then governing national emergencies, without consulting Congress or even his cabinet, Nixon could issue secret executive orders, imprison any violator of those orders for a year without trial, censor all mail crossing the U.S. border, take over any radio or television broadcast station and control its programming, suspend any Federal Communications Commission regulation, control any reading material published in a foreign language, forbid U.S. citizens to enter Canada or Mexico without a passport, permit drug squads to use U.S. Navy vessels, stay "court proceedings endangering the security of naval operations," prohibit photos and drawings "of properties of the military establishment" (relevant to news reports of military involvement in drug law enforcement), control compensation for property loss due to "noncombat activities of the Armed Forces" (such as drug law enforcement), seize or control any foreign flag vessel in U.S. waters, use the Public Health Service in any way (relevant to civil commitments), award and amend government contracts without regard to normal contract law, have the General Services Administration dispose of "surplus property" without advertising or bids, suspend any banking activity, control installment loans by merchants, control property transfers, confiscate any property owned by aliens, seize any real estate that the federal government had previously conveyed to public or private owners, and take "measures as he considers necessary to suppress . . . unlawful combination, or conspiracy."[93] By June 1971 Nixon had available the final draft of a drug crisis speech announcing a national emergency, but he then became distracted by unauthorized release of the so-called Pentagon Papers, secret documents about the Vietnam War.[94] He did not proclaim a drug emergency.

Afterward, Nixon expanded his earlier vision of a personal police force. In September 1972, he told White House counsel John Dean to keep a file on Nixon's enemies: "I want the most comprehensive notes on all those who tried to do us in. . . . They were doing this quite deliberately and they're asking for it and they are going to get it. We have not used the power in this first four years as you know. We have never used it. We have not used the Bureau and we have not used the Justice Department but things are going to change now."[95] Instead of declaring a national emergency, Nixon now devised plans for a new agency in the Justice Department to be called the Drug Enforcement Administration. Epstein noted that it would have "authority to request wiretaps and no-knock warrants, and to submit targets to the Internal Revenue Service; and, with its contingent of former CIA and counterintelligence agents, it had the talent to enter residences surreptitiously, gather intelligence on the activities of other agencies of the government, and interrogate suspects."[96] Epstein further noted:

> If Americans could be persuaded that their lives and the lives of their children were being threatened by a rampant epidemic of narcotics addiction, Nixon's advisors presumed they would not object to decisive government actions, such as no-knock warrants, pretrial detention, wiretaps, and unorthodox strike forces. . . . This in turn required the artful use of the media to propagate a simple but terrifying set of

stereotypes about drug addiction: the addict-dealer would be depicted as a modern-day version of the medieval vampire, ineluctably driven to commit crimes and infect others by his insatiable and incurable need for heroin. The victims would be shown as innocent youth, totally vulnerable to the vampire-addict.[97]

In March 1973 Nixon asked Congress to approve his plan to create the Drug Enforcement Administration, a plan largely developed by ODALE's director.[98] A puzzled House Committee on Government Operations reported, "The plan was hastily formed. . . . Administration witnesses were able to give the subcommittee only a bare outline of the proposed new organization and its functions. Important questions were left unresolved."[99] The committee was concerned "whether the proposed new Drug Enforcement Administration would impair the traditional separation between investigative and prosecutive activities; whether the internal mechanisms for maintaining security and for monitoring performance in the new agency would be sufficiently strong and independent enough to guard against corruption."[100] The committee urged Congress to prevent creation of the DEA.[101] Nonetheless, as Nixon expected, Congress approved his plan to "fight drugs." BNDD and ODALE were now combined into the DEA. Over objection from FBI Director J. Edgar Hoover, Nixon announced, "I intend to see that the resources of the FBI are fully committed to assist in supporting the new Drug Enforcement Administration."[102] ODALE's deputy director became DEA's head.[103] At the time, a perplexed student of drug law enforcement reported, "Although ODALE is allegedly defunct, its function presumably absorbed by the Drug Enforcement Administration, in reality it lingers on. Federal money is still being channeled to ODALE offices, and its personnel continue to operate. The details of the curious history of ODALE have yet to be untangled."[104] Only with revelations of Watergate investigations did that history begin to emerge. Exposure of criminal activities by so many designers of the DEA forced them from government office, and federal bureaucrats who did not share Nixon's criminal dreams took over the DEA, running it as a legitimate law enforcement agency. A top federal law officer, who had opposed Nixon's conspirators, later mused in relief, "If not for Watergate, can you imagine what they would have done with the Drug Enforcement Agency?"[105]

President Jimmy Carter fought drug abuse as one of many problems faced by the nation, but did not encourage public panic. His successors Ronald Reagan and George Bush, however, renewed Nixon's fear campaign, thereby encouraging citizens to accept "emergency" actions that would go against the better judgment of a contented and confident populace.

In the name of drugs, Reagan quickly removed prohibitions against the CIA acting as a domestic law enforcement agency and directed the CIA to help enforce U.S. drug laws.[106] In addition to "former" CIA employees who had long been working within the DEA, the CIA created a Counter Narcotics Center.[107] In 1986 Reagan issued a secret National Security Decision Directive declaring drug trafficking to be military threat against America.[108] That directive formed a basis for invoking war powers.

Reagan did not invoke war powers against drug users, but his administration did establish mechanisms that could permanently alter the governance of America if a president were to declare a national emergency. Reagan administration officials devised mechanisms allowing the president to suspend the Constitution, declare martial law, replace state and local governments with military commandants, and put opponents of such actions in concentration camps without trial. During the Iran-Contra hearings Representative Jack Brooks (D-TX) attempted to delve into this plan but was admonished by joint committee chairman Senator Daniel Inouye (D-HI): "I believe the question touches upon a highly sensitive and classified area. So may I request that you not touch upon that, sir?"[109] A day later Senate Intelligence Committee chairman David Boren (D-OK) assured citizens that selected members of Congress had secretly discussed Reagan's plan. Public information about the plan is limited, but one student of the matter noted that it

> was written to be part of an executive order that President Reagan was to sign and keep secret until "necessary." If either Presidents Reagan or Bush have signed such an executive order, . . . incarceration of millions of innocent people could begin at the outset of . . . presidential declaration of a national emergency. To this day, the exact provisions written into the executive order—and whether or not the order was ever signed—remain unknown.[110]

President Bill Clinton continued federal efforts against drug abuse but cooled the rhetoric used by Nixon, Reagan, and Bush. Perhaps Clinton's assorted goals were not impeded by the Constitution. Nonetheless, we have seen war powers used to incarcerate large numbers of blameless Japanese-American citizens targeted by hate and fear propaganda, incarceration approved by the Supreme Court. We have seen congressional approval of such actions in the Emergency Detention Act of 1950 and congressional deference to Reagan's judgment in his martial law plan. We have seen drugs defined as a military threat, and indeed, under Reagan the Defense Department deployed units to assist civilian law enforcement efforts. We have even seen federal officials justify mass incarceration of Japanese-Americans as a way of keeping them from harm; an argument that could be used to protect drug users from mobs, disease, or poverty.

And we should not finish our discussion of war powers without noting their successful use by drug war zealots who implemented national beverage alcohol prohibition. In September 1917, William Anderson, a director of the Anti-Saloon League of America, saw that war powers could be used to create Prohibition regardless of constitutional guarantees that permitted Americans to drink: "An emergency, by opening a short cut which avoids the necessity for settling a lot of technical questions, enables the doing of certain desirable things with less delay and less friction than would be possible under normal conditions."[111]

Anderson's phraseology was delicate, but his colleagues grasped its meaning. The first use of war powers by Prohibitionists was in passing the Lever Food and Fuel Control Act,[112] In the guise of conserving grains and fruits for the war effort, distilled spirits could no longer be manufactured or even imported. Moreover, the president could limit or eliminate beer and wine manufacturing as well.

The second use of war powers by Prohibitionists was in enacting the War-Time Prohibition Act,[113] signed by the president soon after the war ended. Noted one student of the subject, "War powers afforded the sole constitutional basis for this statute."[114] The law said it would stay in effect "until the termination of demobilization, the date of which shall be determined and proclaimed by the President."[115] Thereby war powers imposed Prohibition after hostilities ceased until a constitutional amendment could create permanent Prohibition. Proponent Senator John Shafroth (D-CO) noted that this "war measure" had been sought for years prior to the war, and opportunity was now at hand to impose Prohibition through war powers without resort to constitutional amendment.[116] The ruse was transparent but effective. Said the *Philadelphia Record*, "Prohibitionists have made their fight upon the grounds that abolition of alcohol was a war-time necessity. There are many who have felt . . . they were insincere in this; that they merely seized a war-time opportunity to make the enforcement of their will upon others a peace-time permanency."[117] The *New York Times* complained of "prohibition as a war measure, enacted by Congress after the actual, if not formal, end of the war."[118] The *St. Louis Post-Dispatch* fumed, "The only shadow of legality attaching to the bill arises from far-fetched interpretations on the extent of the extra Constitutional war powers of Congress. But this bill did not gain the approval of Congress until the war from which a temporary extension of the congressional power is theoretically derived had already reached a de facto end."[119] The subterfuge was clear to President Woodrow Wilson, but he decided to use war powers as a sop to drys, whose support he needed on other measures.[120] He saw alcohol users as expendable.

In autumn 1919, Prohibitionists used war powers a third time when passing Title I of the Volstead Act.[121] Title I gave the Treasury and Justice Departments power to enforce the War-Time Prohibition Act through injunctions against violators. "The genius of this provision was that once an injunction had been issued, subsequent violations were punishable as contempt of court, with no right to jury trial. Landlords were made liable for penalties incurred by their tenants, and the property could be sold to collect any fines."[122] A careful student of that law notes, "It was universally conceded that Title I rested solely on the war powers."[123]

Yet courts had no complaint about implementing war powers against alcohol users in peacetime. Moreover, the president can veto a joint congressional resolution terminating a national emergency. If Congress fails to override the veto with a two-thirds vote, the president can continue governing through emergency powers despite opposition from a majority of Congress.[124] Federal courts tend to take the president's word about the need for a state of emergency, refusing even to demand supporting data.[125]

A stroke of the president's pen can incarcerate every illicit drug user in the United States and every person who opposes such action. This has not happened. But if such mass internment can happen, with full approval from all three branches of federal government, one wonders what will happen the next time a White House regime combines the drug war with an obsession for "national security measures" against persons who oppose the president's policies.

5

ANNIHILATION

Killing is the ultimate element of the destruction process.

Years of hate propaganda against a group of ordinary people promotes a climate of public opinion supporting demands that victims be prohibited from living in ordinary society. Such a climate also promotes demands that victims be prohibited from living at all. And once a society accepts that latter premise, mass murder is no harder to organize than any previous element of the destruction process.

We know this from historical experience. In an earlier book, I showed why mass murder evolved from a war on Jews, a group of ordinary people. Early German perpetrators of the war on Jews condemned any suggestion that victims should be killed. After fifty years of hate propaganda and social discrimination, however, killing became an easy choice in a European country that cherished ideals of Western civilization. In the United States, mass murder is no more impossible than mass incarceration. Necessary legal doctrines grow in strength, as does the necessary climate of public opinion. Unlike Germans, however, Americans have the advantage of knowing what happens if the destruction process is allowed to continue. We can choose to stop the madness if we just say no.

Although Nazi death camps provide the most enduring image of annihilation, camps were not the first annihilation technique used by Nazis. Death squads hunted victims, individuals were beaten by thugs, disease was promoted as medical treatment was withheld, unemployment and other despairs promoted suicide, childbearing was discouraged both by law and by poisoning family life. As we shall see, all of those techniques have been used by drug warriors, and still we hear cries to go further. The call to kill millions of drug users is now rhetoric, but such calls were once mere words in Germany as well. We have seen how more and more persons and organizations have a growing stake in the war on drug users. That stake powers the war and helps its intensity to grow. Given the ultimate consequence of escalation, we would do well to consider the force that promotes it, a force I call bureaucratic thrust.

BUREAUCRATIC THRUST

The peril of bureaucratic thrust in the war on drug users is illustrated by the war on Jews. Two careful students of assorted Nazi regulations found them to be "the collective product of bureaucratic experts on the 'Jewish Question'; the existence of the job itself being sufficient to give discriminatory measures their own momentum." The students added:

> If one reads the welter of decrees and regulations, it is possible to come to the conclusion that they were the product of improvisation, or of the ambition, careerism, and rivalries of the bureaucrats responsible for "Jewish questions" in the ministries and agencies of the party. The pettiness of many of these measures also indicates the self-propelling momentum of bureaucrats whose jobs and professional expertise were inextricably bound up with solving the "Jewish question". In looking at the matter in this way, however, one runs the risk of overlooking both the motivating force behind these measures, and how decisions were made within a fundamental ideological consensus. Put simply, no voices were heard from the top arguing in any other direction; indeed, on the contrary they mapped out the general line which the specialists fleshed out in detail. . . . The effect was systematically devastating for those against whom these measures were directed. The Jews were discriminated against; their human rights were abrogated; they were physically isolated from the non-Jewish population, and totally eliminated from economic and professional life. It did not require much more bureaucratic ingenuity to summon, detain in collection points, and finally deport people who had no rights.[1]

Bureaucratic thrust helps explain a curiosity noted by another student of the Holocaust. "Use of the Jewish problem for empire building took forms other than those employed by Goebbels, Goering, or Streicher. The least harmful of those forms included the establishing of research institutes devoted to investigation of Jewish matters." Nonetheless, "policy continued to be made without the benefit of the institutes' 'experts' or their advice."[2] Those research institutes produced findings of dubious value, but even sterling research would have had little relevance to bureaucrats building empires. The war on Jews intensified because so many warriors stood to gain from it, regardless of whether Jews were a problem. Likewise, drug warriors do not need to know whether the "drug problem" is getting better or worse; either way the public will be told that war efforts need to be intensified to build on success or stave off defeat. The same thinking was revealed by internal documents of the SS. In spring 1934 a report to Himmler "reviewed the Jewish problem, not in the propaganda clichés used by most Nazis, but in the hard cold terms of the real situation," namely the need to keep agitating the public about the Jewish problem in order to retain support for further measures in which the SS would play a larger role. "As important as its commitment to anti-Semitism was the SS's engagement in the general struggle for power. To have ignored the Jewish problem would have been tantamount to surrendering a basic weapon in the arsenal available for the waging of this power struggle."[3]

Where budgets, jobs, and personal prestige depend on stronger efforts against a targeted group of ordinary people, the only limit on sanctions against victims is provided by law. But when prosecutors, judges, and legislators all obey commands of an executive branch directing the war, law becomes yet another weapon of oppression instead of a shield for the blameless. The outcome of a war without limit has to be total destruction.

Another element of bureaucratic thrust is seen as drug warriors exaggerate their accomplishments. At one time federal authorities were embarrassed to announce seizures of X number of ounces or pounds of drugs because the weights were so puny. So announcements instead began referring to seizures of "enough drugs to supply X number of doses," a measurement that could be massaged to make ten pounds of pure heroin supply as many thousands of "cut" doses as authorities needed in order to make the seizure look impressive. The same tactic is used with "street value" of drug seizures. Street value reflects costs that have not yet been incurred when a drug supply is seized before reaching the street. If a hundred pounds of some drug can be produced for $500 by an illicit laboratory, the loss to the drug trade is $500 if the supply is confiscated from the lab—not the $100,000 that street corner dealers would gross from the same supply. Regardless of how a particular seizure is measured (pounds, doses, street value) the amount of drug is the same. But the measurement chosen to describe a seizure can make a drug squad look like it is doing far more than it really is. The arbitrary nature of such measurement was demonstrated in our previous chapter when an Arizona drug squad boasted of generating $3 million in forfeiture income by providing 13 tons of marijuana to dealers. "Street value" math shows the squad provided marijuana worth $125 million. The squad's return on its investment looks less impressive in such context. Police use street value math only when its exaggerated numbers promote support for drug squads, and street value math thereby becomes an important element of bureaucratic thrust.

Body counts promote bureaucratic thrust. Numbers of "drug-related" arrests can balloon if officers start citing suspects for misdemeanor possession that would have previously been ignored when a suspect was stopped for a traffic violation. Or "drug-related" arrests can balloon if every arrested person is given a urine test regardless of why the person was arrested (marijuana use can be detected for weeks after the substance was last used). Or operators of a "treatment" program can announce that clients have doubled or tripled in number—a measurement that conveniently ignores whether treatment succeeds or (in the case of misdemeanor offenders ordered to purchase treatment) whether treatment is even needed.

Body counts give drug squads an inherent advantage over other police divisions when competing for funds. "Patrol division detectives must await the report of a felony before they can take action. . . . Entire evenings may pass when patrolling [division] detectives do nothing other than drive a car slowly around a city for eight hours."[4] Murder squads are not allowed to arrange murders; arson squads are not allowed to arrange arsons. In contrast, drug squads can facilitate crimes they "solve," using informants to arrange felonies on demand. In addition to serving as general agents provocateur, informants can persuade friends to do things that friends would not do for a stranger.[5] That police practice inflates the perceived size of the drug problem while making narcotics officers appear more productive in making arrests. "When law enforcement agencies themselves become major purchasers of narcotics, they make someone like Gomez a much more important-appearing dealer than he would have been had not close to twelve thousand dollars of narcotics been purchased from him by the State. . . . Narcotics police inevitably are part of the 'dope rings' they themselves help to create."[6] By including drug offenses in arrest statistics, police appear far more efficient in clearing crimes than if performance were judged on convictions for burglary or auto theft. The more drug laws, the more efficient police can appear.

Perhaps the nadir of bureaucratic thrust was illustrated by comments from a senior federal drug war official who said a major drug war accomplishment by President Bush was to raise federal drug war expenditures from $5.5 billion when he took office to $11 billion in 1991.[7] Drug warriors present bureaucratic thrust itself as drug war success. And perhaps for drug warriors, such a criterion is the most meaningful measurement.

Bureaucratic thrust also broadens criteria used to identify victims, thereby increasing their number. Part of the expansion occurs through defining ever more drugs as illegal: In recent years federal officials sought to make steroids illegal, criminalizing thousands of athletes who were previously considered role models for youth. Another part of expansion exploits technology, allowing smaller levels of drugs and their metabolites to be detected. A week after smoking marijuana, a person can be apprehended as a criminal even though the person's behavior is as normal as a nonuser's. In the 1950s such a person would never have been a suspect; technology rather than observable conduct now targets a victim. By expanding both the number of illegal drugs and the means to detect their presence in a human body, persons who were once left alone are swept up. The effect is to strip civil liberties from more and more citizens, making it easier and easier for government officials to act on any subject without regard to the public's desires.

One irony of bureaucratic thrust is that it can transform perpetrators into victims. In Germany, as the genealogical definition of Jew expanded, so did technical capabilities of genealogical research. Some Nazis thereby became Jews and received the anti-Jewish sanctions they had advocated. Also, German companies that voluntarily dismissed Jewish employees later found themselves under government order to dismiss Jews.[8] The drug war produces the same transformations of perpetrators into victims. Broader definitions and higher technology can change drug warriors into drug users. So too do private and public employers find themselves threatened with loss of federal contracts and funding if drug-using employees are tolerated. Employers who voluntarily started sanctions to attack drug-using workers must now continue and expand those sanctions to protect themselves from the government.

Harsher laws are an important result of bureaucratic thrust. One element here is politics, as noted by a group of ordinary Americans in the 1940s:

> There are a great many individuals who would not like to see wholesale evacuation of Japanese, but who dare not jeopardize their own positions by speaking up at this time. Understandably, they do not care to lay themselves open to the charges of the vociferous minority that they are un-American and "Jap-lovers."
>
> . . . The Japanese issue has become one that apparently is without the "other side," and politicians find it a most convenient football to be kicked around without fearing any sort of counter-reaction developing from the opposition. In other words, the Japanese issue is an ideal punching bag which politicians can pummel in the limelight of public approval without experiencing any sort of political retaliation. Such irresponsible tactics have done much to inflame public opinion. It might also be pointed out that any officeholder, who remained silent on this issue, could expect to be attacked by those who covet his office.[9]

While speaking about that situation, a former California Republican nominee for the U.S. Senate noted, "Apparently most of our politicians think they can

increase their popularity be attacking these people who have very few defend-
ers."[10] Like the war on Japanese-Americans, the war on drug users is a godsend
for politicians, who portray themselves as tough without ever having to take the
risks that real toughness requires. Some legislators have privately told me that
humane reform of drug law would benefit the nation but have publicly demanded
harsher laws. These drug warriors fear the public while cynically seeking to
capitalize on public fear. And then these same politicians, who are too cowardly
to stand up for their beliefs, are lauded for their "courageous" stance against
drugs. As fearful government "leaders" simply run in front of a mob whose
anger they stoke, a feedback loop develops in which politicians and citizens try
to outdo each other in demands for more sanctions against victims.

Harsher laws are also promoted by treating a felony arrest as more important
than a misdemeanor. As more drug offenses are changed from misdemeanor to
felony, arrests for those offenses become more important even though the
proscribed act itself does not change. The more important those arrests become,
the more important are jobs producing those arrests. So members of drug squads
become more important, meriting increases in budget and personnel. That is one
reason why law enforcement officers seek harsher drug laws.

Another reason is that harsher laws give drug squads more leverage when
sweating a suspect, putting officers in a better position to trade leniency for
information. The harsher the penalty, the more leniency is worth to a suspect.
Probably more information is bought through plea bargaining than through
money.[11] The point of draconian penalties is not to invoke them but to increase
the vigor of interrogations. The tougher the law, the easier life is for headquarters detectives. (But not for members of field patrols. As drug laws get
tougher, so do dealers, because the more timid ones drop out. Harsh laws
advocated by desk personnel put street cops in greater danger.)

A sinister aspect of bureaucratic thrust is that a rising number of victims can
be portrayed as a worsening of the drug user problem. As drug users increase
in number despite measures applied against them, calls for harsher measures gain
support. A major reason that the war on Jews turned lethal is that despite success
at running Jews out of Germany, the number of Jews within the Reich expanded
as the Reich itself expanded. The Jewish "problem" was perceived as worsening
no matter what harshness was applied against victims, and the same perception
is growing among supporters of the war against drug users. "That unqualified
promises should ultimately yield attempts at an unqualified solution does not
appear illogical, at least not in retrospect. Perhaps one should not be surprised
that a movement which writes a segment of humanity out of the human race
should eventually give birth to a policy of physical extermination." So said a
distinguished student of the Holocaust.[12] Said another, "The destruction process

was a development which began with mild measures and ended with drastic action. The victims never remained in one position for long. There were always changes, and the changes were always for the worse."[13]

Having considered how bureaucratic thrust promotes annihilation, let us consider how the drug war begins the process of annihilation by poisoning human relations.

HUMAN RELATIONS

The drug war's most potent poison sickens family life. German laws not only forbade intermarriage between Jew and Aryan but promoted divorce of such couples. Nonetheless, many couples resisted. An Aryan woman married to a Jew "raved about the happiness of her married life. 'I would not hesitate to marry my husband all over again. No pure Aryan could have made me happier. He couldn't possibly have become a brute by legislation.'"[14] This wife did not allow Nazi law to turn her against her husband; she was loyal to him no matter what the authorities said she should do. Perhaps the drug brings forth similar examples of nobility, but publicity and praise more typically go to spouses who betray a partner. A "Teacher of the Year" was fired after she shirked her civic duty by failing to turn in her husband for marijuana use.[15] In 1994 the husband of the Jackson County, Missouri, prosecutor was arrested for misdemeanor possession of marijuana while visiting another county. His wife had been building her political career through the drug war, and now portrayed herself as victimized by a deceitful husband who admitted occasional marijuana use. Irony dripped from the news media's acceptance of her "spin" on events. Stories were similar to domestic violence coverage, which traditionally portrays the perpetrator as victim ("Despairing Husband Kills Wife, Boyfriend"). This prosecutor was presented as harmed by a husband she demeaned and victimized through her prosecutions of harmless people for responsible marijuana use. And not a whisper appeared in the news media about her 1992 admission of her own marijuana use.[16] Before her husband's trial, the wife announced he was guilty.[17] One of my friends bumped into the husband's lawyer and expressed surprise at their failure to mount any defense. My friend says the lawyer replied, "I don't have any say in how this case is being handled." The wife sacrificed her husband's well-being to protect her political career, as a means to retain political power. Comments I heard from citizens lauded the wife for "standing up to the creep." But hurting a harmless spouse against his will in order to gratify oneself is not admirable. It is perverse. It is shameful. Such is the drug war's insidious attack on the core of family values.

The drug war also attacks child custody. The most familiar attack is in divorce proceedings where illicit drug use, however mature and responsible it may be, is cited as criminal conduct endangering a child. A variation occurs when a pregnant woman is discovered using illicit drugs. New Jersey law permits the state to take custody of a fetus if authorities believe the woman is harming proper fetal development.[18] Such action "amounts to sentencing a woman to jail for the duration of her pregnancy."[19] Some judges, and not just in New Jersey, jail any pregnant defendant believed to be using illicit drugs.[20] Aside from the devastating effect that such action can have on the woman's children (most pregnant prisoners are mothers of juveniles),[21] the lethal irony in such action is that mortality among infants born in jails and prisons is higher than among those born in freedom.[22] Newborns whose body fluids show evidence of illicit maternal drug use can be classified as abused and be taken from their mothers forthwith.[23] One social services administrator admitted that such practices "put the state in the position of destroying families as the quick-and-easy answer to the drug epidemic."[24] Such destruction is magnified when the woman used the illicit drug medicinally: An inaccurate story circulating among women unable to afford health care claimed that cocaine shortens and eases childbirth. An infant was taken from a mother who, on recommendation from a nurse, used marijuana to ease childbirth[25] (a therapeutic practice once endorsed in the *Journal of the American Medical Association* as being effective without harming mother or infant).[26] A Brooklyn bank clerk lost custody of her infant because a prescription drug the mother took on her doctor's order yielded a false positive drug test. Only after a grueling struggle was she able to get her child back.[27]

In another attack on family integrity, drug police asked the Missouri legislature to make marijuana possession a child abuse felony if the substance were found in a home where a child lived or visited.[28] With this "investigative tool," drug squads could threaten to have juvenile authorities take custody of children if parents refused to incriminate themselves. Such a tool hardly seems necessary. A runaway teenager told Missouri authorities that she left home because of her parents' drug use. Police told the parents that their daughter had been found, and asked them to meet with officers. Upon arrival at the courthouse, police subjected the parents to lengthy interrogation about their alleged drug use and refused to let them leave. Meanwhile, a drug squad was tearing apart their house. No drugs or drug paraphernalia were found. The daughter's story was a fabrication. Under relentless grilling, the mother admitted that she was a former marijuana user. No criminal charges were filed against either parent, but juvenile authorities then sought custody of the teenager and threatened to seek custody of their other children unless the parents "voluntarily" agreed to undergo drug abuse counseling and surprise urine testing. To prevent breakup of their family, the parents agreed.[29]

The drug war can transform family arguments into family tragedies. After bickering between parents and their teenager daughter about her choice of friends, the teen told police that her parents used and cultivated marijuana at home. Based upon the daughter's information, police searched the home. Although they found some marijuana plants, police were uncertain they had a good case. So they told the mother that unless she confessed to felony cultivation of marijuana, authorities would remove the daughter from the home. To protect her daughter, the mother confessed to a crime carrying a twenty-year sentence. Fortunately the mother received probation instead of imprisonment, but the daughter was horrified at the havoc wrought by her moment of anger.[30] Noting box office appeal in another incident where a girl had her parents arrested for drug use, a Hollywood producer declared, "The normal situation is parents are trying to keep young people off drugs."[31] A disgusted observer commented, "Thanks to Nancy Reagan, parents denouncing their children to the police was already *normal* in the American family in the 1980s."[32] "I admire the girl," said a neighbor.[33]

Even schools participate in destruction of families. Schools nationwide invite the police-sponsored Drug Abuse Resistance Education (DARE) program to give talks to students. A U.S. congressional report described these lecturers as "patrol-hardened, veteran police officers" who "shore up the classroom teacher's anti-drug instruction."[34] A U.S. Justice Department manual notes, "In addition to their formal classroom teaching, DARE officers spend time on the playground, in the cafeteria, and at student assemblies to interact with students informally. . . . Sudents occasionally tell the officer about . . . relatives who use drugs. The officer refers these cases to the school principal or to appropriate resources in the community."[35] The DARE program includes a "suggestion box" where students can deposit reports of persons using drugs. In front of a class a DARE officer read aloud one such note: "Someone in my family is doing drugs and I'm worried that if I say anything it will make it worse." He then asked the class what can happen if an illegal drug is consumed. "You could die," replied one student. Noting that family members who use drugs risk death, the officer then declared, "It's probably OK to get them into trouble, if that's going to happen." If any students were worried about parental drug use, the DARE officer said, they should discuss the situation with a trusted adult. "I'm more than willing to do that," he told the children.[36] One headline declared, "Twelve-Year-Old DARE Graduate Turns in Dad."[37] After attending a DARE presentation, a ten-year-old child told police that his parents had cocaine in the family home. Police asked the child for consent to search the home, the child gave it, and the parents were arrested.[38] Parents of a teenage girl were jailed after she informed her

DARE officer that they were growing marijuana at home.[39] A nine-year-old exploring his parents' bedroom dialed 911 upon finding a small quantity of methamphetamine. Employers fired both his parents, the father was sent to jail for simple possession, and foreclosure proceedings were proposed against the family home.[40] An eight-year-old girl told her teacher about her stepfather's cultivation of marijuana at home. The teacher notified police, who arrested the man. "After the incident, the child went to the school counseling clinic where she was 'devastated' and in tears, according to Short Elementary School Principal Flo Jones."[41] An eleven-year-old DARE student turned in her parents for using marijuana. The mother lost both her jobs even though charges against her were dropped, and the father was convicted of cultivation. Even though the daughter was now living in a drug-free environment, her grades declined and she became unsociable. Reflecting on how her "help" affected her family, the girl declared, "I would never tell again. Never. Never."[42] When a student mentioned her parents' marijuana use to a teacher, the teacher informed police, who then removed the child from class and interrogated her without the parents' knowledge. After getting the child to sign a statement that large quantities of marijuana and other drugs were in the house, a drug squad ransacked the residence and uncovered less than an ounce of marijuana and no other controlled substances at all. Legal expenses, on top of medical expenses from the father's cancer treatment, forced the family into bankruptcy.[43] When a junior high school student turned in her parents after hearing an anti-drug user talk in 1986, Nancy Reagan declared, "She must have loved her parents a great deal."[44] Schools also urge students to report friends who are drug offenders. "You'd be astonished at how well the students are cooperating," said an assistant principal at a small town Texas high school. "Some have even turned in their best friends."[45] Drug czar William Bennett assured Miami, Florida, middle school students, "It isn't snitching or betrayal to tell an adult that a friend of yours is using drugs and needs help." He explained, "It's an act of true loyalty—of true friendship."[46] The school principal declared, "We have positively brainwashed our student body."[47] Attorneys and social service workers across the country have identified a less publicized function of police drug education officers, who enter schools with "a surveillance function, identifying 'at-risk' youth for later drug enforcement attention."[48]

Teaching children to hate ordinary persons targeted by government and confusing children by telling them that family love and national patriotism require them to turn in parents to authorities were keystones of public school education in the Nazi regime. "It isn't their harsh methods which the young have to be so strong to resist. It is their soft ways of confusing good with evil which resolve the power to resist." That observation came from a twelve-year-old anti-Nazi in

1934.[49] "All children are defenseless receptacles, waiting to be filled with wisdom or venom by their parents and educators," mused a repentant Hitler Youth officer decades after the Third Reich ended. "I carry a lingering resentment against Hitler and our educators who allowed us to fall into his grip."[50]

American educators seldom allow students to hear alternatives to drug squad views. An exception was a high school teacher who invited a DEA representative and me to make a joint presentation. The teacher told me that not only did the DEA spokesman refuse to face me, but four different DEA detectives contacted the instructor and urged him to withdraw his invitation to me. The teacher said the DEA told him he was wrong to expose high school students to a felony drug abuser seeking to recruit young people into the drug culture. The DEA's claims about me were fabrications, of course, and the instructor refused to withdraw his invitation, but I wonder how many public high school teachers resist such pressure. The DEA promised to send someone to the class the day after I came. I suggested that class members ask the DEA person why he rejected an opportunity to refute me on the spot. The kids responded instantly: "He's afraid." "He knows you have facts." "He just wants to scare us, and knows he can't succeed if you're in the room with him." Several students stated forthrightly that I had not advocated drug use at all; I had simply explained alternative ways of viewing the drug situation and presented ways of influencing drug-taking behavior without putting people in jail. Such is the information that the DEA wants to prevent teenagers from knowing.

TREATMENT

Just as "education" can be perverted to promote annihilation of victims, so too can "treatment." We have already examined some perils that emerge when persons are defined as both criminal and sick, and we shall examine more in this section. The German experience, however, raises the question of who needs treatment at all. Jewish neurologist Arnold Merzbach studied hundreds of Jewish children during the first eighteen months of the Nazi regime. In the first half of 1933 he found "restlessness, irritability, and increased squabbling. Some youths were refusing to eat; the more intellectual ones were sleeping fitfully and given to brooding." Similar behavior continued throughout the year "as well as many neurotic symptoms." He noted "older children thought themselves objects of special attention when outdoors."[51] We typically find Jewish adults, too, drawing into themselves, exhibiting despair, and developing problems in relating with people as one formerly supportive group after another (employers, insurers, landlords, police) prevented them from living normally in society. These sorts of Jewish behavior mimic the "drug user personality," suggesting that the behavior may be a response to persecution from society rather than an expression of someone's inherent personality—particularly since most users of socially approved drugs such as alcohol and nicotine do not exhibit "drug user symptoms" despite those drugs' potency and danger. In many cases, the proper treatment of drug users may simply be to cease persecuting them.

We have already considered the question of whether therapy is appropriate when a "bill of attainder" has declared someone to be sick without medical diagnosis. We have not, however, considered whether such therapy is criminal. A drug user who must choose between therapy or jail has no free will, no more than did "genetically defective" Germans when they chose between sterilization or a concentration camp. Prosecutors at the Nuremberg Military Tribunal contemptuously rejected Nazi claims that "patients" in such a position made voluntary choices.[52] Tribunal prosecutors not only cited as criminal the German Justice Ministry's persecution of normal people through involuntary medical treatment[53] but cited as criminal the ministry's arbitrary classification of normal people into an asocial status.[54] American legal tradition long held that people have a right to refuse medical treatment and that involuntary treatment is assault.[55]

Drug warriors, however, have eroded that right by defining drug users as both sick and criminal. Although American medical practitioners define anyone who takes drugs without a doctor's order as sick,[56] mere sickness is insufficient grounds to punish drug users. In a key decision, the U.S. Supreme Court warned drug warriors, "Even one day in prison would be a cruel and unusual punishment for the 'crime' of having a common cold."[57] So drug warriors evade that decision by declaring citizens to be criminal if they disregard drug warrior rules on what substances citizens may ingest—the same disregard that defines those citizens as sick. Criminals lose many rights possessed by ordinary citizens, and defining ordinary conduct as criminal was one of the most effective weapons in the Nazi repertoire; many concentration camp inmates were incarcerated for "criminal" acts that are normal conduct in a free society. In the United States, people classified as both criminal and sick can be subjected to harsh sanctions disguised as therapy, sanctions that would be illegal if imposed as punishment for illness.

One classic Nazi sanction used by drug warriors is prevention of birth. The sanction is imposed in several ways: by making pregnant drug users afraid to seek prenatal care, by denying drug abuse treatment to pregnant drug users who seek it, by threatening to imprison female drug users if they become pregnant, by imprisoning pregnant drug users unless they have an abortion, and by seizing any children born to female drug users. All these practices discourage drug users from having children. Discouraging birth is a key step in the annihilation stage of the destruction process.

Law enforcement involving alteration of a woman's body inevitably leads authorities to enroll medical personnel in the drug war as auxiliary police. Those who do not volunteer are drafted through laws requiring health care providers to report pregnant patients who use illicit drugs. Reporting is not uniform, however. In one Florida county, health care providers were ten times more likely to turn in pregnant African-American users than pregnant white users.[58] Almost all victims turned in by a South Carolina hospital were African-American.[59] The American Civil Liberties Union found that eighty percent of pregnant women prosecuted for drug use were African-American,[60] even though pregnant women of other racial and ethnic backgrounds were just as likely to be drug users.

Civic duty impels prosecutors to distort the intent of drug laws in order to squeeze maximum punishments. When a newborn's drug screen was positive, a North Carolina mother was prosecuted for assaulting her child with a deadly weapon—her body.[61] Women have also been prosecuted for distributing drugs to a minor via the umbilical cord in the few moments between birth and severing of the cord. Judges have noted the dubious legal basis of such prosecutions.[62] Considering that such women have sometimes unsuccessfully sought drug abuse treatment during their pregnancy,[63] the moral basis of prosecutions is even more dubious. A judge ordered one woman convicted in such a prosecution to submit to drug abuse therapy—therapy denied to her when she sought it during her pregnancy.[64] After a Kentucky woman gave birth to an infant diagnosed with neonatal abstinence syndrome, she was convicted of child abuse (taking drugs while pregnant), and sentenced to five years incarceration.[65] A young mother in Greenville, South Carolina, received a three-and-a-half-year prison sentence for child neglect because she used cocaine while pregnant. Another mother in that same city received a ten-year sentence because she had failed to complete a drug abuse treatment program. Not only were child neglect charges filed against a teenage mother in Greenville when her infant failed a drug test, the grandparents were also charged with child neglect because the mother had used drugs;[66] as in Nazi Germany, the mother's relatives were held responsible for her conduct. Such drug war prosecutions are expanding to the limit of their legal logic. Wyoming emergency room personnel treating a pregnant woman who had been battered by her abusive husband found she had ingested alcohol. Police arrested her in the emergency room and took her to jail on charges of child abuse for using a drug (alcohol) that endangers fetal development.[67] Prosecutors commonly indict pregnant women for drug use upon receiving reports generated by injuries received from abusive male partners.[68]

Acting on reports forwarded from physicians at a university hospital in South

Carolina, police routinely arrested and jailed drug-using patients who were pregnant or who had recently given birth.[69] In Butte County, California, the prosecuting attorney required hospitals to test newborns for illicit drugs, with positive results to be used for prosecuting mothers as drug abusers rather than child abusers.[70] The prosecutor said victims could choose between drug abuse treatment or ninety days in jail. Butte County treatment facilities, however, could not be reached through public transportation, and any woman who arrived discovered a waiting list that blocked treatment. In the whole state, only five full-time programs enrolled women, who then might have to wait six months before a treatment slot opened.[71]

Even getting on a waiting list is a major accomplishment for pregnant drug users. As the 1990s began, one survey reported that pregnant users could obtain no treatment or referrals from two-thirds of hospitals serving big cities. Half of New York City's drug treatment programs excluded pregnant women, a figure climbing to two-thirds if pregnant users were on Medicaid. Child care was unavailable from nearly all New York City programs that did accept pregnant users, a drawback preventing most from obtaining treatment.[72]

Prosecutors are well aware that treatment facilities cannot accommodate such women, and gladly jail victims even if they beg for treatment. Although prosecutors portray a "jail or treatment" policy as a tool to help drug-using mothers, actually it is a tool to jail drug-using mothers and attack their families—even if the mother is a productive citizen whose drug use is unapparent except through sophisticated chemical analyses of body fluid or tissue.

Transforming doctors into police impedes delivery of medical care. One victim said she would never have revealed drug use to her physician if she had realized she would be prosecuted.[73] Health professionals have recognized that women are reluctant to reveal key elements of medical history when they know governmental authorities may interfere in decisions about caesarean sections,[74] and health professionals have also complained that prohibiting doctors from discussing abortion with patients impedes the mutual truthfulness necessary for competent medical care.[75] A patient's knowledge that she may be imprisoned for what she tells a doctor is even more devastating to medical care. Although we have been discussing limitations on medical care in the context of fetal development, we should remember that authorities who discourage drug users from seeking medical care encourage them to sicken and die.

Although drug warrior rhetoric claims to desire sound fetal development and healthy newborns, drug warrior actions do the opposite. Seeking prenatal or even drug abuse treatment targets a pregnant drug user for incarceration. The effect of those policies is to deny medical supervision to fetal development and to encourage abortion. Neither of those alternatives promotes healthy full-term pregnancies. Instead, drug warriors work to prevent drug users from having children. Prevention of birth is a technique of annihilating a despised group.

In 1989, U.S. Senator Pete Wilson (R-CA) introduced the Child Abuse during Pregnancy Prevention Act.[76] The measure said newborn drug testing must be used to report mothers to "proper authorities." The measure also offered millions of dollars in federal revenue sharing to states passing laws declaring pregnant drug users to be child abusers if newborns showed any deficit that could be attributed to maternal drug use—provided those state laws included mandatory "medical" incarceration of three years (avoidable only if the woman was judged unlikely to use drugs again *and* was monitored to guarantee she never associated with anyone who used drugs). Senator Wilson's legislation declared that a pregnant woman must avoid illicit drug use if she "chooses to carry a pregnancy to term," language inviting pregnant drug users to seek abortion.

An undercurrent swirls through debate on pregnant drug users. That undercurrent involves what Nazis called "race defilement," the production of defective offspring. Defending an "umbilical drug delivery" conviction, a prosecutor shouted, "The message is that this community cannot afford to have two or three cocaine babies from the same person."[77] When drug-using females are prosecuted solely because they become pregnant, when the biological act of becoming pregnant becomes a crime, when a person's physical body becomes a criminal offense, penetration of that physical body becomes a law enforcement technique. In obedience to court orders, German surgeons sterilized hundreds of thousands of persons to prevent them from passing genetic defects to future generations. Nazis considered one type of drug abuse-alcoholism—to be a genetic illness, and those drug abusers were subject to sterilization.[78]

Some medical researchers now argue that other types of drug abuse are expressions of genetic inheritance, arguments lending support to drug warriors who decry drug use as race defilement endangering fetal development while altering human genes. These drug warriors demand access to women's bodies. Kansas legislation sought to require fertile female drug users to submit to surgical installation of Norplant contraceptives, and similar legislation was introduced elsewhere.[79] One California judge ordered a Norplant inserted into a woman, and a Missouri judge simply issued a probation order forbidding a defendant to become pregnant—with a two-year prison term if she experienced contraceptive failure.[80] For such law enforcement to succeed over victims' protests, medical personnel must enter victims' bodies as police agents rather than therapists. As we have seen, American doctors show little reluctance to undergo such transformation. If American courts were to issue wholesale orders for sterilization, American doctors are no less likely to comply than were their German forebears. When speaking of urine tests for drug use in uncooperative teenagers, two physicians supporting the drug war declared, "Because trust among patient, parent, and physician never existed in the first place, we believe that in cases such as the aforementioned our sincere concern for the well-being of our patient justifies a breach of the privilege of informed consent."[81] The drug war inspires physicians to view patient consent as a "privilege" rather than a legal right, a "privilege" that may be disregarded when a medical professional has "sincere concern." The limit of that principle's logic extends far beyond the drug war. In the 1980s judges routinely ordered pregnant women to have C-sections against their will even though the women were never found incompetent to make decisions about their bodies.[82] In 1987 hospital officials urged a caesarean section upon a pregnant woman suffering from lung cancer. Her own doctors believed the operation would kill her. She refused consent, a decision endorsed by her physicians and family. Hospital officials then obtained a court order compelling her to submit. The ten-week premature baby quickly expired, as did the mother.[83]

In addition to women, children are a special target of drug warriors seeking to impose therapy on unwilling recipients. Issues surrounding involuntary therapy were illustrated by Straight, Inc. Although Straight, Inc., was no longer functioning when this book was written, it received high praise from senior drug warriors such as Nancy Reagan and President George Bush. President Bush declared, "Organizations like Straight give us added strength in waging the war against drugs."[84] He appointed the program's founders, Joseph Zappala and Mel Sembler, to be ambassadors to Spain and Australia. Straight ran drug treatment centers in several cities.

Straight's medical director described "any adolescent who is depressed, underachieving in school, or argumentative and belligerent" as showing symptoms of marijuana use.[85] The doctor listed other teen drug signs: "boredom," "restlessness," "impulsiveness," "disrespectful," "unable to delay immediate gratification."[86] Unsurprisingly, children with no drug problems were in Straight's "drug abuse" program.[87] Straight's medical director said, "For legal reasons, adolescents remain clients" rather than "patients."[88]

One mother paid private detectives to kidnap her teenage son in New Mexico. They put him in leg irons and drove him overland 1,700 miles to a Straight facility. A teenage girl was riding in a car with her mother when they stopped at a gas station. Her father and two other men entered the vehicle and subdued her while she was taken to Straight. One teen thought his parents were taking him to Disney World and wound up at Straight instead.[89] One youth said abductors raked him barefoot and bloody across a Straight facility's grounds while handcuffed.[90] In the words of Straight's medical director, most teenagers were "convinced by parental pressure to enter treatment."[91]

Upon arrival children were restrained in a small room. Any who attempted to leave might be beaten by "peer counselors,"[92] teens already at Straight. Peer counselors barraged newcomers with questions about drugs and sex: "How does it feel masturbating inside a woman?"[93] A teen who resisted answering was diagnosed as having a bad attitude, indicating need for treatment. One who denied being a drug abuser was called a liar needing treatment. A child who, after hours of pressure, finally "confessed" to drug abuse was found to need treatment. Such determination might be made by another teen in the Straight program.[94] Straight's medical director freely admitted the program was "supervised, in the main, by skilled nonphysicians and recovering peer counselors."[95]

Fred Collins was forced to disrobe while "nonphysicians and recovering peer counselors" probed his anus, mouth, and ears.[96] Straight used sleep deprivation to weaken resistance to "treatment"; one girl was harassed eighty hours around the clock,[97] and Collins routinely slept four hours or less per night.[98] Food deprivation was another technique. When Collins escaped from Straight the six-foot two-inch youth weighed about 130 pounds, looking "like a concentration camp survivor."[99] A lawsuit on behalf of a female client noted that Straight put one girl on a diet of peanut butter and water for twenty-nine days.[100] Still another technique was physical degradation. Straight routinely forced large numbers of teens, of both sexes, to sit for hours in a room until puddles of their urine accumulated in their chairs.[101] While at such "therapy" sessions, some attenders mutilated themselves.[102] A Straight doctor and his research colleagues noted this mutilation "caused the staff to feel angry and demoralized. In an attempt to stop the girls from carving themselves, countermeasures included public ridicule."[103] "Public ridicule"—such was the therapy applied to people exhibiting a classic sign of despair and low self-esteem. Children held against their will at Straight were also subjected to dubious medical research, a story beyond the scope of this book.[104] Published results of such research, however, provide further documentation of conditions at Straight. *American Journal of Diseases of Children* notes that children there "were not permitted to receive mail, gifts, or visitors. Clients were under direct surveillance 24 hours a day, seven days a week."[105] Teenagers subjected to medical experiments at Straight were frightened: *American Journal of Diseases of Children* describes "possible confounding effects on cognitive processing and concentration ability by emotional states of fear, anxiety, or depression."[106]

Teens who resisted "therapy" were spat upon, punched, thrown to the ground, yanked back and forth by their hair, gagged with feminine hygiene pads. "Clients" complained of broken noses. "Peer counselors" fractured seven ribs of one teen. Court testimony named the male director of one Straight facility as personally applying such "therapy" to one teenage girl.[107]

Clients found themselves unable to terminate "treatment." Straight promised Fred Collins that he could leave after fourteen days; when he sought to leave he was held and did not escape until 134 days after he entered Straight.[108] Jeffrey McQuillen testified that he was forcibly restrained when he decided to terminate therapy. Although tied with a rope, he leaped from a car, fought a pursuer, and managed to escape.[109] Alex Zak said he was knocked down and restrained when he tried to depart after a staff member tore apart his written application to leave the program and tossed the confetti in Zak's face. Arletha Schauteet escaped and hid at a friend's house. The teen's mother lured her outside near midnight, whereupon two men and a woman jumped the daughter, pulled her screaming into a car, and sped her back to Straight.[110] Collins, McQuillen, Zak, and Schauteet were teens but were also adults. They were not civilly committed. They had a legal right to leave Straight at any time, but Straight personnel refused to let them leave.[111] Hope Hyrons testified in federal court that when she protested that she had a legal right to leave Straight, the facility director said, "I don't give a damn about your legal rights."[112] Federal litigation determined that Straight engaged in false imprisonment.[113]

We have already seen that police and ordinary citizens respond with indifference when confronted with the suffering of persons accused of illicit drug use. This indifference is shared by physicians and scientists. I once wrote to two scientific journals after they reported research conducted upon clients at Straight, telling the journals about sufferings experienced by research subjects. I received no reply from the editor of *Science News*. The editor of *American Journal of Diseases of Children* said his publication had no editorial policy requiring judgment of programs that were discussed in research published by the journal, and that he personally had no comment about my concerns.[114] In contrast, peers of a physician who conducted medical research on Straight clients publicly praised his determination when studying drug abuse, lauding his intensity as "almost a compulsion."[115] Indeed, in order to detect teen cannabis smokers, that researcher urged veterinarians to give household pets urine tests for passive inhalation of marijuana smoke and complained about veterinarians failing to heed his advice.[116]

I wonder if no one would be curious about juvenile asthma sufferers who received therapy that deprived them of sleep and broke their ribs. I wonder if no one would be curious about juvenile cardiac patients who received therapy requiring them to sit in pools of their urine while they mutilated themselves. Somehow I think such conditions would prompt investigation.

I suspect that the reason for the scientific community's indifference about Straight is that its "clients" had smoked marijuana. I believe many scientists and medical practitioners view such teenagers as depraved. Depraved persons are often considered worthy of punishment. Do medical practitioners think teenagers at Straight were getting what they deserved? If no bigotry existed against marijuana users, I cannot imagine that the scientific community would be unperturbed by conditions at Straight. I do not believe those conditions were created by psychotics. The things were done by ordinary persons, persons who simply had a strong belief in the necessity to do something and lacked concern about side effects of getting the job done. We see such people all around us. If we look closely enough, we may even see them when we look into a mirror.

INFLICTION OF DEATH

The most sinister stage of annihilation in the destruction process is infliction of death, whether by direct methods or indirect. Indirect methods include drug prohibition itself, which encourages violence when users buy drugs. Another indirect infliction of death is unemployment. Drug warriors demand that employers dismiss competent drug-using workers, and we know that death rates rise with unemployment rates. One estimate holds that every percentage point increase in the U.S. unemployment rate yields 30,000 premature deaths.[117] Still another indirect method is hounding drug users until they commit suicide, easy enough when drug abuse itself is often an expression of self-destruction. Even normal persons whose drug use is not abusive may choose suicide rather than endure harsh legal sanctions. A Montana couple convicted of marijuana cultivation attempted to flee authorities. Immediately after being apprehended, both attempted suicide; the husband failed but the wife succeeded in hanging herself in her jail cell.[118] Police arrested a California couple because the man grew marijuana that his seventy-one-year-old partner used to relieve back pain and depression. Prosecutors offered to go easier on her if she would turn state's evidence against her partner; she chose suicide instead.[119] Violent prison conditions promote death, as do poor nutrition and disease (such as tuberculosis spread by prison overcrowding).[120] Drug warriors also promote fatal disease in free society; denying sterile needles to intravenous drug users encourages spread of AIDS. President Bush excused such a policy by denying that such spread of AIDS was a medical problem; instead he called it a "behavior problem." In essence he gave drug users a simple choice: Behave as he wanted, or he would make them dead.

Just as doctors and government agents may force patients to undergo "therapy" that is anticipated to be fatal (as in the woman who was forced to have a caesarean section), so too do doctors and drug squads cooperate to withhold therapy vital to prolongation of life. We saw a forfeiture squad take a family home because a mentally disturbed boy threatened suicide if his parents disturbed his marijuana patch. The drug squad acted as if the parents should have let their son kill himself rather than tolerate his marijuana cultivation. A counselor advised parents of another troubled youth to build trust in the family by refraining from searching his room. When authorities arrested the teen, they found LSD in his room, a discovery resulting in forfeiture of the house. The prosecutor explained, "The responsibility a parent has to deal with a child's criminal activity is substantial. If they neglect or choose not to exercise that control, the state's response should be forfeiture of the property used in the criminal activity."[121] When following a recommended course of psychological treatment can cost a family its home, parents are discouraged from seeking help for troubled children. Indeed, by seeking medical care for a drug-abusing child (whether the treatment advice is followed or not), parents thereby admit knowledge of drug abuse by a house resident, an admission that can be grounds for forfeiting the house.[122] Forfeiture can also discourage a pregnant drug user from seeking prenatal care in a state where doctors are required to report positive drug screens to government authorities. Forfeiture is a powerful means of limiting access to health care.

Withholding health care can promote death. Some patients and practitioners claim that marijuana eases muscle spasms, thereby easing nausea suffered by patients receiving treatment for AIDS or cancer. For those patients the reported effects of marijuana are life or death matters. Intense nausea and vomiting can cause patients to discontinue AIDS or cancer therapy, or diminish appetite so much that malnourishment leads to further afflictions. Medical marijuana users report enhanced appetites, increasing both their strength and longevity. Other medical claims are made as well.[123] Withholding marijuana from some patients may promote their deaths, as may incarceration of those patients. No regional jails have treatment facilities matching those of regional hospitals.

Controversy surrounds medical use of marijuana. Although not all questions about marijuana's therapeutic effects have been answered, some practitioners find current evidence sufficient to recommend the substance. Regardless of whether such advice is good, the doctor violates no law by giving it. But patients who follow that advice are subject to prosecution, and once the threshold of illegality is crossed, supplemental charges can ratchet up penalties. For example, if a patient accused of misdemeanor possession has a legally registered pistol in the house, under federal law the patient becomes an armed drug offender, a felony with five years' mandatory imprisonment. In our discussion of civic duty we saw examples of such merciless prosecutions.

In 1993 and 1994 drug law reformers in Missouri proposed an end to prosecuting patients who possessed a misdemeanor amount of marijuana on their doctor's advice. This change in criminal law did not make marijuana a prescription drug, did not even say it had medical value. It changed the legal status of people, not the drug. Testimony against this criminal law reform did not come from drug squads but from the Missouri State Medical Association. I heard its spokesperson say that without FDA approval of marijuana's medical use, practitioners who recommend it are unethical, unprofessional, and incompetent. The word used to describe an unprofessional and incompetent doctor is "quack." The spokesperson testified that so many Missouri physicians want to make marijuana available (that is, so many Missouri doctors are quacks) that the only way to stop this behavior is through law. To prevent doctors from recommending marijuana use, he said, it was crucial for doctors to know their patients would be jailed for following the advice. Punishing patients was a deterrent to bad medical practice.

The medical association spokesperson rushed away after his testimony and I was unable to discuss it with him. I wrote to him asking for clarification but got no reply. To me, his point meant patients should be jailed in order to discipline their physicians. Via telephone, one of the spokesman's senior colleagues assured me that this was the organization's stance. The doctor even added that any patient stupid enough to use marijuana deserved jail. I objected, arguing that patients should not be punished for following their doctor's advice. The senior physician replied that jail would send a message to patients, a message that they should get competent doctors.

This desire to jail sick people "for their own good" reveals that health is not the concern; despite controversy on medical benefits of marijuana, no doubt exists that incarceration harms health. Normally physicians are on fire against patients who refuse to follow a practitioner's advice without question, but in opposing the criminal law reform, the medical association argued that patients should pick and choose among their doctor's instructions.

I believe the association's stance was motivated not by concern for patient health but by bigotry against persons who use marijuana recreationally. A medical association member who helped shape the group's stance on this issue told me straight up, "There is the religious view (my own opinion) that this stuff is harmful." If the concern were patient health, the association would support criminal penalties against doctors who recommend marijuana rather than against patients who comply with their doctor's advice. By opposing change in current law, thereby opposing punishment for doctors and supporting punishment for patients, the medical association sought to control doctors' therapeutic advice by punishing their patients.

Whether someone should go to jail is not a medical issue. Doctors would howl if defense attorneys demanded that medical handbooks list marijuana as an approved medicine, but some doctors have no problem with thwarting defense attorneys who seek a criminal code change to protect blameless citizens. Not only do physicians enlist as law enforcement agents, now they help devise the criminal laws they enforce.

Not all drug war fatalities die of bullet wounds. Some may die when medicine is withheld despite pleas from victims' physicians and nurses.

Until now we have been discussing indirect means of killing illicit drug users. Medical personnel have demonstrated not only willingness but eagerness to help jail drug users; would physicians who are willing to extinguish patients' liberty be willing to extinguish their lives? In Nazi Germany the answer was yes.

> Doctors were never *ordered* to murder psychiatric patients and handicapped children. They were *empowered* to do so, and fulfilled their task without protest, often on their own initiative. Hitler's original memo of October 1939 was not an order . . . , but an empowerment . . . , granting physicians permission to act. In the abortive euthanasia trial at Limburg in 1964, Hefelmann testified that "no doctor was ever ordered to participate in the euthanasia program; they came of their own volition."[124]

We have no reason to believe that personalities of German physicians differ markedly from those of American colleagues.

Medical personnel have no monopoly on exploiting biological facts to cause harm. During Prohibition days, the federal government ordered industrial alcohol supplies poisoned in order to harm anyone using them for beverage purposes, even though alcohol consumption was legal. A student of Nixon administration drug control efforts found that CIA agents assigned to the Office of National Narcotics Intelligence (ONNI) proposed poisoning supplies of illicit cocaine to sicken and kill users. Their plan was disapproved.[125] Later another plan, to poison marijuana supplies with paraquat, was approved. This has become a highly publicized law enforcement technique. Marijuana users who smoke supplies laced with paraquat might risk severe lung damage. The Bill of Rights forbids maiming of lungs as a punishment for citizens duly convicted of using marijuana, but police hatred of marijuana users generates imposition of an extralegal penalty of poisoning on them—even in states where marijuana smoking is decriminalized. If government agents believe their actions will injure a citizen engaged in lawful conduct they dislike, and that injury becomes fatal, they may be immune from prosecution. But private citizens who did such things would be indicted for murder.

We do know that law enforcement personnel kill persons suspected of drug law violations. Some killings are incidental, such as in the case of the California millionaire shot in a forfeiture raid and the innocent man whose heart failed when a Boston drug squad wrongfully stormed his residence. Some killings, however, are deliberate. How death squads could be considered "law enforcers" is baffling, but courts have sanctioned kidnap squads whose actions appear just as illegal. Whether courts would be less receptive to approving death squad activity is uncertain. More certain, however, is the fact that victims of death squads are unlikely to ask for court relief. So the question of death squad legality may never arise, let alone be settled.

Drug warriors are circumspect about death squads. A senior Nixon drug war official admitted that U.S. drug agents shot five suspected drug dealers in Mexico, although those deaths may have been incidental to a botched kidnap squad mission.[126] Nixon's director of the Bureau of Narcotics and Dangerous Drugs, however, told Nixon's top White House drug war advisor Egil Krogh that assassination was the only effective way to stop major dealers. The BNDD director later excused his remarks as intended to illustrate the impossibility of using murder as a law enforcement tool, but scholar Edward Jay Epstein found that the influential White House drug adviser G. Gordon Liddy supported an assassination program. Indeed, Epstein found that the White House asked BNDD to prepare such a program.[127] Krogh admitted that such killings were accomplished in Southeast Asia, and his assistants implied that killings were more widespread, particularly in Latin America. Epstein found Nixon drug control advisor Howard Hunt to be active in the Latin American murders. Dr. J. Thomas Ungerleider, member of a government commission studying marijuana, reported a conversation with BNDD officials: "There was some talk about establishing hit squads (assassination teams), as they are said to have in a South American country. It was stated that with 150 key assassinations, the entire heroin refining operation can be thrown into chaos. 'Officials' say it is known exactly who is involved in these operations but can't prove it."[128] Without proof of their suspicions, Nixon drug warriors found murder to be more efficient than trials. An assistant to Henry Kissinger confirmed that "black stuff" had been "expedited."[129] A CIA colonel freely admitted that he joined the BNDD to head death squad operations.[130] Howard Hunt recommended the colonel to BNDD,[131] and a Watergate burglar recalled Hunt telling him about the White House organizing death squads "ostensibly to assassinate narcotics leaders."[132]

When Epstein interviewed Nixon officials, he found that "the assassination bureau was not a subject that any of the former employees of BNDD or the White House desired to discuss."[133] We do not know whether drug warrior death squads disbanded after Nixon left office. The history of U.S. government secret operations after World War II suggests that such a program would have continued and perhaps even expanded. During the presidency of former CIA

Director George Bush, the National Security Council reportedly prepared approval for death squad murders of suspected drug dealers.[134] America's top drug police officer William Bennett declared that ethically no trial is required before killing citizens suspected of drug dealing.[135] The next day Bennett said of drug dealers, "You deserve to die."[136] (In law a "dealer" can be someone who hands a marijuana cigarette to a friend.) Bennett expressed satisfaction over the murder of "drug dealers" whose guilt was never proven in court.[137] In 1992 the Jackson County, Missouri, prosecutor's office declared that "fleeing felons" could be summarily shot.[138] If doubt existed about whether a fleeing citizen was a felon, the issue could be settled if police recovered a packet of thirty-six grams of marijuana from the dead person's coat pocket. We can be sure that only felons will be shot.

With senior drug warriors supporting secret death squads and public lynchings, we should not be surprised if warriors also advocate formal executions. Los Angeles Police Chief Daryl Gates had national influence on drug war strategy and tactics. The DARE program he founded and designed has been adopted nationwide. In 1990 he advised the U.S. Senate about the "'casual user' and what you do with the whole group. The casual user ought to be taken out and shot, because he or she has no reason for using drugs."[139] Gates later emphasized that "he was not being facetious" and declared marijuana users to be guilty of treason.[140] Calling Gates "one of the all-American heroes,"[141] President Bush continued rhetoric used by Ronald and Nancy Reagan, rhetoric inflaming public opinion by portraying drug users as murderers. A county prosecutor building his reputation on the drug war told me that citizens at neighborhood meetings had shifted their anger away from drug dealers and instead blamed users for havoc caused by drug houses and open air markets. More than one person has told me that the answer to the drug problem is to poison illicit supplies. Such persons are unlikely to oppose formal executions.

Would it be possible for authorities to implement the program recommended by DARE founder Gates, to round up and shoot every tenth man, woman, and child in the United States? At one time the answer would have been a resounding "NO!" But we have seen how measures demanded by drug warriors are used to punish citizens innocent of any crime (innocent even by admission of drug warriors administering punishment). We have seen courts bow to drug warrior demands and extinguish civil liberties that once made such abuses impossible. We have seen drug users hounded from jobs, homes, and communities as an orchestrated nationwide campaign of hate rhetoric portrayed them as bums, perverts, and murderers deserving to die. We have seen judges and the public approve military incarceration of blameless men, women, and children in concentration camps. Necessary mechanisms for mass killing are clicking into place as senior drug warriors demand a war to the death. We do not know if they will achieve their death wish. Before the American public succumbed to the war on drug users, mass murder was neither thinkable nor possible in the United States. Now it is both.

Readers who have not devoted considerable study to both the German war on Jews and the American war on drug users may see no possibility of death camps in the United States. But the potential has emerged. I cannot forget a warning from a distinguished student of the Holocaust: "Total integration requires complete acceptance. So long as that acceptance is withheld from a group of people, those people will live more or less peacefully in a state of equilibrium between ultimate incorporation and final annihilation."[142]

CODA: THE CREATION OF UTOPIA

Men are not afraid of outspokenness if they really care about a thing. Nor women either. Where there is ardor of soul against a condition, people defy danger, courting martyrdom. Death is an experience common to each of us. Stirred to defense of a conviction, men and women gladly give their lives. They are not halted by threat of arrest or torture where feeling is strong enough. People the world over suffer, even die, gladly for any cause they really cherish. The Germans are no cowardly exception different from the rest of mankind. I had known too many of them to conclude this. I found . . . their failure to stand by kin and neighbors astounding.

Nora Waln[1]

The "Final Solution" would not have been possible without the progressive steps excluding the Jews from German society which took place in full public view, in their legal form met with widespread approval, and resulted in the dehumanisation of the figure of the Jew. It would not have been possible without the atmosphere of hostility which was met only by apathy and widespread indifference. And it would not have been possible, finally, without the silence of the church hierarchies, . . . and without the consent ranging to active complicity of other prominent sections of the German élites —the bureaucracy of the Civil Service, leading sectors of industry, and the armed forces. Ultimately, therefore, dynamic hatred of the masses was unnecessary.

Ian Kershaw[2]

This book argues that drug users in America are victims of a destruction process. Having offered evidence for that assertion, I wish to conclude by suggesting why this destruction process is underway.

Although I believe drug use is normal and that most harm associated with illicit drug use comes from law rather than pharmacology, I also believe that drug abuse can cause problems for individuals and for society as a whole. Why, however, has our society relied so heavily on criminal statutes to address this situation?

We can address a great social problem without using criminal law. Unemployment is a classic example. The Soviet Union passed laws against "social parasites"; citizens either held a job or went to jail. We could take the same approach. Instead of offering training or welfare to the jobless, we could offer prison. If convicted of being unemployed, the criminals might get probation for a year while they looked for a job. If they were hired, the conviction could be erased from their record; otherwise, after a year the convicted jobless could go into labor battalions building public works. We could use criminal sanctions to eliminate unemployment and welfare.

Yet we choose not to. Just because unemployment is legal, that does not mean we condone it. It simply means we believe that police and prisons are not the best way to address that social problem, even though a high correlation exists between unemployment and crime. Rather than blaming unemployment on the jobless, we choose to see the cause of our unemployment rate in factors beyond the control of any individual. We seek to reduce unemployment by building business prosperity rather than by building prisons. We view unemployment as a sign of sickness in our society rather than as evidence of sickness in individual citizens. We do not give the jobless a choice between prison or enrolling in programs to cure a mental attitude that supposedly caused them to become unemployed when the factory closed.

Criminalizing unemployment would be asking criminal sanctions to accomplish something that law was never designed to accomplish. We can easily see that giving police more and more money to stop unemployment would be ineffective.

It is harder for us to see that criminalizing drug use asks criminal sanctions to accomplish something that law was never designed to do. We view drug use as a police matter simply out of tradition. It has been handled by police for so long that we accept mere tradition as part of the natural order of things.

Such unquestioning acceptance makes us susceptible to assertions that more and more police powers are needed to eliminate illicit drug use. Hidden within that acceptance is still another treacherous assertion, that illicit drug use must be *eliminated*, that no amount can be tolerated. We comfortably tolerate an unspecified but noticeable level of unemployment. Ditto poverty, automobile accidents, insufficient health care, reduced public transit availability, limits on public mobility of physically handicapped citizens, even burglary and car theft. As a society we are simply unwilling to do what is necessary to reduce those problems below assorted levels, let alone eliminate them entirely. Arguably, attacking any of those problems with unlimited resources might fail to eliminate them. Unquestionably, police power and resources can never eliminate drug use. Such a goal is impossible.

Nonetheless, drug warriors have established and maintained a national consensus that America must become free of drug use. By accepting an impossible goal and by accepting the idea that it must be achieved through police power, citizens relinquish more and more rights and revenue to police upon demand by drug war leaders. Continued acquiescence to these escalating demands should create a police state.

I believe authoritarians are manufacturing and manipulating public fears about drug use in order to create a police state where a much broader agenda of social control can be implemented, using government power to determine what movies we may watch, determine who we may love and how we may love them, determine whether we may or must pray to a deity. I believe the war on drug users masks a war on democracy.

After all, what is the vision of a Drug-Free America? Millions in prison or slave labor, and only enthusiastic supporters of government policy allowed to hold jobs, attend school, have children, drive cars, own property. This is the combined vision of utopia held forth by Nancy Reagan, Ronald Reagan, George Bush, William Bennett, Daryl Gates, and thousands of other drug warriors. News media and "public interest" advertising tell us this is the America for which all good citizens yearn.

We have seen how drug war rhetoric transforms drug users into scapegoats. Voters in my county passed a sales tax devoted exclusively to the drug war; those funds have hired a staff person for my neighborhood association. Even peeling paint and unkempt lawns are now the fault of drug users.

> In 1941, instead of annihilating the Red Army which refused to be annihilated and continued fighting, one could kill helpless Jews. . . .
> Instead of driving away the Anglo-American fliers, one again could kill Jews: after the first RAF bombardment of Cologne, 258 Jews in Berlin were lined up in the Gross-Lichterfield barracks and shot "in reprisal."
> In other words, while the actual fighting foes were out of reach, Germany could kill, as savages do, the images of the foes, the Jews. But in this case the images, too, were people of flesh and blood.[3]

For authoritarians a crucial benefit of scapegoating is that directing public anger toward scapegoats assures continuance of public anger, because problems creating fear and anger thereby remain unaddressed and will continue. In contrast to a confident and contented citizenry, a fearful and angry citizenry is more susceptible to authoritarian demands. Scapegoats are crucial for maintaining social turmoil needed by authoritarians.

> It was the Jews who helped hold Hitler's system together—on the practical as well as the ideological level. The Jew allowed Hitler to ignore the long list of economic and social promises he had made to the SA, the lower party apparatus, and the lower middle classes. By steering the attention of these groups away from their more genuine grievances and toward the Jew, Hitler succeeded in blunting the edge of their revolutionary wrath, leaving him freer to pursue his own nonideological goals of power in cooperation with groups whose influence he had once promised to weaken or even destroy. An ideological retreat on the Jewish issue in these circumstances was impossible. . . . The continued search for a solution to the Jewish problem allowed Hitler to maintain ideological contact with elements of his movement for whom National Socialism had done very little.[4]

If drug users are scapegoats, then attempts to reform drug laws are of little value. The need for scapegoats will thwart most reform attempts, and successful attempts will fail to address underlying social discontents that authoritarians feed upon. "What National Socialism has done and is doing with its propaganda is to take advantage of the soft spots in the social body. . . . There is class struggle from above and below; there are religious and racial antagonisms, clashing economic interests, competing political groups. . . . National Socialism propaganda cannot be beaten by a democratic super-propaganda, but only by a superior democratic policy that eliminates the soft spots."[5] Authoritarians can best be defeated by eliminating problems they exploit.

Unfortunately, not all authoritarians seek to be leaders; many more yearn to be followers. Democracy involves acceptance of personal responsibility for what goes wrong as well as what goes right in America, involves personal willingness to devote time, energy, and money in building up strengths while tearing down weaknesses in our neighborhoods, communities, and nation. Many citizens find such responsibility too daunting and gladly support politicians who promise to take on that responsibility and make decisions on citizens' behalf. Happiness is far easier to achieve under a dictatorship than in a democracy; in a dictatorship the only measure of good citizenship is obedience. If citizens do what they are told, they know they are good. As long as they never stretch far enough to touch the walls of their cage, they feel free as ever.

A good German reflected, "What began under Hitler in 1933 and ended in a world afire 12 years and 50 million casualties later, was the result of acquiescence in the discrimination against less than one percent of our population."[6] If one group of ordinary people merits attack, it is easy to find other groups of ordinary people to attack as well, at home and abroad. The Constitution of the United States and its Bill of Rights were designed to prevent government officials from ever molesting ordinary people as they pursued quiet enjoyment of their lives. "Think of the music, not the notes," said Pablo Casals.[7] During my initial encounters with American prosecutors' and courts' parsing of statutory and constitutional language, I thought officials were looking so hard at fragments of phrases that they had lost the melody and rhythm of the music. Only later did I realize their approach was necessary to deny what everyone could hear. The officials were not being dense or small minded. They, too, could hear the music composed by the Founding Fathers. Drug warriors, using the only available means to shut their own ears, are yanking individual notes from the printed score, examining them minutely, trying to ignore the flow of music swirling around us all. But music cannot be ignored. Prosecutors and courts can ban it, but still it will be played.

NOTES

ITT = *In These Times*
KCS = *Kansas City Star*
KCT = *Kansas City Times*
LAT = *Los Angeles Times*
NYT = *New York Times*
 PP = *Pittsburgh Press*
SLPD = *St. Louis Post-Dispatch*

Citations such as "NMT 1234-PS" are to documents in Nuremberg Military Tribunal proceedings. All such cited documents may be found in two collections printed by the United States government. The first is Office of United States Chief Counsel for Prosecution of Axis Criminality, *Nazi Conspiracy and Aggression* (referred to in notes as Red, with the appropriate volume number). The second is *Trials of War Criminals Before the Nurenberg Military Tribunal* (referred to as Green). Often, a reader need only use the indexes of the two collections to find cited materials. Where useful, however, a particular series (Red or Green) is specified along with volume and page numbers. "Tolan Committee" refers to U.S. House, Select Committee Investigating National Defense Migration.

FRONT MATTER

1. Jaspers, "Fight," 251-52.

Preface: THE DESTRUCTION PROCESS

1. Weyrauch, "Gestapo," 596.
2. Hilberg, *Destruction*, 762.

Chapter 1: IDENTIFICATION

1. Weinreich, *Hitler's*, 242.

2. Blum, "Background," in Blum et al., *Society*, 11-12.

3. Blum, "Student," in Blum et al., *Students*, 77-78; Brill and Christie, "Marihuana," 713; Mellinger et al., "Drug," in Kandel, *Longitudinal*, 167-69, 172-73.

4. Pope, Ionescu-Pioggia, and Cole, "Drug," 588-91; Johnston, *Drugs*, 193, 218; Beyerstein, "Mandatory," in *Faces*, 5. Similar findings for adults are noted in Zinberg, *Drug*, 216. See also Nicholson and Duncan, "Is," in Taylor and Small, *Crucial*.

5. Kolb, *Drug*, 10-11. See also 105.

6. Chein et al., *Road*, 358.

7. Weil, *Natural*, 58. See also Platt and Labate, *Heroin*, 171; Biernacki, *Pathways*, 6, 36; Stephen Waldron statement and testimony, U.S. House, Select Com. on Crime, *Improvement*, 287, 291; Craig Reinarman comments in Raymond, "Researchers," A6–A7, A10–A11.

8. Quoted in Trebach, *Great*, 345.

9. Peele, *Love*, 35; Schur, *Narcotic*, 151; Cutting, "Morphine," 39-41.

10. Platt and Labate, *Heroin*, 171; Biernacki, *Pathways*, 6, 36; Weil, *Natural*, 57-58; Zinberg, *Drug*, 157, 162.

11. Jaffe, "Drug," in Goodman and Gilman, *Pharmacological*, 7th ed., 542.

12. Weil, *Natural*, 87; Kagel, Battalio, and Miles, "Marihuana," 373, 390.

13. Sutton, "Effects," 442. See also Crancer et al., "Comparison," 851-54; McBay and Owens, "Marijuana," in Harris, *Problems 1980*; Owens, McBay, and Cook, "Use," 378.

14. McGlothlin and Arnold, "LSD," 49; Jaffe, "Drug," in Goodman and Gilman, *Pharmacological*, 7th ed., 564.

15. Researchers around the world have confirmed this. See Viani et al., "Drug," 145-51 (Italy); Winsløw, "Drug," 531-40 (Denmark); and Comitas, "Social," in Rubin, *Cannabis*, 119-32. See also Biernacki, *Pathways*, 55; Duster, *Legislation*, 9; Morgan, *Yesterday's*, 8; Crothers, *Morphinism*, 31; Rublowsky, *Stoned*, 138, 191; Schur, *Narcotic*, 28; Morgan, *Drugs*, 31; Kolb, *Drug*, 76; Zinberg and Lewis, "Narcotic," 992; Zinberg and Jacobson, "Natural," 38; Earle, "Opium," 445; Blair, "Relation," 288. For more on normalcy of drug users see data throughout Miller, *Case*.

16. For examples see Duster, *Legislation*, 117-28; Hubert S. Howe testimony, U.S. Senate, Judiciary Subcom., *Illicit*, 1339; Grinspoon and Bakalar, *Marihuana*, 152-53.

17. Jaffe and Martin, "Opioid," in Goodman and Gilman, *Pharmacological*, 7th ed., 498.

18. Jaffe, "Drug," in Goodman and Gilman, *Pharmacological*, 6th ed., 547.

19. Horgan, "Test," 18.

20. Smart, "Drinking," 731.

21. Horgan, "Test," 18.

22. Kaestner, "Effect," 381.

23. Gill and Michaels, "Does," 419.

24. Crouch et al., "Critical," in Gust and Walsh, *Drugs*, 183.

25. Sheridan and Winkler, "Evaluation," in Gust and Walsh, *Drugs*, 209-10.

26. Parish, "Relation," 44-47. See also Beyerstein, "Mandatory," in *Faces*, 3-4.

27. Register and Williams, "Labor," 435.

28. For older reports see Kolb, *Drug*, 10-11, 76; King, *Drug*, 18; Cutting, "Morphine," 39-41; Morgan, *Yesterday's*, 8; Crothers, *Morphinism*, 31; Schur, *Narcotic*, 28; Morgan, *Drugs*, 31; Earle, "Opium," 445; Blair, "Relation," 288.

29. *KCS*, Oct. 11, 1992, K4. See also Heymann, *Woman*, 301-2.

30. Ames, "Clinical," 976; Chopra and Chopra, "Use," 13; Comitas, "Social," in Rubin, *Cannabis*, 119-32; *Manchester Guardian Weekly*, Dec. 10, 1989, 24; Dreher, *Working*, 133, 173, 175, 179-85, 197; Page, Carter, and De Frenkel, "Marihuana," in Carter, *Cannabis*, 155-56; Musto, *American*, 72; Stanley, "Morphinism," 753; Grinspoon and Bakalar, *Cocaine*, 21, 99; Simonton, "Increase," 556; "Cocaine," 1729; Wright, *Report*, 49; *NYT*, March 12, 1911, V, 12; Morgan, *Yesterday's*, 4; Szasz, *Ceremonial*, 192; Louria, *Overcoming*, 33; Rublowsky, *Stoned*, 173; Blum, "History," in Blum et al., *Society*, 108; Sanders, "Doper's," 72; Brill and Hirose, "Rise," 179-94; Kato, "Epidemiological," 591-621; Hemmi, "How," in Sjöqvist and Tottie, *Abuse*, 148, 161 (discussion); Ishii and Motohashi, "Drug," 105-14; Henderson, *Waiting*, 183.

31. Quoted in *Christian Science Monitor*, Feb. 2, 1990, 2.

32. Office of National Drug Control Policy, *National*, p. 11.

33. Arntzen, "Some," 424-25; Rublowsky, *Stoned*, 88. Fredborg, *Behind*, 194-95, gives an example from wartime Berlin. Dicks, *Licensed*, 150, describes the same sort of activity among Nazi prisoners of war.

34. Brecher and Editors of *Consumer Reports*, *Licit*, 227 n.; Rublowsky, *Stoned*, 88. Heck, *Burden*, 27, 175, also reports women prostituting themselves for tobacco in postwar Germany, but in the context of acquiring a valued barter item.

35. Feldman, "PCP," in Feldman, Agar, and Beschner, *Angel*, 30, 39-50; Blum, "Drugs," in Blum et al., *Society*, 289; Fauman and Fauman, "Psychiatric," in Petersen and Stillman, *PCP*, 186; Marsella and Hicks, "Phenomenological," in ibid., 203, 205-6; Thombs, "Review," 327; Wish, "PCP," in Clouet, *Phencyclidine*, 179, 187.

36. Gordon, *Return*, 109.

37. For recent summaries of scientific research about drugs and crime see Miller, *Case*, and Alexander, *Peaceful*.

38. *Drug Policy Action*, Jan./Feb. 1991, 2; Brownstein, "Demilitarization,"

in Trebach and Zeese, *Great*, 115; Alexander, *Peaceful*, 192–93. See also Siegel, *Intoxication*, 182-83, 309-10; Bower, "Drugs," 393.

39. Smith, "Cocaine," 117; Erickson et al., *Steel*, 136-37.

40. National Institute, *National*, 23, 35, 83, 89.

41. Office of National Drug Control Policy, *National*, 25.

42. Quoted in *KCT*, Sept. 19, 1989, B1.

43. Quoted in *KCT*, Nov. 8, 1989, A1.

44. 21 U.S.C.A. § 885(d) (1981).

45. *LAT*, Oct. 21, 1994, A1, A27; *NewsBriefs*, Nov. 1994, 16.

46. Courts have ruled that male drug squad members can be punished for adultery if they seduce female suspects and arrest those suspects after using the sexual relationship to encourage the females to violate drug laws. Nonetheless, drug squad officers who face scrutiny for such sexual conduct cite 21 U.S.C. § 885(d) as granting them immunity from prosecution. See Matje v. Leis, 571 F.Supp. 918 (S.D. Ohio 1983); U.S. v. Flannigan, 31 M.J. 240 (C.M.A. 1990). Female undercover operatives, however, are allowed to use sexual relationships to encourage men to violate drug laws. See Wisotsky, "Crackdown," 913.

47. Burleigh and Wippermann, *Racial*, 40.

48. Wayburn, "Fallacies," in Trebach and Zeese, *Great*, 236.

49. Alexander, *Peaceful*, 79-80.

50. Stallman v. Youngquist, 531 N.E.2d 355, 359 (Ill. 1988).

51. Quoted in Proctor, *Racial*, 304.

52. Ibid., 240.

53. Ibid., 248.

54. Ibid., 240.

55. Grunberger, *12*, 120.

56. Quoted in ibid., 122. See also Kirchheimer, "Criminal," 444-45, 459.

57. Kirchheimer, "Criminal," 448; Picton, "Justice," 440.

58. Bennett, "Notes," 374-75.

59. Quoted in Grunberger, *12*, 122.

60. *KCS*, Oct. 2, 1991, C1, and Dec. 17, 1991, B1.

61. *NewsBriefs*, June 1992, 9.

62. Quoted in *Carrollton* (Missouri) *Daily Democrat*, Jan. 24, 1992, p. 1.

63. *KCS*, Oct. 23, 1992, C3.

64. Quoted in Szasz, *Our*, 79.

65. Quoted in Trebach, *Great*, 124.

66. Memo to Members of the Rockhurst Community, Sept. 9, 1994.

67. *Wall Street Journal*, May 18, 1994, A1, A5, and May 26, 1994, C1, C6; *NewsBriefs*, Nov. 1994, 25-26.

68. Merlo, "Prosecuting," in Trebach and Zeese, *New*, 219.

69. Green, *Doped*, 60.

70. Bonavoglia, "Ordeal," 196-97.

71. LaCroix, "Birth," 585.

72. S.B. 190, 86th General Assembly.

73. Lifton, *Nazi*, 25; Proctor, *Racial*, 103; Waln, *Reaching*, 174.

74. Sugarman and Powers, "How," 3326.

75. *New Times*, Nov. 19, 1992, p. 11.

76. Gieringer, "Urinalysis," in Trebach and Zeese, *Strategies*, 80.

77. Green v. State, 390 S.E.2d 285 (Ga. App. 1990).

78. Dicks, *Licensed*, 264.

79. S.B. 190, 86th General Assembly. State-mandated medical advice, in which physicians are forbidden to give advice on the basis of their professional evaluation of the individual patient's case, is not limited to "drug education." During the 1990s, many physicians were forbidden to discuss abortion when counseling pregnant patients.

80. *KCS*, Nov. 30, 1993, A6; Vallance, *Prohibition's*, 13.

81. Anslinger and Oursler, *Murderers*, 169, 175-76, 181-82.

82. King, "Report," in Trebach and Zeese, *Drug Policy*, 10.

83. DiChiara, "Changing," in Trebach and Zeese, *Great*, 306.

84. Kaplan, *Marijuana*, 8.

85. Quoted in Szasz, *Ceremonial*, 215-16. See also *NYT*, Oct. 28, 1980, B1; Primorac, "Cuban," 18; U.S. Senate, Judiciary Com., *DEA Oversight*, 6.

86. *KCT*, June 17, 1989, A1, A18.

87. Harmelin v. Michigan, 111 S.Ct. 2680 (1991) at 2705.

88. Thornton, *Economics*, 126.

89. Epstein, *Agency*, 186-87.

90. Quoted in McWilliams, *Ain't*, 544. See also Lewis and Klinenberg, "Taking," in *Faces*, 2-3.

91. *NewsBriefs*, March 1993, 3. See also Gordon, *Return*, 6.

92. Quoted in *KCS*, Aug. 9, 1989, A1.

93. Office of National Drug Control Policy, *National*, 10-11.

94. Husak, "Can," in Trebach and Zeese, *Strategies*, p. 94.

95. Quoted in Brownstein, "Demilitarization," in Trebach and Zeese, *Great*, 115.

96. Alexander, *Peaceful*, 267.

97. Bloomquist, *Marijuana*, 367.

98. Ibid., 298.

99. Quoted in ibid., 367.

100. Rosenbaum et al., "Women," in Trebach and Zeese, *Drug Prohibition*, 69.

101. Quoted in *Washington Post*, photocopy hand-dated "c. 11/5/92."

102. Dan Viets to Richard Lawrence Miller, telephone conversation, June 19, 1993.

103. Szasz, *Ceremonial*, 132-33.

104. *KCT*, June 3, 1989, A14.

105. Reagan, *Public*, 1311.

106. Quoted in Szasz, *Our*, 113.

107. As given in Mandel, "Racist," in Trebach and Zeese, *New*, 176.

108. Bush, *Public*, Sept. 12, 1989, 1180.

109. *Rolling Stone*, Oct. 14, 1993, 14.

110. Quoted in Gordon, *Return*, 61.

111. Quoted in Szasz, *Our*, 113.

112. Girard, *Scapegoat*, 16.

113. Quoted in Robinson v. California, 370 U.S. 660, 672 (1962) (Douglas, J., concurring).

114. Quoted in Hilberg, *Destruction*, 662.

115. Nixon, *Public*, Oct. 14, 1970, 844.

116. King, *Drug*, 329; Magruder, *American*, 104; Epstein, *Agency*, 170.

117. For example, see Bulych and Beyerstein, "Authoritarianism," in Trebach and Zeese, *New*, 155, 159.

118. *Congressional Record*, Sept. 11, 1986, H6699.

119. Office of National Drug Control Policy, *National*, 55.

120. *Washington Post*, Jan. 27, 1993, D7.

121. Quoted in *NYT*, March 1, 1988, A16.

122. Bush, *Public*, Sept. 13, 1989, 1180.

123. *Columbia* (Missouri) *Daily Tribune*, May 11, 1991, A5.

124. Jaurigue v. Justice Court, described in Paltrow, "Reproductive," in Trebach and Zeese, *Strategies*, 190.

125. "Pot Hooks You Up with a Whole New Circle of Friends," *KCS*, Aug. 6, 1994, C4.

126. Gordon, *Return*, 33.

127. Reagan, *Public*, 1311.

128. O'Rourke, "Taking," 57.

129. *EXTRA!* May/June 1994, 15.

130. Alexander, *Peaceful*, 343.

131. Quoted in Dicks, *Licensed*, 163.

132. Wiggs, "Treatment," 2376.

133. Zinberg, *Drug* 38-39, 208; Kleber, "Nosology," 58-59; Richards, *Demographic*, 4.

134. Quoted in Weinreich, *Hitler's*, 81.

135. Schleunes, *Twisted*, 5. See also Chargé Gordon to Secretary Hull, April 9, 1933, in U.S. Dept. of State, *Foreign*, 1933, v. 2, 217.

136. *Yellow*, 18.

137. Quoted in diary entry July 20, 1933, Fromm, *Blood*, 124.

138. *Yellow*, 23.

139. Ibid., 22.

140. Gordon, *Return*, 102.

141. "Crack Kills," Jackson County, Missouri, drug squad sales tax election brochure, Citizens Against Drugs.

142. Albert Riederer, prepared remarks at Unitarian Forum, Kansas City, Missouri, March 1, 1992.

143. Quoted in Mandel, "Racist," in Trebach and Zeese, *New*, 176.

144. Rhodes, "Public," 14; Stewart, "Advertising," in Trebach and Zeese, *Strategies*, 149 n. 6.

145. Stewart, "Advertising," in Trebach and Zeese, *Strategies*, 147, 150 n. 35; Cotts, "Hard," 302.

146. Stewart, "Advertising," in Trebach and Zeese, *Strategies*, 148.

147. Ibid., 143.

148. Office of National Drug Control Policy, *National*, 55.

149. Quoted in *Washington City Paper*, Dec. 6, 1991.

150. Diary entry, Aug. 9, 1933 in Fromm, *Blood*, 126.

151. *KCS*, Feb. 20, 1992, NO-6.

152. *NYT*, March 23, 1993, C18.

153. *KCS*, Feb. 15, 1992, B10.

154. Quoted in Rhodes, "Public," 14; see also Stewart, "Advertising," in Trebach and Zeese, *Strategies*, p. 150 n. 38.

155. *KCS*, June 22, 1994, C7.

156. Quoted in *Washington City Paper*, Dec. 6, 1991.

157. *Journal of the American Medical Association* 263 (Feb. 9, 1990): inside back cover.

158. Horgan, "Antidrug," 36.

159. Ibid.

160. Ibid.

161. Quoted in Horgan, "Antidrug," 36.

162. Stewart, "Advertising," in Trebach and Zeese, *Strategies*, 148.

163. Quoted in *KCS*, July 16, 1991, B3.

164. Neumann, *Behemoth*, 436.

165. *KCT*, Aug. 15, 1989, A1, A6.

166. Wardlaw, "Military," in Trebach and Zeese, *Great*, p. 107.

167. Quoted in *KCT*, Aug. 22, 1989, B6.

168. Quoted in ibid.

169. *KCT*, Feb. 6, 1989, A7.

170. *EXTRA!* March 1993, 7.

171. Quoted in *Washington City Paper*, Dec. 6, 1991.

172. Quoted in ibid.

173. *Drug Policy Letter*, Spring 1994, 30-31.

174. Szasz, *Our*, 83.

175. *Drug Policy Letter*, Fall 1994, 32.

176. *KCS*, Aug. 4, 1993, C7.

177. *EXTRA!* Sept./Oct. 1993, 25.

178. *F.E.A.R. Chronicles*, v. 1, no. 5, p. 10.

179. Hager, "Drug," in Trebach and Zeese, *Strategies*, 385-86.

180. Trebach, "'Socialist,'" in Trebach and Zeese, *Strategies*, 112.

181. Beckett, "Pregnant," in Trebach and Zeese, *Strategies*, 186.

182. Koren et al., "Bias," 1440-42. See also Mayes, "Problem," 406-8. Miller, *Case*, 16-17, analyzes other examples of drug war thinking camouflaged by scientific rhetoric.

183. See Proctor, *Racial*, especially 62-63; also Kühl, *Nazi*.

184. Quoted in Roberts, "Cognitive," in Trebach and Zeese, *Great*, 292.

185. Trebach, "'Socialist,'" in Trebach and Zeese, *Strategies*, 112.

186. Quotations from *USA Today*, Oct. 11, 1993, 2A, and Oct. 4, 1994, 2A; *NewsBriefs*, Nov. 1994, 13; *Drug Policy Letter*, Spring 1995, 12–14, 23–24; Ennett et al., "How," 1394-1401.

187. Epstein, *Agency*, 188.

188. Pub. L. 100-690, § 5011, 102 Stat. 4296 (1988).

189. *NewsBriefs*, Dec. 1992, 18.

190. Red I, 298.

Chapter 2: OSTRACISM

1. *NYT*, June 20, 1933, 4.

2. Korematsu v. U.S., 323 U.S. 214, 246-47 (1944) (Jackson, J., dissenting).

3. Gisevius, *To*, 27.

4. McWilliams, *Ain't*, 199-200.

5. Ibid., 203.

6. Dan Viets to Richard Lawrence Miller, telephone conversation, June 19, 1993.

7. Baum, "Drug," 888; *Columbia* (Missouri) *Tribune*, Nov. 21, 1991; *Leaflet* (NORML newsletter), Winter 1992, 12.

8. *Yellow*, 111.

9. NMT NG-901 (Green III, 364-65).

10. *Columbia* (Missouri) *Tribune*, Nov. 21, 1991.

11. Quoted in *Grapevine*, May 7, 1993, 1.

12. *KCS*, Dec. 17, 1991, B1.

13. Dan Viets to Richard Lawrence Miller, telephone conversation, June 19, 1993.

14. U.S. v. Barnet, 667 F.2d 835 (9th Cir. 1982).

15. Osburn, *Spectre*, 115.

16. Ibid., 114-15.

17. *ITT*, Dec. 6, 1989, 5; *ITT*, June 26, 1991, 6; *Drug Policy Letter*, May/June 1991, 9.

18. *Columbia* (Missouri) *Daily Tribune*, April 27, 1990, 1.

19. Quoted in *Drug Policy Letter*, May/June 1991, 9.

20. *Drug Policy Action*, March/April 1991, 1.

21. H.B. 1741, 86th General Assembly, 2d sess.; H.B. 47, 87th General Assembly, 1st sess.

22. Wollstein, "Turning," in Trebach and Zeese, *New*, 90.

23. Luff, "Need," in Trebach and Zeese, *Strategies*, 355.

24. Miller, *Case*, 80.

25. Luff, "First," in Trebach and Zeese, *Drug Policy*, 262-66.

26. Francis M. Mullen, Jr., testimony, U.S. Senate, Judiciary Com., *DEA Oversight*, 15.

27. Jeffrey Harris testimony, ibid., 39.

28. U.S. v. Leon, 104 S.Ct. 3430, 3452 (1984) (dissent).

29. Brinegar v. U.S., 69 S.Ct. 1302, 1313 (1949) (dissent).

30. United States v. Leon, 104 S.Ct. 3405 (1984).

31. Ibid., 3431 (dissent).

32. Ibid., 3456 (dissent).

33. *ITT*, June 26, 1991, 6; *Drug Policy Action*, Fall 1991, 5-6.

34. U.S. v. Verdugo-Urquidez, 494 U.S. 259, 265 (1990).

35. Boyd v. U.S., 116 U.S. 616, 635 (1886).

36. People v. Rochin, 225 P.2d 1 (1950); Rochin v. People, 72 S.Ct. 205 (1952).

37. U.S. v. Montoya De Hernandez, 105 S.Ct. 3304 (1985); Ostrowski, "Thinking," in Boaz, *Crisis*, 60.

38. U.S. v. Montoya De Hernandez, 105 S.Ct. 3304, 3315, 3320 (1985) (dissent).

39. Doe v. Renfrow, 475 F.Supp., 1012 (N.D. Ind. 1979); Doe v. Renfrow, 631 F.2d 91 (7th Cir. 1980); Doe v. Renfrow, *cert. denied*, 451 U.S. 1022.

40. *KCS*, May 13, 1989, A1, A20. See also *NYT*, Aug. 19, 1986, I, 14; Acton v. Vernonia 23 F.3d 1514 (1994); Schaill v. Tippecanoe, 864 F.2d 1309 (7th Cir. 1988).

41. *KCT*, April 19, 1989, A9.

42. Miller, *Case*, 117.

43. Szasz, *Our*, 80.

44. Ibid.

45. Office of National Drug Control Policy, *National*, 126.

46. Zimring and Hawkins, *Search*, 131.

47. Florida v. Bostick, 111 S.Ct. 2382, 2393 (1991) (dissent).

48. Osburn, *Spectre*, 9.

49. *NewsBriefs*, March 1993, 5-6.

50. Brinegar v. U.S., 69 S.Ct. 1302, 1313-14 (1949) (dissent).

51. Skolnick, *Justice*, 146.

52. "Drug Agents More Likely to Stop Minorities," *PP*, Aug. 11-16, 1991, reprint, p. 12.

53. Brinegar v. U.S., 69 S.Ct. 1302, 1313-14 (1949) (dissent).

54. State v. Kerwick, 512 So.2d 347, 348-49 (Fla. App. 4 Dist. 1987).

55. Brinegar v. U.S., 69 S.Ct. 1302, 1313-14 (1949) (dissent).

56. Florida v. Bostick, 111 S.Ct. 2382, 2390 (1991) (dissent).

57. Figures and quotation in "Drug Agents More Likely to Stop Minorities," *PP*, Aug. 11-16, 1991, reprint, p. 14.

58. *NYT*, March 20, 1990, B6.

59. U.S. v. Montoya De Hernandez, 105 S.Ct. 3304, 3319 (1985) (dissent).

60. People v. Rochin, 225 P.2d 1, 3 (1950).

61. *NewsBriefs*, Feb. 1993, 8.

62. Skolnick, *Justice*, 221.

63. Illinois v. Gates, 103 S.Ct. 2317 (1983). To get a search warrant, drug squads must "verify" the anonymous tip in some way, but the verification standard is low. For example, if a tip says that illegal drugs are in a two-story house at a particular address, and the squad confirms that the house has two stories, that is enough to verify the anonymous tipster's reliability and to permit a raid.

64. Gellately, *Gestapo*, 138-39.

65. Quoted in Porter, "Blow," 84.

66. Alexander, *Peaceful*, 39. This example is from Canada's drug war, demonstrating that such abuses are not inherent to the United States but rather are inherent to a destruction process.

67. Domanick, "Field," 39.

68. Alexander, *Peaceful*, 39-41. This example is from Canada's drug war.

69. *KCS*, June 15, 1991, A1, A20.

70. Quoted in Engelmann, *In*, 45, 88.

71. Quoted in Henry, *Victims*, 118.

72. *F.E.A.R. Chronicles*, Aug. 1992, 7.

73. Grantland, *Your*, 110.

74. *F.E.A.R. Chronicles*, Nov. 1993, 7.

75. *NewsBriefs*, Feb. 1993, 7.

76. Epstein, *Agency*, 17-18.

77. Ibid., 18.

78. Ibid. These three Illinois searches were without search warrants.

79. *KCS*, April 4, 1989, A1, A7, and April 5, 1989, B1. The FBI raiders were seeking evidence of illegal gambling, but the example is included here as illustrative of the genre.

80. Skolnick, *Justice*, 144.

81. Quoted in Kirkpatrick, *Prosecution*, 39.

82. Quoted in NMT 1759-PS (Red IV, 303). The incident is also described in NMT L-198 (Red VII, 1028).

83. Dan Viets to Richard Lawrence Miller, telephone conversation, June 19, 1993.

84. Quoted in *San Francisco Examiner*, July 3, 1994, A12.

85. *The Match*, Summer 1993, 10.

86. *NewsBriefs*, Jan. 1993, 6.

87. *F.E.A.R. Chronicles*, May 1993, 1.

88. *Drug Policy Letter*, July/Aug. 1994, 3; *NYT*, March 28, 1994, A1, A9.

89. Lusane, *Pipe*, 46; Zeese, "Waging," in Trebach and Zeese, *Drug Prohibition*, 192-93.

90. Florida v. Royer, 460 U.S. 491, 493 n. 2 (1983).

91. Florida v. Bostick, 111 S.Ct. 2382 (1991); *NYT*, March 20, 1990, A1, B6; "Drug Agents More Likely to Stop Minorities," *PP*, Aug. 11-16, 1991, reprint, p. 12; "Government Seizures Victimize Innocent," *PP*, Aug. 11-16, 1991, reprint, p. 6.

92. U.S. v. Westerbann-Martinez, 435 F.Supp. 690, 692-93 (E.D.N.Y. 1977).

93. Florida v. Royer, 460 U.S. 491, 493 n. 2 (1983); U.S. v. Smith 574 F.2d 882, 883 (6th Cir. 1978).

94. U.S. v. Andrews, 600 F.2d 563, 566 (6th Cir. 1979); U.S. v. Westerbann-Martinez, 435 F.Supp. 690, 693 (E.D.N.Y. 1977).

95. U.S. v. Himmelwright, 551 F.2d 991, 992 (5th Cir. 1977).

96. "Drug Agents More Likely to Stop Minorities," *PP*, Aug. 11-16, 1991, reprint, p. 14.

97. Ibid.

98. Ibid.

99. Ibid.

100. Ibid.

101. Ibid.

102. Florida v. Royer, 460 U.S. 491, 493 n. 2 (1983); U.S. v. Westerbann-Martinez, 435 F.Supp. 690, 693 (E.D.N.Y. 1977).

103. U.S. v. Sokolow, 808 F.2d 1366, 1370 (9th Cir. 1987).

104. U.S. v. Smith, 574 F.2d 882, 884-85 (6th Cir. 1978); Jones v. U.S., 819 F.Supp. 698, 702 (M.D.Tenn., 1993).

105. U.S. v. Sokolow, 808 F.2d 1366, 1370 (9th Cir. 1987).

106. Wisotsky, "Crackdown," 915.

107. U.S. v. Himmelwright, 551 F.2d 991, 992 (5th Cir. 1977).

108. U.S. v. Holtz, 479 F.2d 89, 96 (9th Cir. 1973) (dissent).

109. *SLPD*, Oct. 11, 1991, A6.

110. *NewsBriefs*, July 1992, 6; *NewsBriefs*, Sept.–Oct. 1994, 6-7; *Springfield* (Missouri) *News-Leader*, Aug. 20, 1993, B1, B2; Schlosser, "Reefer," 60.

111. Dan Viets to Richard Lawrence Miller, telephone conversation, Jan. 25, 1995 (referring to "Green Merchant" cases of 1990).

112. U.S. v. Sokolow, 808 F.2d 1366, 1367, 1370 (9th Cir. 1987).

113. *ITT*, Sept. 25, 1991, 6.

114. Ibid.

115. California v. Carney, 105 S.Ct. 2066 (1985).

116. Wisotsky, "Crackdown," 915.

117. *Jefferson City* (Missouri) *Post-Tribune*, May 24, 1991, 6.

118. *SLPD*, April 30, 1991, 10.

119. Ibid.

120. Wisotsky, "Crackdown," 915.

121. U.S. v. Mallides, 473 F.2d 859, 860 (1973).

122. Ibid.

123. U.S. v. Montoya De Hernandez, 105 S.Ct. 3304, 3313 n. 2 (1985) (dissent).

124. Ibid.

125. U.S. v. Holtz, 479 F.2d 89, 96 (9th Cir. 1973) (dissent).

126. U.S. v. Van Lewis, 409 F.Supp. 535, 538 (E.D. Mich., S.D. 1976); U.S. v. Smith 574 F.2d 882, 883 (6th Cir. 1978).

127. U.S. v. Mendenhall, 446 U.S. 544, 547 n. 1 (1980); U.S. v. Chambliss, 425 F.Supp. 1330, 1332 (E.D. Mich., S.D., 1977).

128. U.S. v. Sanford, 658 F.2d 342, 343 (5th Cir. 1981).

129. U.S. v. Fry, 622 F.2d 1218, 1219 (5th Cir. 1980); State v. Reid, 255 S.E.2d 71 (Ga. App. 1979), vacated and remanded Reid v. Georgia, 448 U.S. 438 (1980).

130. U.S. v. Sanford, 658 F.2d 342, 343 (5th Cir. 1981).

131. U.S. v. Fry, 622 F.2d 1218, 1219 (5th Cir. 1980).

132. U.S. v. Buenaventura-Ariza, 615 F.2d 29, 31 n. 5 (2d Cir. 1980).

133. Ibid.; U.S. v. Westerbann-Martinez, 435 F.Supp. 690, 692 (E.D.N.Y. 1977).

134. U.S. v. Buenaventura-Ariza, 615 F.2d 29, 31 n. 5 (2d Cir. 1980); U.S. v. Smith 574 F.2d 882, 883 (6th Cir. 1978).

135. U.S. v. Craemer, 555 F.2d 594, 595 (6th Cir. 1977).

136. Ibid.

137. U.S. v. Andrews, 600 F.2d 563, 566 (6th Cir. 1979).

138. U.S. v. Fry, 622 F.2d 1218, 1220 (5th Cir. 1980).

139. U.S. v. Sullivan, 625 F.2d 9, 12 (4th Cir. 1980).

140. Ibid.

141. U.S. v. Craemer, 555 F.2d 594, 595 (6th Cir. 1977).

142. U.S. v. Moore, 675 F.2d 802, 803 (6th Cir. 1982).

143. U.S. v. Sanford, 658 F.2d 342, 343 (5th Cir. 1981).

144. U.S. v. Mendenhall, 446 U.S. 544, 547 n. 1 (1980).

145. U.S. v. McCaleb, 552 F.2d 717, 720 (6th Cir. 1977).

146. U.S. v. Sokolow, 808 F.2d 1366, 1367, 1370 (9th Cir. 1987).

147. U.S. v. Fry, 622 F.2d 1218, 1220 (5th Cir. 1980).

148. U.S. v. Price, 599 F.2d 494, 496 (2d. Cir. 1979); U.S. v. Vasquez, 612 F.2d 1338, 1340 (2d. Cir. 1979).

149. Florida v. Royer, 460 U.S. 491, 493 n. 2 (1983).

150. "Drug Agents More Likely to Stop Minorities," *PP*, Aug. 11-16, 1991, reprint, p. 14.

151. Florida v. Royer, 460 U.S. 491, 493 n. 2 (1983).

152. U.S. v. Sullivan, 625 F.2d 9, 12 (4th Cir. 1980).

153. U.S. v. Ballard, 573 F.2d 913, 914 (1978); U.S. v. Westerbann-

Martinez, 435 F.Supp. 690, 692 (E.D.N.Y. 1977).

154. U.S. v. Fry, 622 F.2d 1218, 1220 (5th Cir. 1980).

155. U.S. v. Smith, 574 F.2d 882, 883-84 (6th Cir. 1978); U.S. v. Chambliss, 425 F.Supp. 1330, 1333 (E.D. Mich., S.D., 1977).

156. U.S. v. Price, 599 F.2d 494, 496 (2d. Cir. 1979).

157. U.S. v. Moore, 675 F.2d 802, 803 (6th Cir. 1982).

158. U.S. v. Mendenhall, 446 U.S. 544, 547 n. 1 (1980); U.S. v. Vasquez, 612 F.2d 1338, 1340 (2d. Cir. 1979).

159. U.S. v. Buenaventura-Ariza, 615 F.2d 29, 31 (2d Cir. 1980).

160. Bernstein, "Fourth," 1003 n. 93; State v. Reid, 255 S.E.2d 71, 72 (1979), vacated and remanded; Reid v. Georgia, 448 U.S. 438 (1980).

161. "Drug Agents More Likely to Stop Minorities," *PP*, Aug. 11-16, 1991, reprint, p. 13.

162. U.S. v. Montoya De Hernandez, 105 S.Ct. 3304, 3313 n. 2 (1985) (dissent).

163. U.S. v. Ballard, 573 F.2d 913, 914 (1978); U.S. v. Chambliss, 425 F.Supp. 1330, 1333 (E.D. Mich., S.D., 1977).

164. Lending, "Drug," 353.

165. Ibid.

166. U.S. v. Smith 574 F.2d 882, 883 (6th Cir. 1978).

167. U.S. v. Chambliss, 425 F.Supp. 1330, 1333 (E.D. Mich., S.D., 1977).

168. U.S. v. Elmore, 595 F.2d 1036, 1039 n. 3 (1979).

169. *SLPD*, April 30, 1991, 10.

170. Ibid.

171. Ibid.

172. U.S. v. Fry, 622 F.2d 1218, 1219 (5th Cir. 1980).

173. U.S. v. Escamilla, 560 F.2d 1229, 1233 (5th Cir. 1977).

174. Florida v. Royer, 460 U.S. 491, 493 n. 2 (1983). See also U.S. v. Westerbann-Martinez, 435 F.Supp. 690, 693 (E.D.N.Y. 1977).

175. Skolnick, *Justice*, 123.

176. Ibid., 144.

177. For the latter, see Green v. State, 390 S.E.2d 285 (Ga. App. 1990).

178. Rochin v. People, 72 S.Ct. 205, 213 (1952) (concurring).

179. Becker and Hora, "What's," in *Faces*, 8 n. 41; *NYT*, Jan. 21, 1994, A12.

180. Leary v. U.S., 395 U.S. 6 (1969).

181. Marchetti v. U.S., 390 U.S. 39, 58-59 (1968).

182. *KCT*, Aug. 26, 1989, A7; *KCS*, Dec. 31, 1993, C1, C8.

183. Department v. Kurth, 114 S.Ct. 1937 (1994).

184. In re Kurth, 986 F.2d 1308, 1310 (1993).

185. U.S. v. Hall, 730 F.Supp. 646 (M.D.Pa. 1990).

186. Quoted in *F.E.A.R. Chronicles*, May 1993, 5.

187. H.B. 86, 87th General Assembly, 1st sess.

188. 1941 RGBl. I, 722, art. 8, quoted in NMT NG-715.

189. Green III, 25, #29. Some aspects of seizures were also characterized as war crimes (Green III, 22, #17).

190. U.S. v. Marshall, 532 F.2d 1279 (1976).

191. *KCS*, June 5, 1991, C1.

192. *KCS*, June 2, 1993, C1, C2.

193. Pub. L. 98-473, 98 Stat. 1976 (1984).

194. Rankin, "Effect," 641-55.

195. I am indebted to Witosky, "Crackdown," for alerting me to this situation.

196. U.S. v. Jin Fuey Moy, 241 U.S. 394 (1916), 402.

197. Blockburger v. U.S., 284 U.S. 299, 304 (1932).

198. Drug czar William Bennett, who long advocated an authoritarian philosophy of government for the United States, told a group of Southern Baptists that drug abuse "is a product of the Great Deceiver." He said, "We need to bring these people in need the God who heals." Noting that many drug abuse patients call crack "the devil," Bennett declared, "This has come up too often to be ignored." (Quoted in *Free Inquiry*, Fall 1990, 39.)

199. Szasz, *Our*, 43.

200. Quotations from ibid., 117.

201. Green III, 47.

202. Red I, 244.

203. NMT 2232-PS (Red IV, 882-83); Marx, *Government*, 145.

204. NMT 2232-PS (Red IV, 883). Such immunity also extended to actions by the SA and SS (NMT 1216-PS; Red Supp. A, 1101-13, 1121-34).

205. Viets, "Human," in Trebach and Zeese, *New*, 32.

206. People v. Barris, 500 N.Y.S.2d 572, 581 (A.D. 4 Dept. 1986); U.S. v. U.S. Currency, 895 F.2d 908 (2nd Cir. 1990).

207. Miller, *Case*, 75.

208. Transcript in Kirkpatrick, *Prosecution*, 41-43.

209. Trebach, *Great*, 130.

210. Ibid. See also Trebach and Zeese, "Can," in Trebach and Zeese, *Strategies*, 268.

211. Green v. State, 398 S.E.2d 360 (Ga. 1990).

212. Beyerstein, "Mandatory," in *Faces*, 2.

213. Quoted in U.S. Sentencing Commission, *Special*, p. 99.

214. "Kicking the Prison Habit," *Newsweek*, June 14, 1993, 32.

215. Bloom, Lind, and Owen, "Women," in Taylor and Small, *Crucial*; *EXTRA!* May/June 1994, 7.

216. Quoted in *NewsBriefs*, Feb. 1993, 9. See also Gordon, *Return*, 33; McWilliams, *Ain't*, 242.

217. Quoted in *NewsBriefs*, May 1993, 13.

218. Skolnick, "Some," 3177.

219. Quoted in *KCS*, Sept. 12, 1993, A18.

220. U.S. v. Davis, 864 F.Supp 1303 (N.D.Ga. 1994); U.S. v. Clary, 846

F.Supp. 768 (E.D.Mo 1994).

221. Quoted in *KCS*, Sept. 12, 1993, A18.

222. 21 U.S.C.A. § 841 (Supp. 1994); McPherson, "News," 5.

223. See Lillie-Blanton, Anthony, and Schuster, "Probing," 993.

224. State v. Russell, 477 N.W.2d 886 (1991); *KCS*, Dec. 14, 1991, A6.

225. U.S. v. Clary, 846 F.Supp. 768, 770 (E.D.Mo. 1994).

226. O'Rourke, "Taking," 61.

227. U.S. v. Clary, 846 F.Supp. 768, 790 (E.D.Mo. 1994).

228. Quoted in *EXTRA!* April/May 1992, 5.

229. *Drug Policy Action*, Fall 1991, 5.

230. For example, see Red I, 226, and Green III, 96.

231. 1941 RGBl. I, 759-61, quoted in NMT 2746-PS (see particularly Red V, 387).

232. NMT 2967-PS.

233. Green III, 19.

234. 21 U.S.C.A. § 841 (Supp. 1994); Baum, "Drug," 887; Wollstein, "Turning," in Trebach and Zeese, *New*, 90.

235. King, "Report," in Trebach and Zeese, *Drug Policy*, 26-27.

236. Grinspoon, "Marijuana," in Trebach and Zeese, *Drug Prohibition*, 162.

237. Schlosser, "Reefer," 55.

238. Baum, "Drug," 887.

239. Tarlow, "RICO," 312-13, 402.

240. Calder v. Bull, 3 U.S. (3 Dall.) 386, 390 (1798). See also Fletcher v. Peck, 10 U.S. (6 Cranch), 138 (1810).

241. 18 U.S.C.A. § 1014 (Supp. 1994); Pub. L. 101-73, § 963, 103 Stat. 183, 504 (1989); *F.E.A.R. Chronicles*, July 1994, 1, 13-14.

242. U.S. v. 403 1/2 Skyline Dr., 797 F.Supp. 796 (C.D.Cal. 1992).

243. Quoted in *F.E.A.R. Chronicles*, July 1994, 13-14.

244. Quoted in *Columbia* (Missouri) *Daily Tribune*, May 11, 1991, 5A.

245. U.S. Sentencing Commission, *Special*, 90; *Drug Policy Letter*, March/April 1991, 7.

246. Quoted in U.S. Sentencing Commission, *Special*, 93, 96.

247. Quoted in Stewart, "Are," in Trebach and Zeese, *New*, 38.

248. Ibid.

249. *KCS*, April 19, 1991, C3. The U.S. attorney in that case disagreed: "This system is much better than allowing some unelected parole board to substitute its judgment." Just who elected the U.S. attorney is unclear.

250. *Drug Policy Letter*, Spring/Summer 1992, 7. See also *Drug Policy Letter*, March/April 1991, 7.

251. Ebenstein, *Nazi*, 84.

252. Loewenstein, "Reconstruction," 444.

253. California v. Acevedo, U.S. slip op. 17 (1991) (dissent).

254. Florida v. Royer, 460 U.S. 491 (1983).

255. Harmelin v. Michigan, 111 S.Ct. 2680 (1991).

256. Ibid., 2718 (dissent).

257. Furman v. Georgia, 408 U.S. 238, 277 n. 20 (1972) (Brennan, J. concurring).

258. U.S. v. Burton, 894 F.2d 188, 192 (6th Cir. 1990).

259. Stewart, "Are," in Trebach and Zeese, *New*, 38.

260. Quoted in *Leaflet* (NORML newsletter), Fall 1991, 2.

261. Quoted in ibid.

262. Jenks, "Before," in Trebach and Zeese, *Strategies*, 215-16.

263. *Leaflet* (NORML newsletter), Winter 1992, 3.

264. *Leaflet* (NORML newsletter), March 1993, 5; Schlosser, "Reefer," 55; *Drug Policy Letter*, Spring 1995, 17.

265. *F.E.A.R. Chronicles*, Nov. 1993, 15; Grantland, *Your*, 204-5.

266. Schlosser, "Reefer," 55.

267. *PP*, Aug. 11-16, 1991, reprint, p. 7.

268. *PP*, Aug. 11-16, 1991, reprint, pp. 9-10.

269. Quoted in *SLPD*, March 11, 1993, 13.

270. *SLPD*, Dec. 6, 1992, 6A.

271. Grinspoon and Bakalar, *Forbidden*, 100.

272. Pub. L. 101-336, § 510(a), 104 Stat. 327, 375 (1990); 42 U.S.C.A. § 12210(a) (Supp. 1994).

273. Vallance, *Prohibition's*, 115.

274. National Treasury Employees Union v. Von Raab, 109 S.Ct. 1384, 1400 (1989) (dissent).

275. Ibid., 1401 (dissent).

276. Fraenkel, *Dual*, 47.

277. *The Times*, July 19, 1934, 13.

278. *NYT*, April 6, 1936, 1.

279. Quoted in Müller, *Hitler's*, 66. See also Marx, *Government*, 145.

280. *KCS*, Oct. 23, 1992, C3.

281. Chapman v. U.S., 111 S.Ct. 1919 (1991); *Drug Policy Action*, Fall 1991, 4-5.

282. Daniel J. Dodson to Richard Lawrence Miller, telephone conversations, June 15, 1993, and July 23, 1993.

283. Chapman v. U.S., 111 S.Ct. 1919 (1991); *NewsBriefs*, Oct. 1992, 9.

284. U.S. Sentencing Commission, *Guidelines*, § 2D1.1.(c), p. 86.

285. Rosenthal, "Growers," in Trebach and Zeese, *New*, 122.

286. Harmelin v. Michigan, 111 S.Ct. 2680, 2716 (1991) (White, J., with Blackmun, J., and Stevens, J., dissenting). See also People v. Konyack 471 N.Y.S.2d 699 (A.D. 3 Dept. 1984); People v. LaPorta, 393 N.Y.S.2d 118 (1977).

287. U.S. Sentencing Commission, *Guidelines*, § 2D1.1.(c), p. 86.

288. Hutto v. Davis, 454 U.S. 370 (1982).

289. *KCS*, Dec. 20, 1991, C2.

290. Johns, "Legalization," in Trebach and Zeese, *Great*, 17.

291. Harmelin v. Michigan 111 S.Ct. 2680 (1991).

292. *Columbia* (Missouri) *Daily Tribune*, May 11, 1991, 5A.

293. Stewart, "Are," in Trebach and Zeese, *New*, 39.

294. *Columbia* (Missouri) *Tribune*, Nov. 14, 1991, 2.

295. *KCS*, Jan. 23, 1993, C3.

296. *NewsBriefs*, Jan. 1993, 15.

297. U.S. v. Boney, 977 F.2d 624, 636 (D.C. Cir. 1992).

298. *KCS*, Feb. 17, 1993, C1, C8.

299. *KCS*, Dec. 28, 1991, A6.

300. U.S. v. Smith, 991 F.2d 802, 1993 WL 125394 (8th Cir. (Ark.)).

301. *Drug Policy Letter*, March/April 1991, 8.

302. Baum, "Drug," 887; *KCS*, April 25, 1991, C3, May 16, 1991, C3, and Sept. 20, 1992, B2.

303. *Drug Policy Letter*, March/April 1991, 8.

304. Quoted in ibid.

305. Green III, 49.

306. Quoted in Stewart, "Are," in Trebach and Zeese, *New*, 38.

307. Baum, "Drug," 887.

308. Franz Gürtner, "Administration," in *Germany*, 85.

309. Stewart, "Are," in Trebach and Zeese, *New*, 39.

310. Dan Viets to Richard Lawrence Miller, telephone conversation, June 19, 1993.

311. Green III, 22, paragraph 16.

312. Green III, 25, paragraph 28.

313. Stewart, "Are," in Trebach and Zeese, *New*, 38.

314. Sager, "State," 52-53.

315. Stewart, "Are," in Trebach and Zeese, *New*, 38.

316. Viets, "Human," in Trebach and Zeese, *New*, 33.

317. *KCS*, Nov. 28, 1992, C7.

318. Müller, *Hitler's*, 160.

319. *NYT*, March 1, 1991, B4; Finkelman, "War," in Trebach and Zeese, *New*, 118.

320. Quoted in *NYT*, March 1, 1991, B4.

321. Quoted in *KCS*, March 13, 1993, A14.

322. Quoted in ibid.

323. Quoted in ibid.

324. Herrera v. Collins, 113 S.Ct. 853 (1993).

325. Ibid., 878 (dissent).

326. *KCS*, July 14, 1993, C1, C8, July 22, 1993, C2, and July 22, 1993, C2.

327. Schlup v. Delo, 11 F.3d 738, 754 (8th Cir. 1993) (Heaney, J., dissenting); *KCS*, Sept. 27, 1993, A1, A8, and Oct. 31, 1993, A1, A16. A few hours before Schlup was to be executed, Missouri governor Mel Carnahan halted

preparations and ordered further administrative inquiry. Subsequently the U.S. Supreme Court agreed that Schlup deserved new judicial proceedings (Schlup v. Delo, slip. op, U.S. LEXIS 701 (1995)); but had the governor refused to act, the Court's subsequent decision would have been moot.

328. Quoted in Dicks, *Licensed*, 98, 100.

329. Quoted in *SLPD*, Feb. 8, 1990, 1, 5. See also *Columbia Missourian*, Feb. 9, 1990, 1A, 8A; *Columbia* (Missouri) *Tribune*, Feb. 13, 1990.

330. *SLPD*, Feb. 9, 1990.

331. Heymann, *Woman*, 375.

332. U.S. v. Alvarez-Machain, 112 S.Ct. 2188 (1992).

333. Ibid., 2199 (dissent).

334. *Drug Policy Action*, Winter 1993, 2.

335. Hohri, *Repairing*, 142-44; Girdner and Loftis, *Great*, 426-27; Weglyn, *Years*, 59-66.

336. Whiting, *War*, 46-47.

337. Green III, 24 (#23 war crimes reference to #11 crimes against humanity), 48 (reference to 1940 RGBl. I, 754 narcotics law).

338. Quoted in Lifton, *Nazi*, 50.

339. Deutsch, "Disfranchisement," in Van Paassen and Wise, *Nazism*, 55.

340. *SLPD*, Feb. 3, 1990, 1.

341. Pub. L. 100-690, § 5301, 102 Stat. 4181, 4310-11 (1988).

342. "Talk," 27.

343. Office of National Drug Control Policy, *National*, 25.

344. *KCT*, Aug. 10, 1989, A12.

345. Wisotsky, "Crackdown," 919.

346. Stewart, "Are," in Trebach and Zeese, *New*, 38.

347. Dan Viets to Richard Lawrence Miller, telephone conversation, June 19, 1993.

348. Shawcross, "Closing Address for the United Kingdom, Great Britain, and Ireland," Red Supp. A, 68.

349. *Christian Science Monitor*, Feb. 2, 1990, 2.

350. H.B. 1095, 86th General Assembly, 2d sess.

351. 1952 N.J. Laws 230, pp. 776-79.

352. Kittrie, *Right*, 229.

353. Gordon, *Return*, 199.

354. Weyrauch, "Gestapo," 570 n. 41.

355. Salerno, "Policeman's," in Trebach and Zeese, *Great*, 65.

356. Bureau of Justice Statistics, *Drugs*, 184.

357. S.B. 460, 86th General Assembly, 2d sess.

358. 42 U.S.C.A. § 1437d(l)(5) (Supp. 1994).

359. Brecher and Editors of *Consumer Reports*, *Licit*, 419-20; Louria, *Overcoming*, 175-76.

360. Cotts, "Year," in Trebach and Zeese, *Strategies*, 85-86.

361. *Great Falls Tribune*, July 17, 1991, 1A.

362. *KCT*, Sept. 1, 1989, A2.

363. *NYT*, Aug. 13, 1935, 6.

364. Müller, *Hitler's*, 133-34.

365. Quoted in ibid., 156.

366. Husch, "Of," in Trebach and Zeese, *Drug Policy*, 232.

367. Beyerstein, "Mandatory," in *Faces*, 1.

368. *KCS*, April 4, 1991, A1, A10.

369. Johnson v. State, 838 P.2d 158, 173, 175 n. 12 (Wyo. 1992).

370. Rushworth v. Gnazzo, Suffolk (Massachusetts) Trial Court, Superior Court Dept., complaint for declaratory and injunctive relief (1991).

371. *SLPD*, Feb. 3, 1990, 5.

372. Com. v. Strunk, 582 A.2d 1326, 1334-35 (Pa. 1990) (Popovich, J., dissenting).

373. Quoted in Müller, *Hitler's*, 157.

374. Hunt and Chambers, *Heroin*, 98-99.

375. *KCS*, Sept. 5, 1991, C8.

376. Private communication to Richard Lawrence Miller.

377. Fraenkel, *Dual*, 28.

378. § 32-44, H.B. 445 (Perfected House Committee Substitute), 86th General Assembly, 1st sess.; *Missouri Lawyers Weekly*, March 18, 1991, 4 (5 M.L.W. 200).

379. Hume, "Reliability," in Trebach and Zeese, *New*, 320-21.

380. Schehr, "Economic," in Trebach and Zeese, *New*, 339.

381. Lusane, *Pipe*, 106-8.

382. Gieringer, "Urinalysis," in Trebach and Zeese, *Strategies*, 78-79.

383. § 32-44, H.B. 445 (Perfected House Committee Substitute), 86th General Assembly, 1st sess.

384. *NYT*, May 25, 1935, 1.

385. *NYT*, Dec. 17, 1935, 18.

386. Decision quoted in *Yellow*, 56-57.

387. The Anti-Drug Abuse Act of 1988 (Pub. L. 100-690, 102 Stat. 4181) requires such clauses from federal contractors. One study found such pressure to be a major factor in workplace drug testing; the study also found that the more power workers had, the less likely their employers would require drug testing (Schehr, "Economic," in Trebach and Zeese, *New*, 340, 341). That finding supports arguments that the war on drug users camouflages efforts to give employers more power over workers; employees whose safety may depend on the competence of fellow workers do not share management's interest in drug testing. Unions may accept drug testing simply as a negotiating ploy when bargaining with employers about other issues (Beyerstein, "Mandatory," in *Faces*, 2).

388. 49 C.F.R. § 219.211(d) (1987)).

389. Marcus, *Rise*, 15.
390. Red VI, 239.
391. Quoted in *KCS*, Jan. 3, 1993, A1.
392. Fraenkel, *Dual*, 90.
393. Roberts, *House*, 263.
394. *Missouri Farm Bureau News*, Jan. 1992, 13-14; *KCS*, May 22, 1995, B-1.
395. *The American Philatelist*, May 1992, 398, 400.
396. Peikoff, *Ominous*, 251; Miller, *Case*, 205 n. 14.
397. Office of National Drug Control Policy, *National*, 10-11.
398. *KCS*, June 16, 1989, 1A; William Bennett interview, "This Week with David Brinkley," telecast by National Broadcasting Company network, Dec. 17, 1989.
399. Quoted in *KCS*, Feb. 12, 1989, 14A.
400. Pichardo, "Viper," in Trebach and Zeese, *New*, 286, 287.
401. *KCS*, Feb. 12, 1989, 14A.
402. Pichardo, "Viper," in Trebach and Zeese, *New*, 287.
403. Red A, 71.
404. Hilberg, *Destruction*, 3-4.
405. Quoted in Massing, *Rehearsal*, 305.

Chapter 3: CONFISCATION

1. Jackson, "Address," 15.
2. In civil forfeiture proceedings, the person we would normally call the "owner" is called "claimant" because the government refuses to recognize the person's ownership of the property. Nonetheless, in this book the term "owner" refers to a person commonly understood as an owner.
3. Bush, "Impact," 1002; Strafer, "Civil," 841; Osburn, *Spectre*, 59.
4. Goldsmith, *Civil*, 2.
5. Osburn, *Spectre*, 59-60; Goldsmith, *Civil*, 18-19; 702 F.2d 1276, 1282; 691 F.2d 725, 728; Grantland, *Your*, 30 n. 59.
6. Myers and Brzostowski, *Drug* (1987), 15.
7. Goldsmith, *Civil*, 18-19; U.S. v. $250,000, 808 F.2d 895, 897 (1st Cir., 1987); U.S. v. A Single Family Residence, 803 F.2d 625, 628 (11th Cir. 1986); One Blue 1977 AMC Jeep v. U.S., 783 F.2d 759, 761 (8th Cir. 1986); *KCS*, Feb. 25, 1992, B6; "Jet Seized, Trashed, Offered Back for $66,000," *PP*, Aug. 11-16, 1991, reprint, p. 31.
8. Myers and Brzostowski, *Drug* (1987), 291.
9. Goldsmith, *Civil*, 18-19.
10. Boyd v. United States, 116 U.S. 616, 634 (1886).
11. One 1958 Plymouth v. Pennsylvania, 380 U.S. 693, 700 (1965).

12. U.S. v. McKee, 26 F. Cas. 1116 (C.C.E.D. Mo. 1877) (No. 15,688).

13. Cohen, "Constitutional," 952.

14. *Congressional Globe*, 37th Cong., 2d sess., April 24, 1862, p. 1809.

15. Ibid., April 19, 1862, p. 1859.

16. Ibid., May 22, 1862, App. p. 167.

17. Ibid., June 25, 1862, p. 2921.

18. Ibid., April 24, 1862, p. 1809.

19. Ibid., April 24, 1862, p. 1811.

20. Ch. LX, 12 Stat. 319 (1861); ch. CXCV, 12 Stat. 589 (1862); J. Res. 63, 12 Stat. 627 (1862).

21. Miller v. U.S., 78 U.S. (11 Wall.) 268 (1871).

22. Boyd v. U.S., 116 U.S. 616 (1886).

23. Ibid., 630.

24. Hoover v. People, 187 P. 531, 533 (1920).

25. Goldsmith-Grant v. U.S., 254 U.S. 505 (1921). The Court reserved judgment on whether railroad cars, ocean liners, and other vehicles of common carriers should be forfeited if a passenger possessed alcohol. Eventually Congress passed an innocent owner defense for common carriers, but those conveyances can still be forfeited if the "owner or person in control (captain, driver, conductor, pilot, etc.) knows of and acquiesces in the illegal use" (Myers and Brzostowski, *Drug* (1987), 86).

26. U.S. v. A Parcel of Land, 884 F.2d 41, 44 (1st Cir. 1989).

27. Carmona v. Ward, *cert. denied*, 439 U.S. 1091, 1096 (1979) (Marshall, J., dissenting).

28. U.S. v. One Single Family Residence, 731 F.Supp. 1563, 1573 (S.D.Fla. 1990).

29. U.S. v. One Single Family Residence, 995 F.2d 1558 (11th Cir. 1993).

30. 18 U.S.C.A. § 1961-1968 (1984).

31. 21 U.S.C.A. § 848 (1981).

32. Kevin D. Rooney to William J. Anderson, March 19, 1981, in GAO, "Asset," 60-61.

33. Markus, "Procedural," 1100 n. 12. Statute 21 U.S.C.A. 881(a)(4) (1994 Supp.) authorizes forfeiture of cars found with marijuana inside them.

34. Pub. L. 91-452, "Statement of Findings and Purpose," 84 Stat. 922 (1970).

35. 18 U.S.C. § 1961(1) (1982).

36. Osburn, *Spectre*, 117 n. 32.

37. U.S. v. Rubin, 559 F.2d 975, 991 n. 15 (5th Cir. 1977).

38. Pub. L. 91-452, § 904(a), 84 Stat. 947 (1970).

39. Sedima v. Imprex Co., 473 U.S. 479, 498 (1985).

40. Coffey, "Selection," 1036.

41. *SLPD*, April 29, 1991, 1, 4.

42. *SLPD*, Oct. 10, 1991, A10. The victim got his property back upon paying a $2,900 settlement fee after the forfeiture.

43. Marrero and Smith, *Introduction*, 3.

44. Myers and Brzostowski, *Drug* (1987), 7, 22.

45. Quoted in *KCS*, April 6, 1991, C8.

46. Ibid.

47. Maxeiner, "Bane," 769 n. 14.

48. U.S. v. McKee, 26 F. Cas. 1116 (C.C.E.D. Mo. 1877) (No. 15,688).

49. State v. One Porsche, 526 P.2d 917, 920 (1974).

50. U.S. v. One 1986 Mercedes, 846 F.2nd 2 (2nd Cir. 1988).

51. *KCS*, Feb. 25, 1992, B1.

52. U.S. v. One (1) 1984 Nissan 300 ZX, 711 F.Supp. 1570 (N.D.Ga. 1989).

53. U.S. v. One 1988 Ford Mustang, 728 F.Supp. 495 (N.D.Ill. 1989).

54. U.S. v. Tax Lot, 861 F.2d 232, 235 (9th Cir. 1988).

55. U.S. v. Premises, 869 F.2d 1093 (8th Cir. 1989).

56. U.S. v. One Parcel, 964 F.2d 814 (8th Cir. 1992).

57. U.S. v. On Leong, 918 F.2d 1289, 1298 (7th Cir. 1990) (Cudhay, J., concurring).

58. Cardozo, *Nature*, 51.

59. U.S. v. Halper, 490 U.S. 435 (1989).

60. *SLPD*, May 2, 1991, 4.

61. *SLPD*, May 3, 1991, 24.

62. U.S. v. Pryba, 900 F.2d 748 (4th Cir. 1990).

63. Quoted in *F.E.A.R. Chronicles*, v. 1, no. 5, p. 9.

64. *NewsBriefs*, Oct. 1992, 10.

65. *F.E.A.R. Chronicles*, v. 1, no. 5, p. 9, and May 1993, 3.

66. People v. Lindner, 535 N.E.2d 829, 833-34 (Ill. 1989); Johnson v. State, 838 P.2d 158, 180 (Wyo. 1992). Those courts' reasoning is supported by U.S. v. Halper 490 U.S. 435 (1989): "A defendant who already has been punished in a criminal prosecution may not be subjected to an additional civil sanction to the extent that the second sanction may not fairly be characterized as remedial, but only as a deterrent or punishment" (448-49), and "When the Government already has imposed a criminal penalty and seeks to impose additional punishment in a second proceeding, the Double Jeopardy Clause protects" (451 n. 10).

67. *KCS*, Sept. 19, 1988, A1, A5.

68. NMT 3051-PS (Red V, 800).

69. *SLPD*, April 29, 1991, 4.

70. Quoted in *SLPD*, May 2, 1991, p. 4.

71. "Government Seizures Victimize Innocent," *PP*, Aug. 11-16, 1991, reprint, p. 5.

72. *NYT*, Oct. 2, 1992, B1.

73. *KCS*, Oct. 3, 1993, A10.

74. *F.E.A.R. Chronicles*, v. 1, no. 5, p. 8.

75. *SLPD*, May 1, 1991, 1, 7.

76. GAO, *Asset Forfeiture: Customs*, passim.

77. *F.E.A.R. Chronicles*, v. 1, no. 5, p. 11; *NewsBriefs*, May 1993, 7, and July 1993, 11; Grantland, *Your*, 39 n. 69; Brenda Grantland to Richard Lawrence Miller, telephone conversation, Jan. 20, 1995. The businesswoman received a two-year prison sentence for possessing less than one ounce.

78. Grantland, *Your*, 41.

79. Myers and Brzostowski, *Drug* (1987), 43; 536 F.2d 1285 (1976).

80. Myers and Brzostowski, *Drug* (1987), 43, 47. The department warned against deliberate illegal seizure due to hazard of lawsuits holding drug squad members personally liable; the warning said nothing about an obligation that law enforcers might have to obey the law.

81. Quoted from U.S. v. One Custom Sport Fisherman, 543 F.Supp. 749 (E.D.Va. 1982).

82. *KCS*, Oct. 3, 1993, A11 (including quotation).

83. *NewsBriefs*, Oct. 1992, 11.

84. Quoted in *SLPD*, Oct. 10, 1991, 7.

85. Myers and Brzostowski, *Drug* (1981), cover; ibid., (1987), cover, 2.

86. NMT 841-PS.

87. Jack Anderson and Michael Binstein, "Forfeiture Program Becoming a Cash Cow," Washington Merry-Go-Round column, Feb. 1993; *F.E.A.R. Chronicles*, Nov. 1993, 12; Grantland, *Your*, 27.

88. *F.E.A.R. Chronicles*, Aug. 1992, 5.

89. NMT 841-PS.

90. Quoted in Osburn, *Spectre*, 2.

91. Grantland, *Your*, 18.

92. Ibid., 23-27; *F.E.A.R. Chronicles*, v. 1, no. 5, pp. 1 (wife quotation), 6, and May 1993, 1 (prosecutor quotation), 8, 10.

93. Osburn, *Spectre*, 1-2.

94. Ibid., 110.

95. *Christian Science Monitor*, Feb. 2, 1990, 2; *KCT*, Dec. 3, 1988, A18. Drug squad attacks on commercial oceangoing vessels resulted in one of the few reforms of tactics. The Anti-Drug Abuse Act of 1988 forbade such seizures if the sole grounds was a crew member having a small amount of drugs for personal use (Pub. L. 100-690, § 6079(d), 102 Stat. 4326 (1988)).

96. U.S. v. $2,355.96, 647 F.Supp. 1460 (E.D.Mo. 1986).

97. Application of Kingsley, 614 F.Supp 219, 226 (D.C.Mass. 1985).

98. Application of Kingsley, 802 F.2d 571, 582 (1st Cir. 1986) (Torruella, J., dissenting).

99. Application of Kingsley, 802 F.2d 571, 576 (1st Cir. 1986).

100. U.S. v. Real Estate, 903 F.2d 490 (7th Cir. 1990).

101. U.S. v. Real Property, 921 F.2d 1551, 1556 (11th Cir., 1991).

102. Osburn, *Spectre*, 119.

103. Quoted in "Talk," 27.

104. *KCT*, Dec. 3, 1988, A1.

105. Osburn, *Spectre*, 61.

106. Smith and Weiner, *Criminal*, 37 n. 43.

107. Red I, 10.

108. *NewsBriefs*, Oct. 1992, 11; Grantland, *Your*, 84-85.

109. Grantland, *Your*, 31-32.

110. "With Sketchy Data, Government Seizes House from Man's Heirs," *PP*, Aug. 11-16, 1991, reprint, p. 27.

111. Coffey v. U.S., 116 U.S. 436 (1886).

112. U.S. v. Dunn, 802 F.2d 646 (2nd Cir. 1986). See also U.S. v. One Assortment, 465 U.S. 354 (1984) and U.S. v. U.S. Currency, 895 F.2d 908, 916 (2nd Cir. 1990). Such a practice evades the long-standing U.S. v. McKee rule by substituting a fiction that civil forfeiture affects property rather than its owner, so the owner is not being punished with a civil sanction.

113. *SLPD*, April 29, 1991, 4.

114. U.S. v. One 1971 Porsche, 364 F.Supp. 745 (E.D.Pa. 1973).

115. Canavan, "Civil," 501 n. 107.

116. Jankowski, "Tempering," 189-91.

117. Grantland, *Your*, 86.

118. Calero-Toledo v. Pearson Yacht, 416 U.S. 663 (1974).

119. Goldsmith and Lenck, *Protection*, 19.

120. Ibid.

121. U.S. v. One 1982 Datsun 200SX, 627 F.Supp 62 (W.D.Pa. 1985), *aff'd mem.*, 782 F.2d 1032 (3d Cir. 1986).

122. U.S. v. One 1978 Chrysler, 531 F.Supp. 32 (E.D.N.Y. 1981).

123. Ibid., 34.

124. U.S. v. One 1957 Oldsmobile, 256 F.2d 931 (5th Cir. 1958).

125. U.S. v. One 1946 Plymouth, 73 F.Supp. 88, 89 (E.D.N.Y. 1946).

126. Devito v. U.S., 520 F.Supp. 127, 130 (E.D.Pa. 1981).

127. Goldsmith-Grant v. U.S., 254 U.S. 505 (1921). This forfeiture was run against a car used to transport an illegal drug, beverage alcohol.

128. "Police Profit by Seizing Homes of Innocent," *PP*, Aug. 11-16, 1991, reprint, pp. 16-17 (including quotation).

129. U.S. v. Two Parcels, 31 F.3d 35, 37, 40 (2nd Cir., 1994).

130. *LAT*, Jan. 12, 1992, K4.

131. U.S. v. Real Property, 940 F.2d 1537, 1991 WL 149509 (9th Cir., 1991); *LAT*, Jan. 12, 1992, K1, K4.

132. U.S. v. 141st Street Corp., 911 F.2d 870 (2d Cir. 1990).

133. U.S. v. Premises, 710 F.Supp. 46 (E.D.N.Y. 1989). This case was unusual because the court said the owner should be compensated for the forfeiture.

134. Grantland, *Your*, 84.

135. Ibid, 60-61.

136. Osburn, *Spectre*, 64-65.

137. U.S. v. Premises, 737 F.Supp. 749 (E.D.N.Y. 1990).

138. Reproduced in U.S. Senate, Com. on Governmental Affairs, *Effective-*

ness, 67.

139. "Police Profit by Seizing Homes of Innocent," *PP*, Aug. 11-16, 1991, reprint, p. 18.

140. Jankowski, "Tempering," 174 n. 43.

141. U.S. v. Angiulo, 897 F.2d 1169 (1st Cir. 1990).

142. Quoted in Grantland, *Your*, 73.

143. *F.E.A.R. Chronicles*, Aug. 1992, 2.

144. *PP*, Aug. 11-16, 1991, reprint, p. 6.

145. U.S. v. Horak, 833 F.2d 1235 (7th Cir. 1987); U.S. v. Kravitz, 738 F.2d 102 (3d Cir. 1984); U.S. v. Rubin, 559 F.2d 975, 992 (5th Cir. 1977) (vacated on other grounds).

146. U.S. v. One 1978 Chrysler, 531 F.Supp. 32 (E.D.N.Y. 1981).

147. Fletcher v. Peck, 10 U.S. (6 Cranch) 87, 138 (1810).

148. U.S. v. Stowell, 133 U.S. 1 (1890).

149. Palm, "RICO," 4 n. 15.

150. GAO, *Asset Forfeiture—A Seldom*, 9; Palm, "RICO," 4 n. 15.

151. NMT 342-PS, par. 6.

152. U.S. v. Campos, 859 F.2d 1233 (6th Cir. 1988); Osburn, *Spectre*, 61.

153. Skorcz, "RICO," 1200-1202, 1218.

154. Jankowski, "Tempering," 165.

155. Osburn, *Spectre*, 61.

156. Ibid., 62 n. 7; *LAT*, Ventura County ed., July 22, 1991, B1.

157. Grantland, *Your*, 119.

158. E.g., see $15 million in damages granted in Ricci v. Key, 662 F.Supp. 1132 (D.Me. 1987).

159. U.S. v. Delco, 772 F.Supp. 1511, 1516-17 (E.D.Pa. 1991).

160. Skorcz, "RICO," 1236.

161. Bush, "Impact," 996.

162. U.S. v. One Piece of Real Estate, 571 F.Supp. 723 (W.D.Tex. 1983); Jankowski, "Tempering," 178-79; Canavan, "Civil," 510-11.

163. Jankowski, "Tempering," 180-82.

164. U.S. v. Four Million, 762 F.2d 895 (11th Cir. 1985).

165. *SLPD*, Oct. 7, 1991, 6-7.

166. Ibid., 6.

167. "Drugs Contaminate Nearly All the Money in America," *PP*, Aug. 11-16, 1991, reprint, p. 15; Jones v. U.S., 819 F.Supp. 698, 719-21 (M.D.Tenn. 1993).

168. Jones v. U.S., 819 F.Supp. 698, 707, 720 (M.D.Tenn. 1993); *F.E.A.R. Chronicles*, v. 1, no. 5, p. 11.

169. Vallance, *Prohibition's*, 41.

170. *SLPD*, Oct. 7, 1991, 7.

171. "Drug Agents More Likely to Stop Minorities," *PP*, Aug. 11-16, 1991, reprint, pp. 12-13.

172. Ibid., 12; *NewsBriefs*, May 1993, 12; Jones v. U.S., 819 F.Supp. 698

(M.D.Tenn. 1993).

173. "Drugs Contaminate Nearly All the Money in America," *PP*, Aug. 11-16, 1991, reprint, p. 15.

174. "Government Seizures Victimize Innocent," *PP*, Aug. 11-16, 1991, reprint, pp. 5-6.

175. "Drugs Contaminate Nearly All the Money in America," *PP*, Aug. 11-16, 1991, reprint, p. 15.

176. "Government Seizures Victimize Innocent," *PP*, Aug. 11-16, 1991, reprint, p. 8. The U.S. Justice Department has contended that even federal courts cannot order return of wrongfully seized cash once it is distributed among law enforcement recipients (U.S. v. $12,390.00, 926 F.2d 801 (8th Cir., 1992).

177. "Police Profit by Seizing Homes of Innocent," *PP*, Aug. 11-16, 1991, reprint, pp. 18-19.

178. *NYT*, May 31, 1993, 10.

179. Quoted in U.S. v. James Daniel Good, 114 S.Ct. 492, 502 n. 2 (1993).

180. Quoted in *NYT*, May 31, 1993, 10.

181. *KCS*, April 6, 1991, C1, C8.

182. Caplin & Drysdale v. U.S., 491 U.S. 617, 629, 629 n. 6 (1989).

183. Kurisky, "Civil," 272-73.

184. Quoted in *KCT*, Sept. 2, 1989, B6.

185. *KCS*, Dec. 16, 1990, B9.

186. *New Times*, June 18, 1992, 13.

187. Quoted in *SLPD*, April 29, 1991, 4.

188. Quoted in *SLPD*, Oct. 6, 1991, 4.

189. Quoted in Baum, "Drug," 887.

190. Jeffrey Harris testimony, U.S. Senate, Judiciary Com., *DEA Oversight*, 37.

191. *KCS*, Jan. 2, 1994, B2.

192. Gallagher, *Management*, 4.

193. U.S. House, Com. on the Judiciary, *Federal*, 105.

194. Report reproduced in U.S. Senate, Com. on Governmental Operations, *Oversight*, 123.

195. Kurisky, "Civil," 272.

196. U.S. Senate, Com. on Governmental Affairs, *Disposition*, 5-6.

197. Grantland, *Your*, 19-20.

198. *KCT*, Dec. 3, 1988, A19.

199. Grantland, *Your*, 20.

200. Ibid., 21.

201. Quoted in *KCS*, Jan. 2, 1994, B2.

202. Dodaro, *Asset*, summary page.

203. NMT 4024-PS.

204. Bettelheim, "Individual," 427.

205. 1941 RGBl. I, 722, quoted in NMT NG-715; Hilberg, *Destruction*, 618.

206. Quoted in *SLPD*, May 5, 1991, 8.

207. Quoted in *SLPD*, May 3, 1991, 24.

208. Quoted in *KCS*, Nov. 22, 1990, C1.

209. Quoted in ibid.

210. Quoted in ibid., C4.

211. Quoted in *KCS*, Dec. 16, 1990, B1.

212. Quoted in ibid., B9.

213. Quoted in *KCS*, Jan. 2, 1994, B2.

214. J. William Gadsby, in U.S. Senate, Com. on Governmental Operations, *Oversight*, 9.

215. Gallagher, *Management*, 2-3.

216. Quoted in Jack Anderson and Michael Binstein, "Forfeiture Program Becoming a Cash Cow," Washington Merry-Go-Round column, Feb. 1993.

217. Quoted in *F.E.A.R. Chronicles*, July 1994, 8.

218. Quoted in ibid., 8.

219. Quoted in ibid., 10.

220. State v. One Porsche, 526 P.2d 917, 920 (1974).

221. "Government Seizures Victimize Innocent," *PP*, Aug. 11-16, 1991, reprint, pp. 4-5.

222. "Talk," 27.

223. Grantland, *Your*, 19-20.

224. *SLPD*, April 28, 1991, 1.

225. "Government Seizures Victimize Innocent," *PP*, Aug. 11-16, 1991, reprint, p. 6.

226. *NYT*, Aug. 2, 1992, 44.

227. Janzen, *Informants*, 21.

228. *LAT*, April 13, 1993, B8.

229. Adoption is authorized by 19 U.S.C.A. § 1616(a)(c) (Supp. 1994) and 21 U.S.C.A. § 881(e)(1)(A) (Supp. 1994).

230. Aylesworth, *Forfeiture*, 10 n.

231. Joseph W. Dean in U.S. House, Com. on the Judiciary, *Federal*, 15-17.

232. Quoted in "35 Arrested Despite Bumbling Ways of Informant," *PP*, Aug. 11-16, 1991, reprint, p. 26.

233. Quoted in *SLPD*, May 5, 1991, 1.

234. Quoted in U.S. Senate, Com. on Governmental Operations, *Oversight*, 28.

235. Aylesworth, *Forfeiture*, 11.

236. Quoted in *F.E.A.R. Chronicles*, July 1994, 8.

237. U.S. Senate, Com. on Governmental Affairs, *Effectiveness*, 2.

238. *SLPD*, May 5, 1991, 1.

239. *SLPD*, April 28, 1991, 6.

240. *KCT*, Sept. 2, 1989, B1.

241. *NewsBriefs*, June 1992, 6.

242. *KCS*, Dec. 16, 1990, B9.

243. *SLPD*, May 5, 1991, 8.

244. "Drug-Fighting Sheriff Puts Compassion before Forfeitures," *PP*, Aug. 11-16, 1991, reprint, p. 36.

245. *F.E.A.R. Chronicles*, May 1993, 9.

246. Quoted in "Government Seizures Victimize Innocent," *PP*, Aug. 11-16, 1991, reprint, p. 5.

247. George J. Terwilliger, III, in U.S. Senate, Com. on Governmental Affairs, *Effectiveness*, 20.

248. Ibid., 23.

249. *NYT*, April 21, 1991, I, 20.

250. U.S. Senate, Com. on Governmental Affairs, *Effectiveness*, 23, 57.

251. *KCS*, Jan. 2, 1994, B2.

252. GAO, *Asset Forfeiture: Noncash*, 4.

253. Quoted in *KCT*, Dec. 3, 1988, A19.

254. Quoted in ibid.

255. Quoted in U.S. Senate, Com. on Governmental Affairs, *Effectiveness*, 1.

256. Myers and Brzostowski, *Drug* (1987), 1.

257. Senate Judiciary Com., *DEA Oversight*, 37.

258. *SLPD*, April 30, 1991, 10; Grantland, *Your*, 72.

259. Janzen, *Informants*, 21.

260. *Liberty* (Missouri) *News*, April 13, 1994, 1.

261. *F.E.A.R. Chronicles*, v. 1, no. 5, p. 11.

262. "Drug Agents More Likely to Stop Minorities," *PP*, Aug. 11-16, 1991, reprint, p. 12.

263. "Government Seizures Victimize Innocent," *PP*, Aug. 11-16, 1991, reprint, p. 7.

264. Quoted in "Crime Pays Big for Informants in Forfeiture Drug Cases," *PP*, Aug. 11-16, 1991, reprint, p. 24.

265. Stolker, Sadighian, and Lenck, *Profile*, 8.

266. U.S. v. Van Lewis, 409 F.Supp. 535, 538 (E.D. Mich., S.D., 1976).

267. *NYT*, April 11, 1990, B5.

268. "Government Seizures Victimize Innocent," *PP*, Aug. 11-16, 1991, reprint, p. 7.

269. U.S. v. $191,910.00, 16 F.3d 1051 (9th Cir. 1994).

270. Quoted in "Crime Pays Big for Informants in Forfeiture Drug Cases," *PP*, Aug. 11-16, 1991, reprint, p. 23.

271. Finder's fees are authorized by 28 U.S.C.A. § 524(c)(1)(B) and § 524(c)(2) (1993).

272. Weyrauch, "Gestapo," 568-69.

273. Grantland, *Your*, 17.

274. "Crime Pays Big for Informants in Forfeiture Drug Cases," *PP*, Aug. 11-16, 1991, reprint, p. 24.

275. Quoted in *F.E.A.R. Chronicles*, no. 4, pp. 10-11.

276. *KCT*, Dec. 3, 1988, A18.

277. Grantland, *Your*, 96 n. 169.

278. Ibid., 85-86; *F.E.A.R. Chronicles*, no. 4, pp. 2-3.

279. Weyrauch, "Gestapo," 565.

280. Skolnick, *Justice*, 142.

281. Ibid.

282. Osburn, *Spectre*, 121.

283. A fastidious reader may argue that federal prosecutors convinced a court to allow the forfeiture after the plea bargain, and therefore it was legal. The same sort of reasoning was used by Nazi prosecutors and judges who underwent trial at Nuremberg, without avail.

284. Osburn, *Spectre*, 65.

285. *SLPD*, April 30, 1991, 10.

286. U.S. v. One (1) 1984 Nissan 300 ZX, 711 F.Supp. 1570 (N.D.Ga. 1989).

287. Laska v. U.S., 82 F.2d 672, 677 (10th Cir. 1936), quoted in Caplin & Drysdale v. U.S., 491 U.S. 617, 626-27 (1989).

288. Vella, "Caplin," 157 (emphasis supplied).

289. Caplin & Drysdale v. U.S., 109 S.Ct. 2667 (1989).

290. Finkelman, "War," in Trebach and Zeese, *New*, 117.

291. U.S. v. Long, 654 F.2d 911 (3rd Cir. 1981).

292. Grantland, *Your*, 41.

293. U.S. Senate, Judiciary Com., *DEA Oversight*, 96.

294. California Transport v. Trucking Unlimited, 404 U.S. 508 (1972); Mine Workers v. Illinois Bar Asn., 389 U.S. 217 (1967); Railroad Trainmen v. Virginia Bar, 377 U.S. 1 (1964); N.A.A.C.P. v. Button, 371 U.S. 415 (1963).

295. U.S. v. Monsanto, 852 F.2d 1400, 1404 (2nd Cir. 1988) (concurring opinion in a highly divided court).

296. U.S. v. Rogers, 602 F.Supp. 1332 (D.Colo. 1985).

297. U.S. v. Brodson, 241 F.2d 107, 115 (7th Cir. 1957) (Finnegan, J., dissenting). Significantly, that judicial attitude was expressed in a forfeiture predating the drug war.

298. Winick, "Forfeiture," 776-77.

299. Morris, "Attorney," 1045.

300. *KCS*, Feb. 4, 1992, B6.

301. *KCS*, Feb. 25, 1992, B1.

302. *F.E.A.R. Chronicles*, Nov. 1993, 6.

303. Osburn, *Spectre*, 86 n. 32.

304. Mennonite Board v. Adams, 462 U.S. 791 (1983).

305. Osburn, *Spectre*, 27-28, 138.

306. U.S. v. $8,850, 461 U.S. 555 (1983).

307. Osburn, *Spectre*, 59.

308. Ibid., 60.

309. Miller, "Foreword," in Osburn, *Spectre*, vi.

310. Goldsmith, *Civil*, 2.

311. Myers and Brzostowski, *Drug* (1987), 228.

312. Trebach, *Great*, 187-89.

313. U.S. Senate, Com. on Governmental Operations, *Oversight*, 4.

314. U.S. Senate, Com. on Governmental Affairs, *Federal*, 76-77.

315. Re Kingsley, 802 F.2d 571.

316. *F.E.A.R. Chronicles*, Aug. 1992, 6.

317. "Drug Agents More Likely to Stop Minorities," *PP*, Aug. 11-16, 1991, reprint, p. 12.

318. *F.E.A.R. Chronicles*, Aug. 1992, 6.

319. Osburn, *Spectre*, 1.

320. Szasz, *Our*, 24-25.

321. *SLPD*, April 28, 1991, 1, 6.

322. Strafer, "Civil," 841; Osburn, *Spectre*, 60.

323. *SLPD*, May 5, 1991, 8.

324. *KCS*, Oct. 3, 1993, A10.

325. "Jet Seized, Trashed, Offered Back for $66,000," *PP*, Aug. 11-16, 1991, reprint, pp. 31-32.

326. "Police Profit by Seizing Homes of Innocent," *PP*, Aug. 11-16, 1991, reprint, p. 19; *F.E.A.R. Chronicles*, Nov. 1993, 3; Grantland, *Your*, 115-18.

327. *Liberty* (Missouri) *Tribune*, Oct. 10, 1990, 4.

328. Osburn, *Spectre*, 85.

329. U.S. Constitution, Art. III, § 3, cl. 2 (see U.S. v. Thevis, 474 F.Supp. 134 (N.D.Ga. 1979) and U.S. v. Grande, 620 F.2d 1026, 1038-39 (4th Cir. 1980)); ch. IX, 1 Stat. 112, 117 (1790), codified at 18 U.S.C. § 3563 (1982) banned forfeiture of estate and was repealed by Pub. L. 98-473, tit. II, chap. II, § 212(a)(2), 98 Stat. 1987 (1984) and later replaced with 18 U.S.C. § 3554 (1988) and 21 U.S.C. § 853 (1988). Perhaps the Grande court, which said repeal of 18 U.S.C. § 3563 would be unconstitutional, was unaware of U.S. Senate, Report no. 617 (91st Cong., 1st sess., 1969, serial 12834-5), which on p. 160 said that RICO invalidated 18 U.S.C. 3563.

330. U.S. House, Judiciary Com., *Comprehensive*, 10-11.

331. Bush, "Impact," 1005.

332. *SLPD*, April 18, 1991, 1, and May 3, 1991, 1, 24.

333. *SLPD*, April 18, 1991, 1, and May 2, 1991, 4.

334. *SLPD*, April 18, 1991, 1.

335. Ibid., 6.

336. *SLPD*, April 29, 1991, 4.

337. Ibid.

338. Ibid.

339. Ibid.

340. Quoted in *SLPD*, April 30, 1991, 10.

341. Gallagher, *Management*, 3.

342. Ibid.

343. *SLPD*, Oct. 9, 1991, 1, 9.

344. "Government Seizures Victimize Innocent," *PP*, Aug. 11-16, 1991, reprint, p. 6.

345. *SLPD*, April 18, 1991, 1.

346. Quoted in *SLPD*, May 4, 1991, 7.

347. *SLPD*, April 30, 1991, 1.

348. *NYT*, Aug. 2, 1992, I, 37.

349. *SLPD*, Oct. 10, 1991, 1, 7.

350. Ibid., A10.

351. Ibid., 7.

352. *NewsBriefs*, Dec. 1992, 23.

353. *SLPD*, Oct. 11, 1991, 6.

354. *KCS*, Oct. 3, 1993, A10, A11.

355. Bryant, *Disclosing*, 8.

356. Gallagher, *Management*, 6.

357. *SLPD*, Oct. 6, 1991, 4.

358. *Washington Post*, Feb. 4, 1993, Classifieds 12.

359. *SLPD*, Oct. 6, 1991, 4 (including quotation); "35 Arrested Despite Bumbling Ways of Informant," *PP*, Aug. 11-16, 1991, reprint, pp. 25-26.

360. *KCS*, Dec. 17, 1991, B1.

361. Red V, 375; Stokes, "German," 176; "Protected," 90; Hoefer, "Nazi," 37.

362. Quoted in "Government Seizures Victimize Innocent," *PP*, Aug. 11-16, 1991, reprint, p. 6.

363. George J. Terwilliger, III, in U.S. Senate, Com. on Governmental Affairs, *Effectiveness*, 20.

364. 113 S.Ct. 2801 (1993).

365. 113 S.Ct. 1126 (1993).

366. Smith and Weiner, *Criminal*, 25

367. Quoted in *F.E.A.R. Chronicles*, Nov. 1993, 10.

368. Oct. 1944–Nov. 1945 (folder 6) War Crimes File, 41, Box 9, Samuel I. Rosenman Papers, Harry S. Truman Library.

369. Green III, p. 25 #28, p. 22 #16, p. 19 #9, p. 23 #21.

370. Lynch v. Household Finance, 405 U.S. 538, 552 (1971).

Chapter 4: CONCENTRATION

1. Bettelheim, "Individual," 440-41.

2. McWilliams, *Ain't*, 87 n.

3. Gordon, *Return*, 30-31.

4. Ibid., 33.

5. Ibid., 31-32; McWilliams, *Ain't*, 10; Baum, "Drug," 886.

6. Baum, "Drug," 886.

7. Reiss, "Military," in Trebach and Zeese, *Great*, 126.

8. House Committee Substitute for H.B. 1334 & 1473, 87th General Assembly, 2d sess.

9. *KCS*, Dec. 31, 1993, C1, C8.

10. S.B. 460, 86th General Assembly, 2d sess.

11. *KCS*, Jan. 29, 1990, 1A.

12. U.S. Senate, Judiciary Com., *DEA Oversight*, 38.

13. *Manchester Guardian Weekly*, June 19, 1994, 20.

14. Lawrence Sherman, quoted in *KCT*, Aug. 3, 1989, A20.

15. Burleigh and Wipperman, *Racial*, 224.

16. Ibid., 226, 239-40.

17. Pub. L. 100-690, § 5301, 102 Stat. 4311 (1988).

18. *KCS*, Aug. 3, 1994, A2.

19. Epstein, *Agency*, 43.

20. Ibid., 39, 43.

21. Quoted in *NYT*, July 18, 1969, 36.

22. Whiting, *War*, 38-39.

23. Fred MacDonald, quoted in Hohri, *Repairing*, 145.

24. Fischer, "West," 277.

25. Ch. III, 1 Stat. 103 (1790); Title XXX, Rev. Stat., § 2169; ch. 3592, 34 Stat. part I, 596 (1906); 8 U.S.C. § 703 (1940); Ozawa v. U.S., 260 U.S. 178 (1922).

26. Thomas and Nishimoto, *Spoilage*, 5.

27. Ibid., 6-7.

28. tenBroek, Barnhart, and Matson, *Prejudice*, 102; Commission on Wartime Relocation and Internment of Civilians, *Personal*, 70.

29. Presidential Proc. 2525, 6 Fed. Reg. 6321 (1941); Presidential Proc. 2526, 6 Fed. Reg. 6323 (1941); Presidential Proc. 2527, 6 Fed. Reg. 6324 (1941).

30. Quoted in tenBroek, Barnhart, and Matson, *Prejudice*, 105.

31. Executive Order 9066, 7 Fed. Reg. 1407 (1942).

32. Weglyn, *Years*, 69; Hohri, *Repairing*, 5-6.

33. Ch. 191, 56 Stat. 173 (1942).

34. Commission on Wartime Relocation and Internment of Civilians, *Personal*, 104 n.-105 n.; Hohri, *Repairing*, 166-67.

35. Korematsu v. U.S., 323 U.S. 214, 235 (1944) (Murphy, J., dissenting).

36. tenBroek, Barnhart, and Matson, *Prejudice*, 110.

37. Mary Tsukamoto in Tateishi, *And*, 7.

38. 7 Fed. Reg. 2601 (1942).

39. 7 Fed. Reg. 3967 (1942).

40. Korematsu v. U.S., 323 U.S. 214, 232 (1944) (Roberts, J., dissenting). See also dissent by Murphy, J., at 233.

41. Ibid., 243-44 (Jackson, J., dissenting).

42. Ibid., 230 (Roberts, J., dissenting).

43. 56 Stat. 173 (1942).

44. Ex parte Endo, 323 U.S. 283, 301 (1944).

45. Ibid.

46. Korematsu v. U.S., 323 U.S. 214, 246-47 (1944) (Jackson, J., dissenting).

47. Linfield, *Freedom*, 94.

48. Japanese, *Case*, 4-5.

49. George P. Clements to John Collier, Feb. 18, 1942, quoted in Hohri, *Repairing*, 133.

50. M. S. Eisenhower, "Memorandum for Members of Congress," April 20, 1942, SV Box 215, Harry S. Truman papers, Harry S. Truman Library.

51. Commission on Wartime Relocation and Internment of Civilians, *Personal*, 11; Weglyn, *Years*, 115-16.

52. Weglyn, *Years*, 115.

53. Tolan Committee, Report 2124, 155.

54. Weglyn, *Years*, 94, 99.

55. H. L. Strobel, Tolan Committee hearings, 11088.

56. James G. Bryant to Richard M. Neustadt, March 12, 1942, quoted in Tolan Committee hearings, 11048.

57. Quoted in Weglyn, *Years*, 97-99.

58. Quoted in Tateishi, *And*, 56.

59. Weglyn, *Years*, 98, 100.

60. Tadashi Tsufura quoted in Hohri, *Repairing*, 182.

61. tenBroek, Barnhart, and Matson, *Prejudice*, 125-26; Nagata, *Legacy*, 9; Tateishi, *And*, xxi, 130. Further rules governed Filipino-Japanese couples and couples with certain types of mixed genealogies (Taylor, *Jewel*, 85-86).

62. Thomas and Nishimoto, *Spoilage*, 91.

63. Quoted in ibid., 94.

64. Quoted in ibid., 94.

65. Quoted in ibid., 97-98.

66. Weglyn, *Years*, 91.

67. tenBroek, Barnhart, and Matson, *Prejudice*, 2.

68. Francis Biddle to Franklin Roosevelt, April 17, 1943, quoted in Weglyn, *Years*, 73, 200.

69. Commission on Wartime Relocation and Internment of Civilians, *Personal*, 9.

70. 7 Fed. Reg. 2601 (1942).

71. Green III, 1076.

72. Quoted in Korematsu v. U.S., 323 U.S. 214, 241 n. 15 (1944) (Murphy, J., dissenting). Similar sentiments were expressed by California Attorney General

Earl Warren (Tolan Committee hearings, 11011).

73. Japanese, *Case*, 58-59, 138.

74. Ibid., 60.

75. Ibid., 81.

76. Korematsu v. U.S., 323 U.S. 214, 225 (1944) (Frankfurter, J., concurring).

77. Ch. 1024, § 100-116, 64 Stat. 1019 (1950).

78. Ibid., § 114.

79. Linfield, *Freedom*, 80.

80. Presidential Proc. 2914, 15 Fed. Reg. 9029 (1950).

81. Linfield, *Freedom*, 130.

82. Epstein, *Agency*, 204.

83. Ibid., 299.

84. Ibid.

85. Ibid., 205 n.

86. Ibid., 207.

87. Ibid., 201.

88. U.S. v. Chambliss, 425 F.Supp. 1330, 1333 (E.D. Mich., S.D. 1977).

89. Egil Krogh, quoted in Epstein, *Agency*, 206.

90. Ibid., 143.

91. Quoted in Kirkpatrick, *Prosecution*, 33.

92. Epstein, *Agency*, 138-140.

93. See following Nixon era U.S. Code provisions: 8 U.S.C. § 1185; 10 U.S.C. § 333, 2304, 2733, 2734, 7224, 7722; 12 U.S.C. § 95a; 18 U.S.C. § 1383; 40 U.S.C. § 484; 41 U.S.C. § 252; 42 U.S.C. § 217, 266; 47 U.S.C. § 606(c); 50 U.S.C. § 191, 1435, app. § 5, 19, 785. See also Senate Special Com., *Emergency*, 9-10, 47-63, 189, 374, 388, 404, 413-14; Senate Special Com., *Executive*, 5, 139; Senate Special Com., Rpt. 1170, 2,4. Some cited U.S. Code emergency provisions could have been activated due to the still-continuing Korean War emergency and the Vietnam War. After Watergate abuses were exposed, Congress repealed some national emergency laws that Nixon would have relied upon, but those laws could be reenacted; they were never declared unconstitutional.

94. Epstein, *Agency*, 203.

95. Conversation, Sept. 15, 1972, *Submission*, 65-66.

96. Epstein, *Agency*, 252.

97. Ibid., 165.

98. U.S. Senate, Com. on Governmental Operations, Rpt. 1039, 55.

99. U.S. House, Com. on Government Operations, Rpt. 228, 2.

100. Ibid., 3.

101. Ibid., 3, 9.

102. Quoted in U.S. Senate, Com. on Governmental Operations, Rpt. 1039, 35.

103. Ibid., 55.

104. Kirkpatrick, *Prosecution*, 29 n.

105. Eugene Rosside, quoted in Epstein, *Agency*, 241.

106. Trebach, *Great*, 141.

107. Schroeder, *Politics*, 136; *ITT*, Sept. 13, 1989, 4.

108. *NYT*, June 8, 1986, I, 1.

109. U.S. Senate, Select Com., Hearings, 122.

110. Linfield, *Freedom*, 167. See also *KCS*, July 5, 1987, A1, A15.

111. Quoted in May, *In*, 63. This was not the first time that zealots had proposed using war powers to accomplish what was otherwise forbidden by the Constitution. Whiting's classic *War Powers under the Constitution* argued that slavery could be ended forever by using war powers during a temporary war.

112. Ch. 53, § 15, 40 Stat. 282 (1917).

113. Ch. 212, 40 Stat. 1046 (1918).

114. May, *In*, 66.

115. Ch. 212, 40 Stat. 1046 (1918).

116. *Congressional Record*, 65th Cong., 2d sess., Aug. 29, 1918, p. 9650.

117. Quoted in May, *In*, 72.

118. *NYT*, Nov. 20, 1918, 14.

119. Quoted in May, *In*, 73.

120. Ibid., 73.

121. Ch. 85, 41 Stat. 305 (1919).

122. May, *In*, 87.

123. Ibid., 88.

124. 50 U.S.C. app. § 1622 (Supp. III, 1985).

125. U.S. v. Reynolds, 345 U.S. 1, 10 (1952); U.S. v. Nixon, 418 U.S. 683, 710-11 (1974); May, *In*, 260.

Chapter 5: ANNIHILATION

1. Burleigh and Wippermann, *Racial*, 84; 94-96.

2. Schleunes, *Twisted*, 171-73.

3. Ibid., 178-79.

4. Skolnick, *Justice*, 139-40.

5. Weyrauch, "Gestapo," 595 n. 110.

6. Skolnick, *Justice*, 161.

7. Szasz, *Our*, 91.

8. Red VI, 37-38.

9. Emergency Defense Council of Seattle Chapter Japanese-American Citizens League, Tolan Committee hearings, 11463-64.

10. Philip Bancroft, quoted in Tolan Committee hearings, 11243.

11. Skolnick, *Justice*, 125.

12. Schleunes, *Twisted*, 5.

13. Hilberg, *Destruction*, 56.

14. Diary entry Feb. 27, 1935, Fromm, *Blood*, 189.

15. *KCT*, Sept. 1, 1989, A2.

16. *KCS*, July 22, 1992, A1, A11, and July 24, 1992, C2.

17. *KCS*, July 26, 1994, B1, and July 29, 1994, A13.

18. 1981 & Supp. 1994 N.J. Laws 30:4c-11.

19. Green, *Doped*, 61.

20. Becker and Hora, "What's," in *Faces*, 1, 7; *KCS*, May 23, 1989, A7.

21. Becker and Hora, "What's," in *Faces*, 6.

22. Ibid., 5.

23. Green, *Doped*, 60-61.

24. Quoted in Willwerth, "Should," 62-63.

25. Letter, *Nation* 249 (1989): 38.

26. "Effects of Alcohol and Cannabis during Labor," *Journal of the American Medical Association* 94 (1930): 1165.

27. Willwerth, "Should," 63.

28. S.B. 9, 86th General Assembly, 1st sess.

29. Viets, "Human," in Trebach and Zeese, *New*, 34-35.

30. Ibid., 35.

31. Quoted in *NYT*, Aug. 22, 1986, A6.

32. Szasz, *Our*, 79.

33. Quoted in *NYT*, Aug. 22, 1986, A6.

34. U.S. House, Com. on Education and Labor, Rpt. 572, 2.

35. Marx and DeJong, *Invitation*, 4.

36. *Drug Policy Letter*, Spring 1995, 14–15.

37. *NewsBriefs*, June 1992, 8.

38. *NewsBriefs*, Nov. 1992, 9.

39. *NewsBriefs*, Feb. 1993, 5.

40. *Drug Policy Letter*, Spring 1994, 30.

41. *NewsBriefs*, Feb. 1993, 16.

42. *Riverfront Times*, Oct. 13, 1993, 2.

43. Viets, "Human," in Trebach and Zeese, *New*, 35.

44. Quoted in Szasz, *Our*, 78.

45. Quoted in Wisotsky, "Crackdown," 915.

46. Quoted in *NYT*, May 19, 1989, I, 12.

47. Quoted in ibid.

48. Gordon, *Return*, 39; *Drug Policy Letter*, Spring 1995, 23.

49. Waln, *Reaching*, 80.

50. Heck, *Burden*, 44, 238.

51. Quoted in Boas, "Shrinking," 256.

52. Green III, 1076.

53. Ibid., 21, #15.

54. Ibid., 20, #10.

55. Schloendorff v. Society of New York Hospitals, 105 N.E. 92 (N.Y. 1914).

56. Kleber, "Nosology," 58-59; Zinberg, *Drug*, 38-39, 208.

57. Robinson v. California, 370 U.S. 660, 667 (1962).

58. Green, *Doped*, 43.

59. *NYT*, Jan. 21, 1994, A12.

60. Green, *Doped*, 44, 57. See also Beckett, "Pregnant," in Trebach and Zeese, *Strategies*, 187.

61. Green, *Doped*, 45. See also Paltrow, "Reproductive," in Trebach and Zeese, *Strategies*, 193; Becker and Hora, "What's," in *Faces*, 4.

62. Muraskin, "Mothers," in Trebach and Zeese, *New*, 213; Paltrow, "Reproductive," in Trebach and Zeese, *Strategies*, 189-91.

63. Beckett, "Pregnant," in Trebach and Zeese, *Strategies*, 187; Paltrow, "Reproductive," in Trebach and Zeese, *Strategies*, 194; *SLPD*, April 20, 1991, 6.

64. Paltrow, "Reproductive," in Trebach and Zeese, *Strategies*, 191.

65. Green, *Doped*, 56.

66. Ibid., 57.

67. Ibid., 55.

68. Paltrow, "Reproductive," in Trebach and Zeese, *Strategies*, 189.

69. *NYT*, Jan. 21, 1994, A12.

70. Green, *Doped*, 44-45.

71. Ibid., 80-81.

72. Ibid., xv, 80-81; Beckett, "Pregnant," in Trebach and Zeese, *Strategies*, 187. See also Paltrow, "Reproductive," in Trebach and Zeese, *Strategies*, 194; Becker and Hora, "What's," in *Faces*, 4; Willwerth, "Should," 63; *NYT*, April 3, 1991, A15; *ITT*, Feb. 7, 1990, 7.

73. *NYT*, April 3, 1991, A15.

74. Green, *Doped*, 36.

75. Sugarman and Powers, "How," 3326.

76. S. 1444, 101st Cong., 1989.

77. *KCS*, Aug. 26, 1989, A6.

78. Proctor, *Racial*, 107.

79. Willwerth, "Should," 62; *KCS*, Feb. 28, 1992, C2.

80. Becker and Hora, "What's," in *Faces*, 2; *KCS*, Sept. 26, 1991, A1, A16.

81. Letter, *Pediatrics* 85 (1990): 232.

82. Kolder, Gallagher, and Parsons, "Court," 1195; *KCS*, Dec. 31, 1993, A1, A9.

83. Green, *Doped*, 34.

84. Quoted in Bradbury and Foley, "American," in Trebach and Zeese, *Strategies*, 271.

85. Schwartz, "Marijuana," 314.

86. Schwartz, "Psychoactive," 205. See also Schwartz, Hoffmann, and Jones, "Behavioral,"266.

87. Description of Group C in Schwartz et al., "Short," 1215; Trebach, *Great*, 19. See also 37, 38.

88. Schwartz, "Reply," 158.

89. Trebach, *Great*, 62, 58, 29. See also *LAT*, March 24, 1990, A1.

90. Trebach, *Great*, 41.

91. Schwartz et al., "Short," 1215.

92. Collins v. Straight, 748 F.2d 916, 918 (1984); Trebach, *Great*, 33, 58.

93. Trebach, *Great*, 32.

94. Ibid., 32.

95. Schwartz, "Reply," 158. See also Bradbury and Foley, "American," in Trebach and Zeese, *Strategies*, 269-70.

96. Trebach, *Great*, 35. See also *Washington Post*, Sept. 30, 1990, B8.

97. Trebach, *Great*, 41.

98. Ibid., 38. See also *Washington Post*, Feb. 3, 1991.

99. Trebach, *Great*, 38, 42. See also *Washington Post*, Sept. 30, 1990, B8, and Feb. 3, 1991; *LAT*, March 24, 1990, A1.

100. *Washington Post*, Oct. 16, 1986, C1.

101. Trebach, *Great*, 38, 42.

102. Schwartz et al., "Self-Harm," 342, 344.

103. Ibid., 344.

104. See Miller, "When," in Trebach and Zeese, *New*, 39-42.

105. Schwartz, Hayden, and Riddile, "Laboratory Detection," 1093.

106. Schwartz et al., "Short," 1215.

107. Trebach, *Great*, 39, 40; *LAT*, March 24, 1990, A1. See also Bradbury and Foley, "American," in Trebach and Zeese, *Strategies*, 271.

108. Collins v. Straight, 748 F.2d 916, 918 (1984); Trebach, *Great*, 34, 39, 41, 44.

109. Trebach, *Great*, 59.

110. Ibid., 57.

111. Straight denied Zak's statement (*LAT*, March 24, 1990, A1).

112. Quoted in Trebach, *Great*, 58.

113. Collins v. Straight, 748 F.2d 916 (1984).

114. Vincent A. Fulginiti to Richard Lawrence Miller, May 31, 1990, author's files.

115. "Richard," front matter.

116. Schwartz and Riddile, "Marijuana," 206; Schwartz, "Comments," 262.

117. *Manchester Guardian Weekly*, Jan. 10, 1993, 3, and June 12, 1994, 9; Morris, Cook, and Shaper, "Loss," 1135-39; Wilkinson, "Divided," 1113-14. See also Bower, "Growing," 24-25; Phillimore, Beattie, and Townsend, "Widening," 1125-28.

118. Viets, "Human," in Trebach and Zeese, *New*, 36-37.

119. Grantland, *Your*, 204-5.

120. Skolnick, "Some," 3177-78.

121. Quoted in Grantland, *Your*, 50.

122. Ibid., 46.

123. Grinspoon and Bakalar, *Marihuana*, is an excellent modern treatment of medical marijuana claims.

124. Proctor, *Racial*, 193.

125. Epstein, *Agency*, 219-20.

126. Ibid., 96-97.

127. Ibid., 141-42.

128. Quoted in ibid., 144.

129. Ibid., 289.

130. Ibid., 146.

131. Ibid., 144.

132. Ibid., 205, 289.

133. Ibid., 289.

134. *ITT*, Sept. 13, 1989, 4, and Nov. 15, 1989, 3; Trebach, "When," in Trebach and Zeese, *Drug Prohibition*, 183.

135. *KCS*, June 16, 1989, 1A.

136. Quoted in Trebach, "When," in Trebach and Zeese, *Drug Prohibition*, 183.

137. William Bennett interview, "This Week With David Brinkley," telecast by National Broadcasting Company network, Dec. 17, 1989.

138. *KCS*, Aug. 29, 1992, C1.

139. Testimony, U.S. Senate, Judiciary Com., *One*, 77.

140. *ITT*, Sept. 19, 1990, 6.

141. Quoted in Domanick, "Field," 39.

142. Hilberg, *Destruction*, 761.

Coda: THE CREATION OF UTOPIA

1. Waln, *Reaching*, 59-60.

2. Kershaw, "Persecution," 289.

3. Weinreich, *Hitler's*, 164.

4. Schleunes, *Twisted*, 261

5. Neumann, *Behemoth*, 437, 438.

6. Heck, *Burden*, 248.

7. Quoted in Karst, "Why," 289.

SOURCES

Where full citations are given in notes, those sources are not repeated here.

BOOKS

Alexander, Bruce K. *Peaceful Measures: Canada's Way Out of the "War on Drugs."* Toronto: University of Toronto Press, 1990.

Anslinger, Harry J., and Will Oursler. *The Murderers: The Story of the Narcotics Gangs*. New York: Farrar, Straus and Cudahy, 1961.

Bakalar, James B., and Lester Grinspoon. *Drug Control in a Free Society*. Cambridge: Cambridge University Press, 1984.

Biernacki, Patrick. *Pathways from Heroin Addition: Recovery without Treatment*. Health, Society, and Policy, edited by Sheryl Ruzek and Irving Kenneth Zola. Philadelphia: Temple University Press, 1986.

Bloomquist, Edward R. *Marijuana: The Second Trip*. Rev. ed. Beverly Hills: Glencoe Press, 1971.

Blum, Richard H., et al. *Society and Drugs: Drugs I: Social and Cultural Observations*. The Jossey-Bass Behavioral Science Series. San Francisco: Jossey-Bass, 1969.

————. *Students and Drugs: College and High School Observations*. The Jossey-Bass Behavioral Science Series and the Jossey-Bass Series in Higher Education (published jointly). San Francisco: Jossey-Bass, 1969.

Boaz, David, ed. *The Crisis in Drug Prohibition*. 2nd ed. Washington: Cato Institute, 1991.

Brecher, Edward M., and the Editors of *Consumer Reports*. *Licit and Illicit Drugs: The Consumers Union Report on Narcotics, Stimulants, Depressants, Inhalants, Hallucinogens, and Marijuana—Including Caffeine, Nicotine, and Alcohol*. Boston: Little, Brown and Company, 1972.

Burleigh, Michael, and Wolfgang Wippermann. *The Racial State: Germany 1933-1945*. Cambridge: Cambridge University Press, 1991.

Cardozo, Benjamin N. *The Nature of the Judicial Process*. New Haven: Yale University Press, 1921.

Carter, William E., ed. *Cannabis in Costa Rica: A Study of Chronic Marihuana Use*. Philadelphia: Institute for the Study of Humane Issues, 1980.

Chein, Isidor, et al. *The Road to H: Narcotics, Delinquency, and Social Policy*. New York: Basic Books, 1964.

Crothers, T. D. *Morphinism and Narcomanias from Other Drugs*. Philadelphia: W.B. Saunders and Company, 1902.

Dicks, Henry V. *Licensed Mass Murder: A Socio-Psychological Study of Some SS Killers*. The Columbus Centre Series. Studies in the Dynamics of Persecution and Extermination. General editor Norman Cohn. New York: Basic Books, 1972.

Dreher, Melanie Creagan. *Working Men and Ganja: Marihuana Use in Rural Jamaica*. Philadelphia: Institute for the Study of Human Issues, 1982.

Duster, Troy. *The Legislation of Morality: Law, Drugs, and Moral Judgment*. New York: Free Press, 1970.

Ebenstein, William. *The Nazi State*. New York: Farrar & Rinehart, 1943.

Engelmann, Bernt. *In Hitler's Germany: Everyday Life in the Third Reich*. Translated by Krishna Winston. New York: Schocken Books, 1986.

Epstein, Edward Jay. *Agency of Fear: Opiates and Political Power in America*. New York: G. P. Putnam's Sons, 1977.

Erickson, Patricia G., et al. *The Steel Drug: Cocaine in Perspective*. Lexington Books. Lexington, Mass.: D. C. Heath and Company, 1987.

The Faces of Change. Washington, DC: Drug Policy Foundation, 1993.

Feldman, Harvey W., Michael H. Agar, and George M. Beschner, eds. *Angel Dust: An Ethnographic Study of PCP Users*. Lexington, Mass.: D. C. Heath and Company, 1979.

Fraenkel, Ernst. *The Dual State: A Contribution to the Theory of Dictatorship*. Translated by E. A. Shils, Edith Lowenstein, and Klaus Knorr. New York: Oxford University Press, 1941.

Fredborg, Arvid. *Behind the Steel Wall: A Swedish Journalist in Berlin 1941-43*. New York: The Viking Press, 1944.

Fromm, Bela. *Blood and Banquets: A Berlin Social Diary*. 1943. Reprint. A Birch Lane Press Book. New York: Carol Publishing Group, 1990.

Gellately, Robert. *The Gestapo and German Society: Enforcing Racial Policy 1933-1945*. Oxford: Oxford University Press, 1990.

Germany Speaks. London: T. Butterworth, Ltd., 1938.

Girard, René. *The Scapegoat*. Translated by Yvonne Freccero. Baltimore: Johns Hopkins University Press, 1986.

Girdner, Audrie, and Anne Loftis. *The Great Betrayal: The Evacuation of the Japanese-Americans during World War II*. New York: Macmillan Company, 1969.

Gisevius, Hans Bernd. *To the Bitter End*. Translated by Richard Winston and

Clara Winston. Boston: Houghton Mifflin Company, 1947.

Goodman, Louis S., and Alfred Gilman. *The Pharmacological Basis of Therapeutics*. 6th and 7th eds. New York: Macmillan Company, 1980 and 1985.

Gordon, Diana R. *The Return of the Dangerous Classes: Drug Prohibition and Policy Politics*. New York: W. W. Norton & Company, 1994.

Grantland, Brenda. *Your House Is under Arrest: How Police Can Seize Your Home, Car, and Business Without a Trial—and How to Protect Yourself.* Burnsville, Minn.: The Institute for the Preservation of Wealth, 1993.

Green, Valerie. *Doped Up, Knocked Up, and . . . Locked Up? The Criminal Prosecution of Women Who Use Drugs during Pregnancy*. Children of Poverty: Studies and Dissertations on the Effects of Single Parenthood, the Feminization of Poverty, and Homelessness, edited by Stuart Bruchey. New York: Garland Publishing, 1993.

Grinspoon, Lester, and James B. Bakalar. *Cocaine: A Drug and Its Social Evolution*. New York: Basic Books, 1976.

———. *Marihuana: The Forbidden Medicine*. New Haven: Yale University Press, 1993.

Grunberger, Richard. *The 12-Year Reich: A Social History of Nazi Germany 1933-1945*. New York: Holt, Rinehart and Winston, 1971.

Heck, Alfons. *The Burden of Hitler's Legacy*. Frederick, Colo.: Renaissance House Publishers, 1988.

Henderson, Bruce Griffin. *Waiting*. New York: Plume-Penguin, 1995.

Henry, Frances. *Victims and Neighbors: A Small Town in Nazi Germany Remembered*. South Hadley, Mass.: Bergin & Garvey, 1984.

Heymann, C. David. *A Woman Named Jackie*. New York: Lyle Stuart, 1989.

Hilberg, Raul. *The Destruction of the European Jews*. 1961. Reprint. Chicago: Quadrangle Books, 1967.

Hohri, William Minoru. *Repairing America: An Account of the Movement for Japanese-American Redress*. Pullman, Wash.: Washington State University Press, 1988.

Hunt, Leon Gibson, and Carl D. Chambers. *The Heroin Epidemics: A Study of Heroin Use in the United States, 1965-75*. Sociomedical Science Series. New York: Spectrum Publications, 1976.

Japanese American Citizens League. *The Case for the Nisei*. N.p.: The League, ca. 1944. [Amicus brief in Korematsu case.]

Johnston, Lloyd. *Drugs and American Youth*. Ann Arbor: Institute for Social Research, University of Michigan, 1973.

Kandel, Denise B., ed. *Longitudinal Research on Drug Use: Empirical Findings and Methodological Issues*. Washington: Hemisphere Publishing Corporation, 1978.

Kaplan, John. *Marijuana—The New Prohibition*. New York: World Publishing Company, 1970.

Kershaw, Ian. *Popular Opinion and Political Dissent in the Third Reich: Bavaria 1933-1945*. Oxford: Clarendon Press, 1983.

King, Rufus. *The Drug Hang-Up: America's Fifty Year Folly*. New York: W. W. Norton & Company, 1972.

Kirkpatrick, Thomas B., Jr. *Prosecution Perspectives on Drugs*. Washington: The Drug Abuse Council, 1975.

Kittrie, Nicholas N. *The Right to Be Different: Deviance and Enforced Therapy*. Baltimore: Johns Hopkins University Press, 1971.

Kolb, Lawrence. *Drug Addiction: A Medical Problem*. Springfield, Ill.: Charles C. Thomas, 1962.

Kühl, Stefan. *The Nazi Connection: Eugenics, American Racism, and German National Socialism*. New York: Oxford University Press, 1994.

Lifton, Robert. *The Nazi Doctors: Medical Killing and the Psychology of Genocide*. New York: Basic Books, 1986.

Linfield, Michael. *Freedom under Fire: U.S. Civil Liberties in Times of War*. Boston: South End Press, 1990.

Louria, Donald B. *Overcoming Drugs: A Program for Action*. New York: McGraw-Hill Book Company, 1971.

Lusane, Clarence. *Pipe Dream Blues: Racism and the War on Drugs*. Boston: South End Press, 1991.

McWilliams, Peter. *Ain't Nobody's Business If You Do*. Los Angeles: Prelude Press, 1993.

Magruder, Jeb Stuart. *An American Life: One Man's Road to Watergate*. New York: Atheneum, 1974.

Marcus, Jacob R. *The Rise and Destiny of the German Jew*. Cincinnati: Union of American Hebrew Congregations, 1934.

Marx, Fritz Morstein. *Government in the Third Reich*. Second edition, revised and enlarged. McGraw-Hill Studies in Political Science, edited by Fritz Morstein Marx. New York: McGraw-Hill Book Company, 1937.

Massing, Paul W. *Rehearsal for Destruction: A Study of Political Anti-Semitism in Imperial Germany*. Studies in Prejudice, edited by Max Horkheimer and Samuel H. Flowerman. American Jewish Committee Social Studies Series, Publication No. 11. New York: Harper & Brothers, 1949.

May, Christopher N. *In the Name of War: Judicial Review and the War Powers since 1918*. Cambridge, Mass.: Harvard University Press, 1989.

Miller, Richard Lawrence. *The Case for Legalizing Drugs*. New York: Praeger, 1991.

Morgan, H. Wyane. *Drugs in America: A Social History, 1800-1980*. Syracuse, N.Y.: Syracuse University Press, 1981.

————, ed. *Yesterday's Addicts: American Society and Drug Abuse 1865-1920*. Norman: University of Oklahoma Press, 1974.

Müller, Ingo. *Hitler's Justice: The Courts of the Third Reich*. Translated by Deborah Lucas Schneider. Cambridge, Mass.: Harvard University Press,

1991.

Musto, David F. *The American Disease: Origins of Narcotic Control*. New Haven: Yale University Press, 1973.

Nagata, Donna K. *Legacy of Injustice: Exploring the Cross-Generational Impact of the Japanese American Internment*. Critical Issues in Social Justice, edited by Melvin J. Lerner and Riël Vermunts. New York: Plenum Press, 1993.

Neumann, Franz. *Behemoth: The Structure and Practice of National Socialism 1933-1944*. 1944. Reprint. 2d ed. with new Appendix. New York: Octagon Books, 1963.

Osburn, Judy. *Spectre of Forfeiture*. Frazier Park, Calif.: Access Unlimited, 1991.

Peele, Stanton, with Archie Brodsky. *Love and Addiction*. New York: Taplinger Publishing Company, 1975.

Peikoff, Leonard. *The Ominous Parallels: The End of Freedom in America*. 1982. Reprint. New York: New American Library, 1983.

Platt, Jerome J., and Christina Labate. *Heroin Addiction: Theory, Research, Treatment*. Wiley Series on Personality Processes, A Wiley Interscience Publication. New York: John Wiley & Sons, 1976.

Proctor, Robert N. *Racial Hygiene: Medicine Under the Nazis*. Cambridge, Mass.: Harvard University Press, 1988.

Roberts, Stephen H. *The House that Hitler Built*. New York: Harper & Brothers, 1938.

Rubin, Vera, ed. *Cannabis and Culture*. The Hague: Mouton Publishers, 1975.

Rublowsky, John. *The Stoned Age: A History of Drugs in America*. Capricorn Books. New York: G. P. Putnam's Sons, 1974.

Schleunes, Karl A. *The Twisted Road to Auschwitz: Nazi Policy toward German Jews 1933-1939*. Urbana: University of Illinois Press, 1970.

Schroeder, Richard C. *The Politics of Drugs: An American Dilemma*. 2d ed. Washington: Congressional Quarterly Press, 1980.

Schur, Edwin N. *Narcotic Addiction in Britain and America: The Impact of Public Policy*. Bloomington: Indiana University Press, 1962.

Siegel, Ronald K. *Intoxication: Life in Pursuit of Artificial Paradise*. New York: Dutton, 1989.

Sjöqvist, Folke, and Malcolm Tottie, eds. *Abuse of Central Stimulants*. New York: Raven Press, 1969.

Skolnick, Jerome H. *Justice without Trial: Law Enforcement in Democratic Society*. New York: John Wiley & Sons, 1966.

Szasz, Thomas. *Ceremonial Chemistry: The Ritual Persecution of Drugs, Addicts, and Pushers*. Rev. ed. Holmes Beach, Fla.: Learning Publications, 1985.

————. *Our Right to Drugs: The Case for a Free Market*. New York: Praeger, 1992.

Tateishi, John. *And Justice for All: An Oral History of the Japanese American Detention Camps*. New York: Random House, 1984.

Taylor, Sandra C. *Jewel of the Desert: Japanese American Internment at Topaz*. Berkeley: University of California Press, 1993.

Taylor, Whitney A., and Kevonne Small, comps. *The Crucial Next Stage: Health Care & Human Rights*. Washington: Drug Policy Foundation, 1994.

tenBroek, Jacobus, Edward N. Barnhart, and Floyd W. Matson. *Prejudice, War and the Constitution*. Japanese American Evacuation and Resettlement, vol 3. Berkeley: University of California Press, 1958.

Thomas, Dorothy Swaine, and Richard S. Nishimoto. *The Spoilage*. Japanese American Evacuation and Resettlement, vol 1. Berkeley: University of California Press, 1946.

Thornton, Mark. *The Economics of Prohibition*. Salt Lake City: University of Utah Press, 1991.

Trebach, Arnold S. *The Great Drug War and Radical Proposals that Could Make America Safe Again*. New York: Macmillan Company, 1987.

Trebach, Arnold S., and Kevin B. Zeese, eds. *Drug Policy 1989-1990: A Reformer's Catalogue*. Washington: The Drug Policy Foundation, 1989.

———. *Drug Prohibition and the Conscience of Nations*. Washington: The Drug Policy Foundation, 1990.

———. *The Great Issues of Drug Policy*. Washington: The Drug Policy Foundation, 1990.

———. *New Frontiers in Drug Policy*. Washington: The Drug Policy Foundation, 1991.

———. *Strategies for Change: New Directions in Drug Policy*. Washington: The Drug Policy Foundation, 1992.

Vallance, Theodore R. *Prohibition's Second Failure: The Quest for a Rational and Humane Drug Policy*. Westport, Conn.: Praeger, 1993.

Van Paassen, Pierre, and James Waterman Wise, eds. *Nazism: An Assault on Civilization*. New York: Harrison Smith and Robert Haas, 1934.

Waln, Nora. *Reaching for the Stars*. Boston: Little, Brown and Company, 1939.

Weglyn, Michi. *Years of Infamy: The Untold Story of America's Concentration Camps*. New York: William Morrow and Company, 1976.

Weil, Andrew. *The Natural Mind: An Investigation of Drugs and the Higher Consciousness*. Rev. ed. Boston: Houghton Mifflin Company, 1986.

Weinreich, Max. *Hitler's Professors: The Part of Scholarship in Germany's Crimes against the Jewish People*. New York: Yiddish Scientific Institute—YIVO, 1946.

Whiting, William. *War Powers under the Constitution of the United States*. 1864. Reprint. 10th ed. A Rio Grande Press Special. Glorieta, N.M.: The Rio Grande Press, 1971.

The Yellow Spot: The Outlawing of Half a Million Human Beings: A Collection of Facts and Documents Relating to Three Years' Persecution of German Jews, Derived Chiefly from National Socialist Sources, Very Carefully Assembled by a Group of Investigators. New York: Knight Publications, 1936.

Zimring, Franklin E., and Hawkins, Gordon. *The Search for Rational Drug Control*. An Earl Warren Legal Institute Study. New York: Cambridge University Press, 1992.

Zinberg, Norman E. *Drug, Set, and Setting: The Basis for Controlled Intoxicant Use*. New Haven: Yale University Press, 1984.

UNITED STATES GOVERNMENT DOCUMENTS

Aylesworth, George N. *Forfeiture of Real Property: An Overview*. Vol. 14 of *Asset Forfeiture*. Washington: Justice Department, 1991. [SuDocs J26.29:14]

Bryant, Wanda G. *Disclosing Hidden Assets: Plea Bargains and Use of the Polygraph*. Vol. 5 of *Asset Forfeiture*. Washington: Justice Department, 1989. [SuDocs J26.29:5]

Bureau of Justice Statistics. *Drugs, Crime, and the Justice System: A National Report*. Washington: Justice Department, 1992. [SuDocs J29.2:D84/3]

Bush, George. *Public Papers of the Presidents of the United States: George Bush, 1989*. Washington: Government Printing Office, 1990.

Clouet, Doris H., ed. *Phencyclidine: An Update*. National Institute on Drug Abuse, Research Monograph Series, no. 64. Rockville, Md.: The Institute, 1986. [SuDocs HE20.8216:64]

Commission on Wartime Relocation and Internment of Civilians. *Personal Justice Denied: Report of the Commission on Wartime Relocation and Internment of Civilians*. Washington: Government Printing Office, 1982. [SuDocs Y3.W19/10:J98]

Department of State. *Foreign Relations of the United States, 1933-1939*. Washington: Government Printing Office, 1949-1955. [SuDocs S1.1: 1933-1939]

Dodaro, Gene L. *Asset Forfeiture Programs: Progress and Problems*. Washington: General Accounting Office, 1988. [SuDocs GA1.5/2:T-GGD-88-41]

Gallagher, G. Patrick. *The Management and Disposition of Seized Assets*. Vol. 3 of *Asset Forfeiture*. Washington: Justice Department, 1988. [SuDocs J26.29:3]

General Accounting Office (GAO). *Asset Forfeiture—a Seldom Used Tool in Combating Drug Trafficking*. Washington: General Accounting Office, 1981. [SuDocs GA1.13:GGD81-51]

———. *Asset Forfeiture: Customs Reports Improved Controls over Sales of Forfeited Property*. Washington: General Accounting Office, 1991. [SuDocs GA1.13:GGD-91127]

———. *Asset Forfeiture: Noncash Property Should Be Consolidated Under the Marshals Service*. Washington: General Accounting Office, 1991. [SuDocs GA1.13:GGD-9197]

Goldsmith, Michael. *Civil Forfeiture: Tracing the Proceeds of Narcotics Trafficking*. Revised. ed. Vol. 1 of *Asset Forfeiture*. Washington: Justice Department, 1992. [SuDocs J26.29:1]

Goldsmith, Michael, and William Lenck. *Protection of Third-Party Rights*. Vol. 12 of *Asset Forfeiture*. Washington: Justice Department, 1990. [SuDocs J26.29:12]

Gust, Steven W., and J. Michael Walsh, eds. *Drugs in the Workplace*. National Institute on Drug Abuse, Research Monograph Series, no. 91. Rockville, Md.: The Institute, 1989. [SuDocs HE20.8216:91]

Harris, Louis S., ed. *Problems of Drug Dependence, 1980: Proceedings of the 42nd Annual Scientific Meeting, the Committee on Problems of Drug Dependence, Inc.* National Institute on Drug Abuse, Research Monograph Series, no. 34. Rockville, Md.: The Institute, 1981. [SuDocs HE 20.8216:34]

Janzen, Sandra. *Informants and Undercover Investigations*. Vol. 13 of *Asset Forfeiture*. Washington: Justice Department, 1992. [SuDocs J26.29:13]

Marrero, Juan C., and David B. Smith, eds. *Introduction to Civil Statutes*. Vol. 1 of *Forfeitures*. Washington: Justice Department, 1984. [SuDocs J1.2:F76/3]

Marx, Eva, and William DeJong. *An Invitation to Project DARE: Drug Abuse Resistance Education*. Program Brief. Washington: Bureau of Justice Assistance, Justice Department, 1988.

Myers, Harry L., and Joseph P. Brzostowski. *Drug Agents' Guide to Forfeiture of Assets*. Washington: Justice Department, 1981. [SuDocs J24.8:D84/6]

———. *Drug Agents' Guide to Forfeiture of Assets*. 1987 ed. Revised by William M. Leuck. Washington: Justice Department, 1987. [SuDocs J24.8:D84/6/987]

National Institute on Drug Abuse. *National Household Survey on Drug Abuse, Population Estimates 1990*. Rockville, Md.: The Institute, 1991. [DHHS Publication No. (ADM) 91-1732]

Nixon, Richard M. *Public Papers of the Presidents of the United States: Richard Nixon, 1970*. Washington: Government Printing Office, 1971.

Office of National Drug Control Policy. *National Drug Control Strategy*. Washington: Government Printing Office, 1989. [SuDocs PrEx1.2: D84]

Office of United States Chief of Counsel for Prosecution of Axis Criminality, International Military Trials. *Nazi Conspiracy and Aggression*. 8 vols. and 3 supplements. Washington: Government Printing Office, 1946. (Red series.)

Petersen, Robert C., and Richard C. Stillman, eds. *PCP: Phencyclidine Abuse: An Appraisal*. National Institute on Drug Abuse, Research Monograph Series, no. 21. Rockville, Md.: The Institute, 1978. [SuDocs HE20.8216:21]

Reagan, Ronald. *Public Papers of the Presidents of the United States: Ronald Reagan, 1988*. Washington: Government Printing Office, 1991.

Richards, Louise G. *Demographic Trends and Drug Abuse, 1980-1995*. Rockville, Maryland: National Institute on Drug Abuse, Research Monograph

Series, no. 35. Rockville, Md.: The Institute, 1981. [SuDocs HE20.8216:35]

Smith, David, and Edward C. Weiner. *Criminal Forfeitures under the RICO and Continuing Criminal Enterprise Statutes*. Washington, DC: Justice Department, 1980. [SuDocs J1.2:R11]

Stolker, Richard, Joseph Sadighian, and William Lenck. *Profile Factors After "Sokolow."* Vol. 10 of *Asset Forfeiture*. Washington: Justice Department, 1989. [SuDocs J26.29:10]

Submission of Recorded Presidential Conversations to the Committee on the Judiciary of the House of Representatives by President Richard Nixon, April 30, 1974. Washington: White House, 1974. [SuDocs Pr37.2:C76]

Trials of War Criminals before the Nuernberg Military Tribunals Under Control Council Law No. 10: Nuremberg, October 1946–April 1949. 15 vols. Washington: Government Printing Office, 1949-1953. (Green series.)

U.S. House. Committee on Education and Labor. *Drug Abuse Resistance Education Act of 1990*. Report. 101st Cong., 2d sess. H. Rpt. 572. Serial 14014.

———. Committee on Government Operations. *Approving Reorganization Plan No. 2 of 1973*. 93rd Cong., 1st sess., 1973. H. Rpt. 228.

———. Committee on the Judiciary. *Comprehensive Drug Penalty Act of 1984*. Report. 98th Cong., 2d sess. H. Rpt. 845, pt. 1. Serial 13593.

———. Hearings. *Federal Drug Forfeiture Activities*. 101st Cong., 1st sess., 1989. [SuDocs Y4.J89/1:101/55]

U.S. House. Select Committee on Crime. Hearings. *The Improvement and Reform of Law Enforcement and Criminal Justice in the United States*. 91st Cong., 1st sess., 1969. [SuDocs Y4.C86/3:L41]

———. Select Committee Investigating National Defense Migration [Tolan Committee]. Hearings. 77th Cong, 2d sess., 1941-1942. [SuDocs Y4.N21/5:M58/pts. 29-31]

———. Report. 77th Cong., 2d sess., 1942. H. Rpt. 2124. Serial 10668.

U.S. Senate. Committee on Governmental Affairs. Com. print. *Disposition of Seized Cash Management in the Customs Service and the Justice Department*. 100th Cong., 1st sess., 1987. S. Rpt. 36. [SuDocs Y4.G74/9:S.prt.100-36]

———. Hearing. *The Effectiveness of the Management of Asset Forfeiture Programs at the Justice and Treasury Departments*. 102d Cong., 1st sess., 1991. [SuDocs Y4.G74/9:S.hrg.102-756]

———. Subcommittee on Federal Spending, Budget, and Accounting. Hearing. *Federal Government's Forfeiture Programs Seized Cash and Forfeited Property Management*. Hearing. 100th Cong., 1st sess., 1987. [SuDocs Y4.G74/9:S.hrg.100-400]

U.S. Senate. Committee on Governmental Operations. Hearing. *Oversight of "High Risk" Asset Forfeiture Programs at the Justice Department and the Customs Service*. 101st Cong., 2d sess., 1990. [SuDocs Y4.G74/9:S.hrg.101-1000]

————. Report. *Federal Narcotics Enforcement*. 94th Cong., 2d sess., 1976. S. Rpt. 1039. Serial 13132.

U.S. Senate. Committee on the Judiciary. Hearings. *One-Year Drug Strategy Review*. 101st Cong., 2d sess., 1990. [SuDocs Y4.J89/2:S.hrg. 101-1206]

————. Subcommittee on Improvements in the Federal Criminal Code. Hearings. *Illicit Narcotics Traffic*. 84th Cong., 1st sess., 1955. [SuDocs Y4.J89/2:N16/1-10]

————. Subcommittee on Security and Terrorism. Hearings. *DEA Oversight and Budget Authorization: Hearing on Drug Enforcement Administration Oversight and Budget Authorization and S. 2320*. 97th Cong., 2d sess., 1982. [SuDocs Y4.J89/2:J97-112]

U.S. Senate. Select Committee on Secret Military Assistance to Iran and the Nicaraguan Opposition and U.S. House, Select Committee to Investigate Covert Arms Transactions with Iran. Hearings. July 10, 13, and 14, 1987. 100th Cong., 1st sess., 1987. [SuDocs Y4.IN8/20: 100-7/pt.2]

U.S. Senate. Special Committee on National Emergencies and Delegated Emergency Powers. Report. 93rd Cong., 2d sess., 1974. S. Rpt. 1170. Serial 13057-8.

————. Report. *Executive Orders in Times of War and National Emergency*. 93rd Cong., 2d sess., 1974. S. Rpt. 1280.

U.S. Senate. Special Committee on the Termination of the National Emergency. Report. *Emergency Powers Statutes: Provisions of Federal Law Now in Effect Delegating to the Executive Extraordinary Authority in Time of National Emergency*. 93rd Cong., 1st sess., 1973. S. Rpt. 549. Serial 13019-5.

U.S. Sentencing Commission. *Guidelines Manual*. Washington: The Commission, 1992. [SuDocs Y3.SE5:8G94/992]

————. *Special Report to the Congress: Mandatory Minimum Penalties in the Federal Criminal Justice System*. August 1991. [SuDocs Y3.SE5:2P37]

Wright, Hamilton. *Report on the International Opium Commission and on the Opium Problem as Seen within the United States and Its Possessions*. Published in *Opium Problem. Message from the President of the United States*. 61st Cong., 2d sess., 1910. S. Doc. 377.

JOURNALS AND PERIODICALS

Ames, Frances. "A Clinical and Metabolic Study of Acute Intoxication with *Cannabis Sativa* and Its Role in the Model Psychoses." *Journal of Mental Science* 104 (1958): 976.

Arntzen, F. I. "Some Psychological Aspects of Nicotinism." *American Journal of Psychology* 61 (1948): 424-25.

Baum, Dan. "The Drug War On Civil Liberties." *Nation* 254 (1992): 886-88.

Bennett, James V. "Notes on the German Legal and Penal System." *Journal of Criminal Law and Criminology* 37 (1947): 368-74.

Bernstein, Steven K. "Fourth Amendment—Using the Drug Courier Profile to Fight the War on Drugs." *Journal of Criminal Law & Criminology* 80 (1990): 996–1017.

Bettelheim, Bruno. "Individual and Mass Behavior in Extreme Situations." *Journal of Abnormal and Social Psychology* 38 (1943): 417-52.

Blair, Thomas S. "The Relation of Drug Addiction to Industry." *Journal of Industrial Hygiene* 1 (Oct. 1919): 284-96.

Boas, Jacob. "The Shrinking World of German Jewry, 1933-1938." *Leo Baeck Institute Year Book* 31 (1986): 241–66.

Bonavoglia, Angela. "The Ordeal of Pamela Rae Stewart." *Ms.* (July/Aug. 1987): 92-95, 196-98, 200-204.

Bower, Bruce. "Drugs of Choice." *Science News* 136 (1989): 392-93.

———. "Growing Up Poor." *Science News* 146 (July 9, 1994): 24-25.

Brill, Henry, and Tetsuya Hirose. "The Rise and Fall of a Methamphetamine Epidemic, Japan 1944-55." *Seminars in Psychiatry* 1 (1969): 179-94.

Brill, Norman Q., and Richard L. Christie. "Marihuana Use and Psychosocial Adaption: Follow-up Study of a Collegiate Population." *Archives of General Psychiatry* 31 (1974): 713.

Bush, Graeme W. "The Impact of RICO Forfeiture on Legitimate Business." *Notre Dame Law Review* 65 (1990): 996–1008.

Canavan, Patricia M. "Civil Forfeiture of Real Property: The Government's Weapon against Drug Traffickers Injures Innocent Owners." *Pace Law Review* 10 (1990): 485–519.

Chopra, I. C., and R. N. Chopra. "The Use of the Cannabis Drugs in India." *Bulletin on Narcotics* 9 (Jan.–March 1957): 13

"The Cocaine Habit among the Negroes." *British Medical Journal* (Nov. 19, 1902): 1729.

Coffey, Paul E. "The Selection, Analysis, and Approval of Federal RICO Prosecutions." *Notre Dame Law Review* 65 (1990): 1035-49.

Cohen, Michael Paul Austern. "The Constitutional Infirmity of RICO Forfeiture." *Washington & Lee University Law Review* 46 (1989): 937–59.

Cotts, Cynthia. "Hard Sell in The Drug War." *Nation* 254 (1992): 300-302.

Crancer, Alfred, et al. "Comparison of the Effects of Marihuana and Alcohol on Simulated Driving Performance." *Science* 164 (1969): 851-54.

Cutting, Windsor C. "Morphine Addiction for 62 Years." *Stanford Medical Bulletin* 1 (Aug. 1942): 39-41.

Domanick, Joe. "Field Marshal Daryl Gates." *Mother Jones* (July/Aug. 1991): 39.

Earle, Charles W. "The Opium Habit: A Statistical and Clinical Lecture." *Chicago Medical Review* 2 (1880): 442-46.

Ennett, Susan T., et al. "How Effective Is Drug Abuse Resistance Education?

A Meta-Analysis of Project DARE Outcome Evaluations." *American Journal of Public Health* 84 (Sept. 1994): 1394-1401.

Fischer, Louis. "West Coast Perspective." *Nation* 154 (March 7, 1942): 276-77.

Gill, Andrew M,. and Robert J. Michaels. "Does Drug Use Lower Wages?" *Industrial and Labor Relations Review* 45 (April 1992): 419.

Hoefer, Frederick. "The Nazi Penal System—II." *Journal of Criminal Law, Criminology, and Police Science* 36 (1945): 30-38.

Horgan, John. "An Antidrug Message Gets Its Facts Wrong." *Scientific American* 262 (May 1990): 36.

———. "Test Negative: A Look at the 'Evidence' Justifying Illicit-Drug Tests." *Scientific American* (March 1990): 18.

Ishii, Akio, and Nobuo Motohashi. "Drug Abuse in Japan." *Addictive Diseases* 3 (1977): 105-14.

Jackson, Robert. "Address." *Proceedings of the American Society of International Law* (1945): 10-18.

Jankowski, Mark A. "Tempering the Relation-Back Doctrine: A More Reasonable Approach to Civil Forfeiture in Drug Cases." *Virginia Law Review* 76 (1990): 165–96.

Jaspers, Karl. "The Fight against Totalitarianism." *Confluence* 3 (1954): 251-66.

Kaestner, Robert. "The Effect of Illicit Drug Use on the Wages of Young Adults." *Journal of Labor Economics* 9 (1991): 381.

Kagel, John H., Raymond Battalio, and C. G. Miles. "Marihuana and Work Performance: Results from an Experiment." *Journal of Human Resources* 15 (1980): 373, 390.

Karst, Kenneth L. "Why Equality Matters." *Georgia Law Review* 17 (1983): 289.

Kato, Masaaki. "An Epidemiological Analysis of the Fluctuation of Drug Dependence in Japan." *International Journal of the Addictions* 4 (1969): 591-621.

Kershaw, Ian. "The Persecution of the Jews and German Popular Opinion in the Third Reich." *Leo Baeck Institute Yearbook* 26 (1981): 261–89.

Kestenberg, Milton. "Legal Aspects of Child Persecution during the Holocaust." *Journal of the American Academy of Child Psychiatry* 24 (1985): 381-84.

Kirchheimer, Otto. "Criminal Law in National-Socialist Germany." *Studies in Philosophy and Social Science* 8 (1939-1940): 444-63.

Kleber, Herbert. "The Nosology of Abuse and Dependence." *Journal of Psychiatric Research* 24 (1990, supp. 2): 57-64.

Kolder, Veronika, E. B., Janet Gallagher, and Michael T. Parsons. "Court-Ordered Obstetrical Interventions." *New England Journal of Medicine* 316 (1987): 1192-96.

Koren, Gideon, et al. "Bias against the Null Hypothesis: The Reproductive Hazards of Cocaine." *Lancet* (Dec. 16, 1989): 1440-42.

Kurisky, George A., Jr. "Civil Forfeiture of Assets: A Final Solution to International Drug Trafficking?" *Houston Journal of International Law* 10

(1988): 239-73.

LaCroix, Susan. "Birth of a Bad Idea: Jailing Mothers for Drug Abuse." *Nation* 248 (1989): 585-88.

Lending, Patricia M. "Drug Courier Profiles in Airport Stops: Legitimate Equivalents of Reasonable Suspicion?" *Southwestern University Law Review* 14 (1984): 353.

Lillie-Blanton, Marsha, James C. Anthony, and Charles R. Schuster. "Probing the Meaning of Racial/Ethnic Group Comparisons in Crack Cocaine Smoking." *Journal of the American Medical Association* 269 (1993): 993-97.

Loewenstein, Karl. "Reconstruction of the Administration of Justice in American-Occupied Germany." *Harvard Law Review* 61 (1948): 419-67.

McGlothlin, William H., and David O. Arnold. "LSD Revisited—A Ten-Year Follow-Up of Medical LSD Use." *Archives of General Psychiatry* 24 (1971): 43-49.

Markus, Eric R. "Procedural Implications of Forfeiture under RICO, the CCE, and the Comprehensive Forfeiture Act of 1984: Reforming the Trial Structure." *Temple Law Review* 59 (1986): 1097-1130.

Maxeiner, James R. "Bane of American Forfeiture Law—Banished at Last?" *Cornell Law Review* 62 (1977): 768-802.

Mayes, Linda C. "The Problem of Prenatal Cocaine Exposure: A Rush to Judgment." *Journal of the American Medical Association* 267 (Jan. 15, 1992): 406-8.

Morris, David M. "Attorney Fee Forfeiture." *Columbia Law Review* 86 (1986): 1021-50.

Morris, Joan K., Derek G. Cook, and A. Gerald Shaper. "Loss of Employment and Mortality." *British Medical Journal* 308 (April 30, 1994): 1135-39.

O'Rourke, P. J. "Taking Drugs—Seriously." *Rolling Stone* (Nov. 30, 1989): 57-58, 61, 63.

Owens, S. Michael, Arthur J. McBay, and Clarence E. Cook. "The Use of Marihuana, Ethanol, and Other Drugs among Drivers Killed in Single-Vehicle Crashes." *Journal of Forensic Sciences* 28 (1983): 372-79.

Palm, Craig W. "RICO Forfeiture and the Eighth Amendment: When Is Everything Too Much?" *University of Pittsburgh Law Review* 53 (1991): 1-95.

Parish, David Charles. "Relation of the Pre-employment Drug Testing Result to Employment Status: A One-year Follow-up." *Journal of General Internal Medicine* 4 (1989): 44-47.

Phillimore, Peter, Alastair Beattie, and Peter Townsend. "Widening Inequality of Health in Northern England, 1981-91." *British Medical Journal* 308 (April 30, 1994): 1125-28.

Picton, Harold. "Justice in Nazi Germany." *Contemporary Review* 156 (1939): 437-46.

Pope, Harrison G., Jr., Martin Ionescu-Pioggia, and Jonathan D. Cole, "Drug Use and Life-Style among College Undergraduates: Nine Years Later." *Archives of General Psychiatry* 38 (1981): 588-91.

Porter, Bruce. "Blow." *Rolling Stone* (July 8, 1993): 84.

Primorac, Max. "The Cuban Drug Connection." *American Legion Magazine* (April 1989): 18.

"Protected by Hitler: An Unbiased Account of a Real Experience." *Current History* (June 1936): 83-90.

Rankin, Anne. "The Effect of Pretrial Detention." *New York University Law Review* 39 (1964): 641-55.

Raymond, Chris. "Researchers Say Debate over Drug War and Legalization Is Tied to Americans' Cultural and Religious Values." *Chronicle of Higher Education* 36 (March 7, 1990): A6-A7, A10-A11.

Register, Charles A., and Donald R. Williams. "Labor Market Effects of Marijuana and Cocaine Use Among Young Men." *Industrial and Labor Relations Review* 45 (April 1992): 435.

Rhodes, Steve. "Public Service, Private Ideologies." *EXTRA!* (July–Aug. 1991): 14.

"Richard H. Schwartz, MD: Practitioner-Researcher." *Clinical Pediatrics* 28 (Dec. 1989): front matter.

Sager, Mike. "The State of Michigan vs. Gary Fannon: A Tragic Miscarriage of Justice Continues." *Rolling Stone* (Sept. 2, 1993): 51-53, 70.

Sanders, Clinton R. "Doper's Wonderland: Functional Drug Use by Military Personnel in Vietnam." *Journal of Drug Issues* 3 (Winter 1973): 71-72.

Schlosser, Eric. "Reefer Madness." *Atlantic Monthly* 274 (Aug. 1994): 45-63.

Schwartz, Richard H. "Comments on Cannabis Intoxication in Pets." *Veterinary and Human Toxicology* 31 (1989): 262.

———. "Marijuana: An Overview." *Pediatric Clinics of North America* 34 (1987): 314.

———. "Psychoactive Drug Use during Adolescence: The Pediatrician's Role." *American Journal of Diseases of Children* 138 (1984): 205.

———. "Reply." *Journal of Pediatrics* 111 (1987): 158.

Schwartz, Richard H., Gregory F. Hayden, and Mel Riddile. "Laboratory Detection of Marijuana Use: Experience With a Photometric Immunoassay to Measure Urinary Cannabinoids." *American Journal of Diseases of Children* 139 (1985): 1093.

Schwartz, Richard H., Norman G. Hoffmann, and Richard Jones. "Behavioral, Psychosocial, and Academic Correlates of Marijuana Usage in Adolescence: A Study of a Cohort under Treatment." *Clinical Pediatrics* 26 (1987): 266.

Schwartz, Richard H., and Mel Riddile. "Marijuana Intoxication in Pets." *Journal of the American Veterinary Medical Association* 187 (1985): 206.

Schwartz, Richard H., et al. "Self-Harm Behavior (Carving) in Female Adolescent Drug Abusers." *Clinical Pediatrics* 28 (1989): 342, 344.

———. "Short-Term Memory Impairment in Cannabis-Dependent Adolescents." *American Journal of Diseases of Children* 143 (1989): 1215.

Simonton, Thomas G. "The Increase of the Use of Cocaine among the Laity in

Pittsburg." *Philadelphia Medical Journal* 11 (1903): 556.

Skolnick, Andrew A. "Some Experts Suggest the Nation's 'War on Drugs' Is Helping Tuberculosis Stage a Deadly Comeback." *Journal of the American Medical Association* 268 (1992): 3177-78.

Skorcz, Elizabeth A. "RICO Forfeiture: Secured Lenders Beware." *University of California at Los Angeles Law Review* 37 (1990): 1200-36.

Smart, Reginald G. "Drinking Problems among Employed, Unemployed and Shift Workers." *Journal of Occupational Medicine* 21 (1979): 731.

Smith, David E. "Cocaine-Alcohol Abuse: Epidemiological, Diagnostic and Treatment Considerations." *Journal of Psychoactive Drugs* 18 (April–June 1986): 117-18.

Stanley, L. L. "Morphinism and Crime." *Journal of the American Institute of Criminal Law and Criminology* 8 (1918): 753.

Stokes, Lawrence D. "The German People and the Destruction of the European Jews." *Central European History* 6 (1973): 167-91.

Strafer, G. Richard. "Civil Forfeitures: Protecting the Innocent Owner." *University of Florida Law Review* 37 (1985): 841.

Sugarman, Jeremy, and Madison Powers. "How the Doctor Got Gagged: The Disintegrating Right of Privacy in the Physician-Patient Relationship." *Journal of the American Medical Association* 266 (1991): 3326.

Sutton, Lawrence R. "The Effects of Alcohol, Marihuana and Their Combination on Driving Ability." *Journal of Studies on Alcohol* 44 (1983): 438-45.

"Talk of the Town." *New Yorker* 67 (April 29, 1991): 27-28.

Tarlow, Barry. "RICO Revisited." *Georgia Law Review* 17 (1983): 291-424.

Thombs, Dennis L. "A Review of PCP Abuse Trends and Perceptions." *Public Health Reports* 104 (1989): 327.

Vella, Anthony G. "Caplin & Drysdale, Chartered, v. United States: Seizing Attorney Fees—Frozen Assets or Frozen Justice? The Sixth Amendment Right to Counsel of Choice Is Given the Cold Shoulder." *Northern Illinois University Law Review* 11 (1990): 157.

Viani, F., et al. "Drug Abuse in Adolescence: Some Remarks on Individual Psychopathology and Family Structure." *Acta Paedopsychiatrica* 42 (Oct. 1976): 145-51.

Weyrauch, Otto Walter. "Gestapo Informants: Facts and Theory of Undercover Operations." *Columbia Journal of Transnational Law* 24 (1986): 553-96.

Wiggs, James W. "The Treatment of Opioid Dependence: Try Prison, It's Cheaper—or Is It?" *Journal of the American Medical Association* 268 (1992): 2376.

Wilkinson, Richard G. "Divided We Fall." *British Medical Journal* 308 (April 30, 1994): 1113-14.

Willwerth, James. "Should We Take Away Their Kids?" *Time* 137 (May 13, 1991): 62-63.

Winick, Bruce J. "Forfeiture of Attorneys' Fees Under RICO and CCE and the

Right to Counsel of Choice: The Constitutional Dilemma and How to Avoid It." *University of Miami Law Review* 43 (1989): 765–869.

Winsløw, Jens J. B. "Drug Use and Social Integration." *International Journal of the Addictions* 9 (1974): 531-40.

Wisotsky, Steven. "Crackdown: The Emerging 'Drug Exception' to the Bill of Rights." *Hastings Law Journal* 38 (1987): 889–926.

Zinberg, Norman E., and Richard C. Jacobson. "The Natural History of 'Chipping.'" *American Journal of Psychiatry* 133 (1976): 37-40.

Zinberg, Norman E., and D. C. Lewis. "Narcotic Usage: I. A Spectrum of a Difficult Medical Problem." *New England Journal of Medicine* 270 (1964): 989-93.

INDEX

About the Author

RICHARD LAWRENCE MILLER is an independent scholar. He is the author of *Heritage of Fear: Illusion and Reality in the Cold War* (1988), *Truman: The Rise to Power* (1985), *The Case for Legalizing Drugs* (Praeger, 1991), and the recently published *Nazi Justiz: Law of the Holocaust* (Praeger, 1995).